MARTYRS IN MEXICO

MARTYRS IN MEXICO

A MORMON STORY OF REVOLUTION AND REDEMPTION

F. LaMond Tullis

Published by the Religious Studies Center, Brigham Young University, Provo, Utah, in cooperation with Deseret Book Company, Salt Lake City.

Visit us at rsc.byu.edu.

© 2018 by Brigham Young University. All rights reserved.

Printed in the United States of America by Sheridan Books, Inc.

DESERET BOOK is a registered trademark of Deseret Book Company.

Visit us at DeseretBook.com.

Any uses of this material beyond those allowed by the exemptions in US copyright law, such as section 107, "Fair Use," and section 108, "Library Copying," require the written permission of the publisher, Religious Studies Center, 185 HGB, Brigham Young University, Provo, Utah 84602. The views expressed herein are the responsibility of the author and do not necessarily represent the position of Brigham Young University or the Religious Studies Center.

Cover and interior design by Madison Swapp and Emily Strong.

ISBN: 978-1-9443-9432-5

Library of Congress Cataloging-in-Publication Data

Names: Tullis, F. LaMond, 1935- author.
Title: Martyrs in Mexico : a Mormon story of revolution and redemption / F. LaMond Tullis.
Description: Provo, Utah : Religious Studies Center, Brigham Young University, 2018. | Includes bibliographical references and index.
Identifiers: LCCN 2017048890 | ISBN 9781944394325
Subjects: LCSH: Church of Jesus Christ of Latter-Day Saints--Missions--Mexico--San Marcos--History. | Monroy, Rafael, 1878-1915. | Morales, Vicente, -1915. | Church of Jesus Christ of Latter-Day Saints--Mexico--Hidalgo--History. | Mormon Church--Mexico--Hidalgo (State)--History. | Mormons--Mexico--Hidalgo (State) | Hidalogo (Mexico : State)--Church history.
Classification: LCC BX8617.M4 T85 2018 | DDC 289.3/7246--dc23 LC record available at https://lccn.loc.gov/2017048890

CONTENTS

Illustrations	vii
Foreword	ix
Acknowledgments	xiii

PART 1: FOUNDING A NEW FAITH IN SAN MARCOS, HIDALGO, MEXICO

1.	Milieu of the Martyrs	1
2.	The Monroys' Curiosity	19
3.	Prelude to the Martyrdoms	51
4.	The Executions	65
5.	The Aftermath	73

PART 2: MATURING THE FAITH IN A MEXICAN VILLAGE

6.	Institutionalizing the Church in San Marcos and Environs	85
7.	San Marcos Mormons Embrace Temporal Progress and Development	129
8.	The Genes of the Martyrs	155
	Afterword	163
	Bibliography	165
	Index	175
	About the Author	181

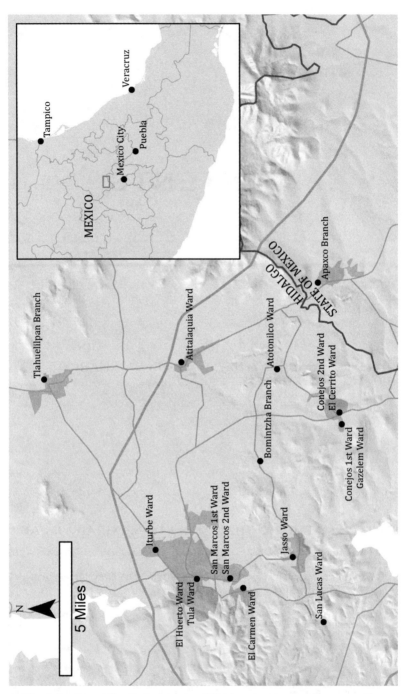

Map 1: Portion of the Mexican state of Hidalgo showing locations near San Marcos where modern LDS congregations were meeting in dedicated chapels. Map courtesy of Brandon Whitney, Think Spatial, BYU.

ILLUSTRATIONS

Map 1. Portion of the Mexican State of Hidalgo — vi

Photo 1. Rafael Monroy, ca. 1911 — 3

Photo 2. María Jesús Mera Pérez de Monroy, ca. 1911 — 5

Photo 3. Monroy family with missionaries and friends, ca. 1922 — 6

Photo 4. Wedding of Rafael Monroy Mera and Guadalupe Hernández Ávalos, 6 January 1909 — 8

Photo 5. Rey Lucero Pratt — 27

Photo 6. Ernest W. Young, Rafael Monroy Mera, and Jovita and María Guadalupe, 11 June 1913 — 29

Photo 7. Monroy family in San Marcos, Hidalgo, ca. 1913 — 31

Photo 8. Isauro Monroy Mera, ca. 1900 — 34

Photo 9. Emiliano Zapata, 1914 — 35

Photo 10. Benito Juárez — 53

Photo 11. Henry Lane Wilson — 56

Photo 12. Making furniture for the first chapel in San Marcos, ca. 1930 — 95

Photo 13. Wedding of Jovita Monroy Mera and Bernabé Parra Gutiérrez,
    13 November 1920   98

Photo 14. Margarito Bautista, 1933   105

Photo 15. San Marcos chapel, August 1925   107

Photo 16. Second chapel at San Marcos, Hidalgo   110

Photo 17. Rey L. Pratt, Isaías Juárez, David Juárez, Benito Panuaya,
    Narciso Sandoval, and Tomás Sandoval, ca. 1931   111

Photo 18. Abel Páez, Isaías Juárez, and J. Reuben Clark Jr., ca. 1931   112

Photo 19. Bernabé Parra preaching in the San Marcos chapel, 1966   113

Photo 20. María Guadalupe Monroy Mera, María de Jesús Mera Vda. de Monroy,
    and Amalia Monroy, 1933   115

Photo 21. Bernabé Parra Gutiérrez, Bernabé Parra Monroy,
    and Benjamín Parra Monroy, ca. 1944   116

Photo 22. George Albert Smith, April 1946   118

Photo 23. New LDS chapel, San Marcos, Hidalgo, 1974   146

Photo 24. Health Services missionary aides, 1974   148

FOREWORD

In a sense, the substance of this monograph took shape in 1975, the year my thirteen-year-old son Michael and I spent the summer pulling a travel trailer from village to town to city in Mexico and Central America. From Colonia Juárez in Mexico's state of Chihuahua to Guatemala City, south of the Isthmus of Tehuántepec, we interviewed scores of members of The Church of Jesus Christ of Latter-day Saints (LDS). Except in the larger towns and cities, there were no hotel—let alone motel—conveniences along the way of our interviews. The small towns we visited were consistent with the historical development of the Church in Mexico and Guatemala, where the faith took root in villages, generally among the poorer classes of people.

As part of the Church's "sesquicentennial history project," I had been commissioned to carry out a large research project on the history of the Church in Latin America.[1] I began my effort in Mexico, but in 1976, I expanded the interviewing to include Brazil, Uruguay, Argentina, Chile, Bolivia, and Peru (where, during 1966–67, I had completed field research for a book).[2]

A large research design for Church history in Latin America notwithstanding, for complicated and certainly idiosyncratic reasons, my effort on Mexico was all that emerged as a publication in book form.[3] Later, I donated my files and interview recordings to the Church History Department.

During our 1975 journey in Mexico, my son and I stopped in San Marcos, Tula, Hidalgo (the focus of this monograph); parked our RV trailer in a vacant lot owned by Bishop Saúl Villalobos and his wife, Violeta Pérez; and from there spent a week doing interviews. Aside from contacts in San Marcos, we visited Church members in San Miguel, Guerrero, Santiago Tezontlale (including the aged Trinidad Hernández), and a few other places in the state of Hidalgo.

Later, in the 1980s, while I was on a business trip to Mexico with my wife Marta Morrill (deceased, 2007), we stopped for Sunday services in San Marcos, renewed acquaintances, and met new members. Then, in the mid-1990s, under the sponsorship of Fernando Gómez and his Museum of Mormon History, we returned with others to the region, including the gravesite in Tula of the martyr Rafael Monroy Mera, where we, as have so many others, paused to pay homage.

All these things foreshadowed events in 2011–15 when my wife Eileen Roundy and I spent a year and a half in Mexico (and two and a half years in follow-up) as Church history missionaries researching and writing pioneer narratives, "fifth Sunday" history lessons, and articles dealing with the history of the Church in Mexico. Spanish versions of many of these are now in the country-specific portal for Mexico of lds.org[4] in the section "Historia de la Iglesia en México." The present work on San Marcos is a continuation of these experiences and efforts.

If one were inclined to concentrate solely on the problems, failures, and shortcomings of people as they traverse time and space, she or he would obtain much information, some of it fundamentally important to our understanding of religions, societies, and peoples. However, we can add more to our understanding by concentrating on how people overcome their problems and, as religious persons, progressively enter a more powerful discipleship. That is the course of this monograph.

Unless otherwise stated in the text or the notes, all translations from Spanish to English are mine.

LaMond Tullis
Spring City, Utah

NOTES

1. I detail this and related matters in my article, "Writing about the International Church: A Personal Odyssey in Mexico," *Journal of Mormon History* 42, no. 4 (October 2016): 1–30.
2. LaMond Tullis, *Lord and Peasant in Peru: A Paradigm of Political and Social Change* (Cambridge, MA: Harvard University Press, 1970).
3. LaMond Tullis, *Mormons in Mexico: The Dynamics of Faith and Culture* (Logan: Utah State University Press, 1987).
4. Lds.org.mx.

ACKNOWLEDGMENTS

Over the years, numerous people have contributed to this monograph. Among the most important are the Church members I interviewed in the state of Hidalgo in May of 1975. Some of them, then advanced in years and now deceased, were among the first members—if not their children—who were old enough to have firsthand memories of some of the early happenings in their villages and nearby environs. Principal people I interviewed are Florencia Cornejo de Trujillo, Trinidad Hernández, Agrícol Lozano Herrera, María Concepción Monroy de Villalobos, Ezequiel Montoya Ortiz, Jorge Montoya, Violeta Pérez de Villalobos, Elena Parra de Pérez, María Elena Pérez Parra, Denia Sion, Emilio Trujillo Linares, Saúl Villalobos, Benito Villalobos Rodríguez, and Efraín Villalobos Vásquez. In 1974, in Provo, Utah, I had an opportunity to interview an aged W. Ernest Young, who played an enormous role in the evolution of the Church in San Marcos.

Aside from these now-deceased members (two or three still remain as of this writing), María Guadalupe Monroy Mera—popularly known as Guadalupe, or just "Lupe"—who died in 1965 at age eighty and was one of the first three members to be baptized in San Marcos, left a meticulously written record that immensely facilitated the writing of this historical narrative. Within her 113 pages (closing in 1944 with an appendix written in 1962) transcribed from her original handwriting, Guadalupe kept the most detailed records one might ever hope to find anywhere of small-village events of interest to the local history of the Church. She also researched supplemental documents and inventoried her memory to prepare her San Marcos narrative, manuscript copies of which are in the L. Tom Perry Special Collections in Brigham Young University's Harold B. Lee Library and in the LDS Church History Library in Salt Lake City.

Guadalupe also kept a voluminous diary containing autobiographical information and additional notes about happenings in San Marcos among the Saints and with her family. For undisclosed reasons, the diary is not available for public access but is closely held for family members. Nevertheless, Minerva Montoya Monroy, a great grandniece, has graciously made relevant pages available to me via facsimile and transcription. In many other ways, Minerva has been immensely helpful to this project, for which I am profoundly grateful.

Additional help of immense importance has come from some of the other descendants of Rafael Monroy, one of the two martyrs in San Marcos, principally through his granddaughter Maclovia Monroy Espejel; her husband, Abel Montoya Gutiérrez; and their children Elder Hugo Montoya Monroy and the previously mentioned Minerva Montoya Monroy. They have collected, collated, and placed on their family web page numerous documents, narratives, and photos dealing with their forebears in San Marcos.[1]

Some of the descendants of Vicente Morales, the other martyr in San Marcos, have also provided biographical information regarding their forebear, particularly Ruth Josefina Saunders Morales de Villalobos, granddaughter of Vicente Morales. Nuria Villalobos and Gustavo López Hidalgo have also provided helpful information.

In 2014, I became acquainted with Laura Smith, who, in the 1970s, served a health-services mission in the state of Hidalgo. Her meticulously tended diary added important details to the Church's health and agricultural-services project in Hidalgo in the 1970s.

More proximately, I have had the good fortune to receive superb substantive and editorial critiques of an earlier version of this monograph from Bradley

ACKNOWLEDGMENTS

Lunt Hill, Matthew Geilman, Clint Christensen, Elder Hugo Montoya Monroy, Richard Thomas, Minerva Montoya Monroy, Sharman Gill, and Susan Stevenson. Their valuable contributions helped correct internal errors or omissions while at the same time providing startling expertise in proofing a text. Eileen Roundy Tullis also helped collect some of the information for this monograph. I am grateful for the work of the Religious Studies Center staff: Thomas A. Wayment, Joany O. Pinegar, Brent R. Nordgren, R. Devan Jensen, Tyler Balli, Mandi Diaz, Kimball Gardner, Megan Judd, Emily Strong, Shannon Taylor, and Madison Swapp.

Of course, while we all can take some credit for this monograph's virtues, I alone must be bear the burden of any factual errors or erroneous interpretations found herein. I have tried faithfully to minimize them to the extent that my abilities have allowed.

NOTE

1. "Linaje Monroy en el estado de Hidalgo, Mexico," https://sites.google.com/site/linajemonroy/rafael-monroy-mera.

PART 1

FOUNDING A NEW FAITH IN SAN MARCOS, HIDALGO, MEXICO

1

MILIEU OF THE MARTYRS

"What bravery! They died with their boots on," remarked one of the Zapatista executioners.[1] He was reflecting almost respectfully on the surreal way that Mormon leaders Rafael Monroy and Vicente Morales had stood to receive the fusillade that pierced their bodies on the evening of 17 July 1915. The terror of facing an execution squad notwithstanding, no cowering, no begging, and no hysterics marred their calm and stalwart resolution to not repudiate their faith. The Zapatista commander had given them that option. The men responded by reaffirming their religious convictions, emphasizing that the only arms they possessed were not the clandestine military weapons they were accused of hiding in the Monroy family store but rather their sacred texts—the Bible and the Book of Mormon—which Monroy carried with him nearly all the time.[2] Monroy was president of the San Marcos Branch of The Church of Jesus Christ of Latter-day Saints. Vicente Morales, Monroy's employee, was also his first counselor.

Whether the slaughterers would have spared the men had Monroy and Morales renounced their faith is now moot. They sealed their fidelity when the executioners fired, when the muzzles of their American-made Winchester M1895 lever-action or Springfield M1903 bolt-action rifles spit out the bullets that silenced their young lives.³

Accounts of the executions are copious, ranging from academic treatises to magazine articles, newsprint, films, sound bites, diaries, journals, and family lore with varying degrees of conformity to the facts, which this monograph attempts to correct,.⁴ With the centennial of the martyrdoms having arrived in mid-2015, more appeared to be forthcoming, including a new feature-length film.⁵ All this notwithstanding, and although the martyrdoms themselves are among the most dramatic events in the history of the Church in Mexico, they had causes and consequences not only for Vicente Morales and Rafael Monroy and their respective families but also for the whole San Marcos Church membership and subsequent converts. Beyond, these events articulated the long process of institutionalizing the Church in San Marcos.

This book scans the background and details of some of those causes and consequences not only for Church members but also for the Church as an institution in San Marcos. Specifically, it reflects on the lives of Rafael Monroy and Vicente Morales as martyrs in their faith and later studies the executions as a reflection not only of the Revolution of 1910–17 but also of the international political economy undergirding it. The monograph examines the conversions of the Monroy family and of Vicente Morales within the context of Mexico's contesting political ideologies and thereafter looks into the aftermath of the martyrdoms for the members in San Marcos. It shows how numerous members eventually rose above their tribulations and substantial personal failings to bequeath to the present-day LDS Church an example of profound personal and institutional fidelity. Finally, it examines how the Church became institutionalized in San Marcos, Tula, Hidalgo.

RAFAEL MONROY MERA (1878–1915)

Before moving to San Marcos in December of 1906, Rafael's immediate family had become relatively well off elsewhere in Hidalgo. Various members worked as hacienda administrators, teachers, and governmental employees. For generations, the Monroy family had striven to be upwardly mobile, to rise from servitude to independence and beyond, and there is evidence of success. For example, Rafael's grandfather Pablo L. Monroy along with Pablo's wife, Porfiria

Photo 1. Portrait of Rafael Monroy done by the studio Napoleón Fotografía in Mexico City, ca. 1911. The venue, attire, and quality of the portrait suggest that the Monroy family was relatively well off economically.
Courtesy of Church History Library.

Vera López, sat in elegant dress around 1875 for a photograph[6] just a decade following the popularizing of the new technology in Mexico during the years of the French intervention (1864–67). (The Austrian emperor Maximilian, who Napoleón III had installed over Mexico, was a boundless fan of photos and circulated many of Empress Carlotta and him to try to legitimize his French-imposed reign.)[7] Moreover, Rafael's grandfather had been able to educate at least some of his fourteen children. His son José Jesús Silvano Monroy Vera, who became Rafael Monroy's father, certainly was literate, as was his sister, Praxedis Monroy Vera, who was, in fact, a schoolteacher in El Arenal, Hidalgo (located forty-five miles northeast of San Marcos). Later, she helped her nieces Natalia and Jovita, Rafael's sisters, to become state-appointed teachers in small villages or hamlets relatively close to the Monroy extended family. As customary for the times, the teenage teachers' students ranged in age from very young (ca. age six) to advanced (ca. age fifteen and sometimes older), all highly desirous to begin their first year of formal education.[8]

Rafael's father was already an administrator of haciendas (*administrador de haciendas*) when he and the much younger María Jesús Mera Pérez (she went by Jesusita to distinguish her name from that of her partner, José Silvano de Jesús) decided to live together, a decision they later solemnized with a formal marriage.[9] Jesusita came from impoverished parents who worked on various *ranchos* in the vicinity. She was unable to attend any school until age thirteen, when she began to remediate her illiteracy. She was keen to study whenever she had a chance, and through the years she became respectably self-taught, although she always claimed not to know how to read or write well.[10]

Thinking about what would be best for the children that Jesusita and her partner expected would bless their home,[11] the couple eventually decided to move to where at least rudimentary educational opportunities existed. Rafael's father resigned his administrative position, and the couple moved to El Arenal, six miles northwest of Actopan, to be near his extended family and the educational resources they nurtured. Rafael's parents-to-be were intent that their yet unborn offspring should have an opportunity to be formally educated in order to rise above the toil of ordinary country life.[12]

With opportunities at hand, members of the Monroy extended family in El Arenal, especially José Silvano de Jesús's sister Praxedis Monroy, taught all the children in El Arenal who were willing to work to become literate, and she and other members of the extended family gave extensive educational help to the children in the extended Monroy family. Accordingly, Rafael and his surviving younger siblings (Natalia, Jovita, Guadalupe, and Pablo) learned to read and write. Tellingly, their parents valued education enough not only to make

Photo 2. María Jesús Mera Pérez de Monroy, known as Jesusita, mother of Rafael Monroy Mera, ca. 1911. Courtesy of Church History Library.

opportunities available but also to free the children from domestic and field chores sufficiently to allow them to pursue it, which was, in the short term, an economic sacrifice for the parents.

Photo 3. Monroy family with missionaries and friends on an excursion, ca. 1922. Amalia Monroy, daughter of Rafael Monroy and Maclovia Flores Pérez, is standing at the left, ca. 1922. Around 1918 she came to live in the Monroy compound in San Marcos, Hidalgo. Courtesy of Maclovia Monroy de Montoya.

Aside from becoming literate, Rafael grew up learning administrative skills from his father and grandfather, experiences that landed him a full administrative title in 1903 at age twenty-four, when his father, then the administrator of the Hacienda del Cedó near Actopan, suddenly died at age fifty. The hacienda owners debated about whom to appoint as the administrative successor. They settled on Rafael.

Conforming to the common practice of the times and certainly following a pattern that his father had set,[13] Rafael began about this time a nearly three-year romantic relationship with Maclovia Flores Pérez that produced two children, Luis and Gerarda (the latter was known as Amalia Monroy after age twelve).[14]

Gerarda (Amalia) was born on 3 October 1906 in Llano Largo, Hidalgo, near the Hacienda del Cedó, where her mother, Maclovia, also was employed.

In late October 1906, shortly after the birth of Gerarda, Rafael resigned as administrator of the Hacienda del Cedó; split with his children's mother, Maclovia; and—along with his mother, Jesusita, and siblings—moved to Tecajique, Hidalgo, for a couple of months. In December 1906, the Monroy family moved to San Marcos. Maclovia remained at work at the Hacienda del Cedó, and her children, Luis and Gerarda, stayed with her.

Gerarda stayed with her mother for twelve years. A year after her mother's death in 1918, Gerarda eventually moved to the custody of her father in San Marcos and was renamed Amalia.[15]

In addition to learning how to be an hacienda administrator from his father, Rafael also learned at least one additional skill from him: the need—if not the art—of cultivating good relations with governmental officials. Indeed, assiduously nurturing relations with Hidalgo's politicians and administrators had been front and center during the family's entire time at the Hacienda del Cedó (1898–1906). Rafael acquired political visibility in the municipality (county) of Tula (in the state of Hidalgo), where authorities gave him various tasks relating to the development of agriculture and irrigation in the region. Any number of locals sought his advice regarding their business and ranching dealings.[16]

Rafael and his brother Pablo, who would soon die in San Marcos at age nineteen,[17] shortly took employment in the valley of Tula—Rafael as a police commander in Tula and Pablo as manager of Tula's municipal slaughterhouse. Their sisters Natalia and Jovita kept their teaching positions but later—along with their sister Guadalupe and mother, Jesusita—joined Rafael in San Marcos, where he had been able to acquire the lands knows as El Godo and El Capulín. Rafael helped Natalia and his mother, Jesusita, establish a store (*tienda*) in San Marcos, which seemed to be every woman's favorite wish.[18] Starting out in rented quarters near San Marcos's central plaza, the family eventually built a home at El Capulín. It was in that house, in what became a *casa de oración*, a house of worship, that the first twentieth-century meetings of the LDS Church in that area took place.[19]

While living in San Marcos, Rafael Monroy developed a romantic relationship with Guadalupe Hernández Ávalos, whom he apparently had known for some time through his extended family. Guadalupe Hernández lived in San

Photo 4. Wedding of Rafael Monroy Mera and Guadalupe Hernández Ávalos, San Agustín Tlaxiaca, Hidalgo, Mexico, 6 January 1909. Courtesy of Maclovia Monroy de Montoya.

Agustín Tlaxiaca, Hidalgo (forty-five miles northeast of San Marcos), and there, in 1909 or 1910, she and Rafael Monroy were married.[20] In due course, they produced a daughter, María Concepción.

TABLE 1: SELECTED GENEALOGICAL CONNECTIONS TO RAFAEL MONROY

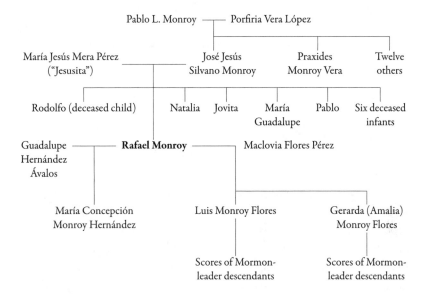

When Rafael and Guadalupe's daughter was two years old, Rafael began to develop an interest in the LDS missionary discussions. He took particular interest not only in the Book of Mormon as a compelling document but also in the Restoration's teachings about God's relationship with his earthly children and his requirement that they repent of their sins and be baptized.

Except for Rafael's wife, who was not happy about all this and had done her best to thwart the missionaries' efforts,[21] the whole Monroy family was mesmerized at Joseph Smith's hand in the Restoration of the gospel of Jesus Christ and, in particular, his work in translating the Book of Mormon. Accordingly, and not surprisingly, Rafael and his sisters Guadalupe and Jovita were baptized in 1913, and soon their mother, Jesusita, joined them. Surprisingly, and despite her early foot dragging, Rafael's wife, Guadalupe, was also baptized a month and a half later.[22] W. Ernest Young had discharged his missionary duties well.[23]

The family's relatively good social and economic status in the community notwithstanding, Rafael, his sisters, and their mother soon felt the scimitar of persecution for having abandoned, in the eyes of their neighbors, the teachings of the community's ancestors to join an alien US church.[24] Associating with foreigners was particularly anathema to the xenophobic Zapatistas from the state of Morelos, whose armed militia would later occupy the village.

Persecution aside, the Monroy home became the Church's meeting place for what would become a gradually increasing number of Mormons in San Marcos. Vicente Morales moved in from Puebla to help.

VICENTE MORALES GUERRERO (1887–1915)

The rapidly assembled insurgent Zapatista firing squad that ended the life of Rafael Monroy Mera in 1915 also terminated that of his cousin-in-law, employee, and counselor in the San Marcos Branch presidency, twenty-nine-year-old Vicente Morales Guerrero.

If in the Zapatista mind a constellation of factors condemned Monroy to a firing squad (his religious persuasion being only one among several), the matter appeared to be less complicated for the Zapatista general regarding Morales. Morales was a Mormon, was therefore pairing with aliens, and was a confidant of the aspiring middle-class Monroy, who would not confess his alleged crimes, no matter the torture. Even worse, Morales would not betray Monroy by doing the confessing himself. That was enough. In those days, examination of evidence was not a hallmark of the Zapatistas' minds except insofar as it affected their own sense of oppression and maltreatment at the hands of Mexico's privileged classes. Spiteful vengeance (*venganza rencorosa*), not to mention indiscriminate vengeance, is a powerful motivator of malevolence. In the Mexican Revolution (1910–17), spiteful and indiscriminate vengeance amply fueled grief and despair as pandemonium enveloped the land like smoke from a million wildfires.

Vicente Morales was born among the indigenous Otomí in the municipality of Alfajayucan, in the state of Hidalgo.[25] He was living in Cuautla, in the state of Morelos, when he became acquainted with the Church, which he joined in 1907 at age twenty. From age seventeen, he had been in a common-law relationship with María Petra Gutiérrez, four years his junior, with whom he had begotten and buried two daughters by 1907. After Vicente and María legalized their union through marriage to facilitate Vicente's baptism (which must have comforted María, given that she had joined the Church in Toluca at age ten), the couple had one more daughter (1909), who, like the others, died before her first birthday. In less than two years thereafter, María herself died (1911) from unrecorded causes, but perhaps related to another pregnancy.

With the family of his first love wiped out, and savaged by unremitting grief and despair, Morales nevertheless cemented himself in the Church by accepting a call as a part-time local missionary when regular missionaries fled Mexico in August of 1913 due to war hostilities.[26] Given his difficulty in speaking the Spanish language (his native tongue being Otomí), his acceptance of a mission assignment to Spanish speakers was of itself quite remarkable.[27] His missionary efforts eventually took him to San Marcos, Hidalgo, where he made several visits. Specifically, from January to March 1914, he and his traveling companions met with the Monroy family on at least three separate occasions to give them postbaptism gospel teachings.

The civil war was displacing hundreds of thousands of people, among them many Mormons, including Casimiro Gutiérrez and Plácida González, the parents of Vicente's deceased wife, María. Toluca, where they had been residing, was either aflame or in rubble, and Casimiro and Plácida, along with their other children, fled to San Marcos and to the community of Mormons there, hoping for safety. After the martyrdoms, Casimiro assumed the office of branch president,[28] but that he and his family were in San Marcos beforehand probably encouraged Vicente to make numerous visits to his parents-in-law as the widower dealt with his grief.[29]

Ultimately, however, there was perhaps a more compelling reason for Vicente to be attracted to San Marcos as a local missionary. Her name was Eulalia Mera Martínez, the seventeen-year-old niece of Rafael Monroy's mother, Jesusita, and therefore Rafael's cousin, who was living in the Monroy compound. Her appearance, typical of a youthful Otomí as revealed in the one extant photo we have seen, was very appealing to Vicente. Indeed, Eulalia was beautiful, had come of age, and was a member of the Church. Although Vicente had lost three children and his wife, and although he was more than a decade older than Eulalia, he nevertheless wondered if the young woman might be interested in him. He was stable, had none of the regular male vices of the day, was a strong member of the Church who was faithful to its teachings, and was considered by some to be quite handsome. They were both of Otomí heritage. So, he wondered.

Around 1912, then-fifteen-year-old Eulalia had moved to San Marcos from the municipal seat of Tula, Hidalgo. Jesusita took her niece in as if she were

TABLE 2: SELECTED GENEALOGICAL CONNECTIONS TO VICENTE MORALES

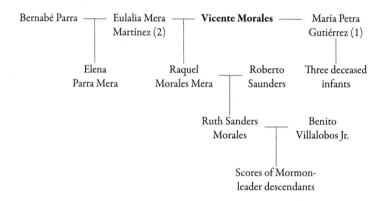

one of her own, a deed Jesusita had done before and would continue to do for others on numerous occasions. Eulalia was not long in her new home before she accepted the Mormon faith and was baptized (1913). By mid-1914, she had taken a liking to Morales, and, within a year, that liking matured. With President Rey L. Pratt's written permission (necessary because Vicente had a missionary calling) delivered from the United States, where he had taken refuge from the civil war, Vicente and seventeen-year-old Eulalia were married in San Marcos in early January 1915, just six and a half months before Morales's execution.[30] In March, when the fratricide of the civil war subsided for a few weeks, they had their marriage registered with civil authority in Tula—at least that part of civil authority that still functioned in Hidalgo.

The wedding celebration held in the Monroy compound was a grand affair. More than fifty people joined the gala. In addition to his extended family from the Rodríguez and Casimiro Gutiérrez clans, Vicente had invited many of his friends and acquaintances from other Church branches where he had served as a local missionary. Even Agustín Haro, the president of the San Pedro Mártir Branch, then in great distress as its members were scattering due to the war, showed up for the celebration.

Afterward, the invitees met in the one activity that always united them whether in celebration or in distress—a testimony meeting. A wedding celebration punctuated by a testimony meeting may seem strange. For the San Marcos members, such meetings were always the highlight of the first Sunday of the month as well as for every other occasion they could conjure up, including funerals and picnics in the countryside.³¹ And, this time, it was a wedding.

When the Zapatista bullets pierced Vicente's body on 17 July 1915, his daughter Raquel was still in utero. Eulalia was five months pregnant when she heard the Zapatista fusillade that killed her husband and her cousin Rafael Monroy. Let us look at the background to these events.

NOTES

1. The Spanish rendition as recorded by Rafael's sister Guadalupe is "¡Qué valor de hombre! ¡Han muerto con sus calzones en su lugar!" María Guadalupe Monroy Mera, "Como llegó el evangelio restaurado al pueblo de San Marcos, Tula de Allende, estado de Hidalgo," *Linaje Monroy en el estado de Hidalgo, México*, 1944, 27, https://sites.google.com/site/linajemonroy/rafael-monroy-mera/como-llego-el-evangelio-restaurado-a-san-marcos; cited hereafter as Monroy Mera, "Como Llegó el Evangelio." (Mexicans generally use two surnames, the penultimate being the paternal surname; the last one, the maternal. People generally go by their paternal surname; thus, the citation is under Monroy but with the maternal name of Mera included in this case for clarification.) With the inclusion of Guadalupe's 1962 appendix, the single-spaced typescript, transcribed from the author's manuscripts, totals 113 pages. As stated in the foreword, Guadalupe kept meticulous records. During the 1990s, Minerva Montoya Monroy, Guadalupe's great-grandniece, transcribed Guadalupe's handwritten text into the referenced typescript that I have used extensively for this writing (https://sites.google.com/site/ linajemonroy/rafael-monroy-mera/como-llego-el-evangelio-restaurado-a-san-marcos). The document details the period 1906–62 and covers events mostly dealing with the Church but also includes Guadalupe's personal ruminations regarding why she witnessed and recorded these events and their consequences. Additionally, certain pages of Monroy Mera's diary, which is not available for public access, have graciously been made available by Minerva Montoya Monroy.

2. An excellent analysis of the events leading up to the executions is Mark L. Grover, "Execution in Mexico: The Deaths of Rafael Monroy and Vicente Morales," *BYU Studies* 35, no. 3 (1995–96): 7–28. See also LaMond Tullis, *Mormons in Mexico: The Dynamics of Faith and Culture* (Logan: Utah State University Press, 1987), 100–103, 109–10.

3. Winchester M1895 lever-action and Springfield M1903 bolt-action rifles were those generally used by Emiliano Zapata's loosely structured revolutionary bands, the *Zapatistas*, and Francisco (Pancho) Villa's revolutionary forces, the *Villistas*. During Mexico's civil war of 1910–17, the Villistas, along with other revolutionary groups, sought to topple the country's federal government and rupture the dysfunctional and feudal society it coercively sustained. At the time of the San Marcos martyrdoms, the Zapatistas and the Villistas were in one of their sometimes-temporary alliances, at least in the state of Hidalgo. The Zapatistas, whose forces occupied San Marcos, appear to have been taking instructions, if not orders, from Villista commanders whose forces had occupied nearby Tula. As for the rifles and who used them, see "Weapons Used in the Mexican Revolution," History Wars Weapons, www.historywarsweapons.com/weapons-used-in-mexican-revolution. For information about the Zapatistas, one of the best is still John Womack, *Zapata and the Mexican Revolution* (New York: Alfred Knopf, 1969). Jim Tuck captures the picturesque Pancho Villa in his book *Pancho Villa and John Reed: Two Faces of Romantic Revolution* (Tucson: University of Arizona Press, 1984). For a general treatment of this period in Mexico's history, see Adolfo Gilly, *The Mexican Revolution* (New York: W. W. Norton, 2005). Readers of Spanish will profit from the diverse essays by prominent scholars in Jaime Ballón Corrés, Carlos Martínez Assad, and Pablo Serrano Álvarez, eds., *El siglo de la Revolución Mexicana*, 2 vols. (Mexico City: Instituto Nacional de Estudios Históricos de la Revolución Mexicana, Secretaria de Gobernación, 2000). A fine multivolume Spanish-language reference work on the revolution is Daniel Cosío Villegas, *Historia de la Revolución Mexicana* (Mexico City: El Colegio de México, 1977–84).

4. Grover, "Execution in Mexico"; Tullis, *Mormons in Mexico*, 100–103, 109–10. Primary sources include Monroy Mera, "Como llegó el evangelio," 25–30; Jesús M. Vda. de Monroy to mission president Rey L. Pratt, 27 August 1915; Rey L. Pratt to Jesús M. Vda. de Monroy, 28 October 1915, from Manassa, Colorado, where he had taken refuge from the Mexican Revolution; and Diary of W. Ernest Young, Appendix I, 669–85. Secondary sources include Rey L. Pratt, "A Latter-day Martyr," *Improvement Era* 21 (June 1918): 720–26; Rey L. Pratt, in Conference Report, April 1920, 87–93; "Two Members Died Courageously for the Truth," *Church News*, 12 September 1959; Jack E. Jarrard, "Martyrdom in Mexico," *Church News*, 3 July 1971; and numerous entries elsewhere based mostly on those previously mentioned. As for films, the visitors' center in Mexico City has a short clip on the assassinations. The most widely known is the somewhat ahistorical video *And Should We Die* (1966), written by Scott Whitaker and produced by Brigham Young University.

5. Kirk Henrichsen has been planning a video. From the preliminary screenplay outline, the outcome will likely be the best film yet on the martyrdoms and their context. Kirk Henrichsen, "Preliminary Screenplay Outline Notes," 19 March 2014. Copy provided by Hugo Montoya Monroy.
6. The photograph appears in "Historia de Rafael Monroy," *Linaje Monroy en el estado de Hidalgo, México*, 1, https://sites.google.com/site/linajemonroy/rafael-monroy-mera/historia-de-rafael-monroy.
7. For a treatise on early photography in Mexico, see Beth Ann Guynn, "A Nation Emerges: 65 Years of Photography in Mexico," Getty Research Institute, http://www.getty.edu/research/tools/guides_bibliographies/photography_mexico/. Napoleon III of France installed the Austrian Archduke Maximilian as emperor of Mexico on 10 April 1864 at the behest of Mexican monarchists and European freebooters, and his reign lasted until 1867, when Mexican nationalists under Benito Juárez captured and executed him. See M. M. McAllen, *Maximilian and Carlota, Europe's Last Empire in Mexico* (San Antonio: Trinity University Press, 2014).
8. Minerva Montoya Monroy to LaMond Tullis, email, 21 September 2016, citing the diary of María Guadalupe Monroy Mera, 31.
9. Following the birth of the fifth of their thirteen children (five of whom survived infancy), the couple was married on 3 June 1886. Common-law unions were the norm at the time, as was profligate infidelity. For example, Rafael's father had unions with at least four other women who bore him children. "Historia de Rafael Monroy."
10. "Biografía de Mamá Jesusita Mera narrada por Minerva Montoya Monroy," typescript, five pages, n.d. Copy provided by Hugo Montoya Monroy, 1 March 2014. Minerva gleaned her information from *El diario de María Guadalupe Monroy Mera*, 6–7. Jesusita said that because of the family's poor economic situation, she was unable to attend school. By this, she meant she could not attend until age thirteen and likely not for more than a year or so afterward. For that reason, she viewed herself as not being able to read well.
11. Children, aside from being loved, were also a culturally valued demonstration of virility and fecundity and were generally considered an economic asset to a family because they could be put to work in the fields around age six.
12. "Historia de Rafael Monroy," 2.
13. "Jesús Monroy had other sexual partners, e.g., Vicenta Ríos, Marciala, Valentina Bisuet y Petra Vera, with whom he had other children." See "Historia de Rafael Monroy," 3.

14. A picture of Agustina Marcelina Maclovia Flores Pérez shows that she was a beautiful young woman. The children were Luis Monroy Flores (1904) and Gerarda Monroy Flores (1906). "Historia de Rafael Monroy," 5.
15. Hugo Montoya Monroy, comments to the author.
16. Monroy Mera, "Como llegó el evangelio," 3.
17. María Concepción Monroy de Villalobos, oral history interview by Gordon Irving, 1974, typescript, James Moyle Oral History Program, Church History Library, 1–2.
18. In her diary, Guadalupe says the store was established for Natalia. Minerva Montoya Monroy to LaMond Tullis, email, 21 September 2016, citing pp. 43 and 48 from the diary.
19. Members from an earlier 1880–81 period are noted (e.g., Jesús Sánchez), although we have not seen any record that indicates they held meetings in San Marcos. "Historia de Rafael Monroy," 14.
20. When Rafael Monroy and Guadalupe Hernández joined in marriage on 8 January 1909 (Hugo Montoya Monroy's date) or 6 Janaury 1910 (María Guadalupe Monroy Mera's date from her diary), Maclovia appeared to give up on any thought of reconciliation with Rafael. She subsequently began a relationship with Santos Ortiz that produced two girls, Juliana and Alfonsa. We do not know if Rafael maintained any communication with Maclovia and his children. However, several fragments in the history of the family indicate that from time to time, Rafael mentioned his children with Maclovia. Hugo Montoya Monroy to LaMond Tullis, 27 February 2014.
21. Grover, "Execution in Mexico," 11.
22. Walter Ernest Young, *The Diary of W. Ernest Young* (Provo, UT: Brigham Young University Press, 1973), 107.
23. On 11 June 1913, W. Ernest Young performed the baptisms, while mission president Rey L. Pratt witnessed the baptisms. Young, *Diary*, 658–60. See also the narrative of Guadalupe Monroy Mera, one of those baptized, in "Como llegó el evangelio," 4–5.
24. Monroy Mera, "Como llegó el evangelio," 3–45.
25. Ruth Josefina Saunders Morales de Villalobos (daughter of Raquel Morales Mera and granddaughter of Vicente Morales) to LaMond Tullis, 11 February 2014. Morales's case illustrates the problem of gathering genealogical information in Mexico. Although one source alleges that Morales was born in Cuautla, there are no extant records. All the recorded vital statistics in Morelos prior to about 1912 were burned during the civil war. Guadalupe Monroy, who knew Morales perhaps as well as anyone except his immediate relatives (who left no records), affirms that he was born in Hidalgo, as stated in the text. Monroy Mera, "Como llegó el evangelio," 7.

As for the Otomíes, they predated the Aztecs, who arrived in the central Mexican plateau around AD 1000. The Otomíes existed in numerous subethnic groups, speaking several and sometimes mutually intelligible variants of the Otomí language. Many of their ancestral customs and language variants prevail into 2018. Their ancient homeland included portions of the present state of Hidalgo, but descendants are now located in major numbers in the states of Hidalgo and Querétaro. Other identifiable and smaller Otomí populations exist in the states of Puebla, México, Tlaxcala, Michoacán, and Guanajuato. For a perceptive discussion of the Otomíes in one area, see Mateo Cajero, *Historia de los otomíes en Ixtenco*, 2nd ed. (Bristol: University of the West of England, Bristol, 2009).

26. The call probably came from Agustín Haro, president of the San Pedro Mártir Branch, which, along with the Ixtacalco Branch, undertook supervision of San Marcos when the full-time missionaries and President Rey L. Pratt fled Mexico. Monroy Mera, "Como llegó el evangelio," 7–48. Haro, whose own work in the Church has become legendary, was Casimiro González's brother-in-law. Saunders Morales to Tullis.

27. Saunders Morales to Tullis. Additionally, accomplished writer Guadalupe Monroy put it this way: Morales "was quite poor and spoke Spanish incorrectly or with a bad pronunciation because his mother tongue was Otomí. He was from Alfayayucan from the state of Hidalgo. Luck had extracted him from there and he had accepted the gospel." (Morales *"era un hermano de humilde condición, hablaba el idioma Español muy incorrectamente o mal pronunciado porque su idioma natal era el otomí. Él era del Pueblo de Alfajayucan del estado de Hidalgo y la suerte lo había sacado de aquellos lugares y había aceptado el Evangelio.*) Monroy Mera, "Como llegó el evangelio," 7.

28. Saunders Morales to Tullis. See also Monroy Mera, "Como llegó el evangelio," 110–11.

29. The record does not disclose when Morales first began his missionary work in San Marcos, but he was there with his companion Juan García on 25 January 1914, when they met with the Monroys. On this occasion, Vicente was known as having the office of deacon and his companion as being a teacher. A month later, he returned with his companion Ángel López and yet a month later with Antonio Pérez. By this time, Vicente held the office of teacher. Others who accompanied him to San Marcos and visited the Monroys were Anacleto Rodríguez and Francisco Rodríguez. Monroy Mera, "Como llegó el evangelio," 7–9.

30. Vicente Morales and Eulalia Mera were married 4 January 1915. Monroy Mera, "Como llegó el evangelio," 13. Further corroboration in Familia Montoya Monroy, "Martirio en México," *Linaje Monroy en el estado de Hidalgo, México*,

17 January 2014, 3, https://sites.google.com/site/linajemonroy/rafael-monroy-mera/martirio-en-mexico.
31. Guadalupe Monroy's extraordinary detail in her records over twenty years includes not only the names of those who bore their testimonies in these meetings but also summaries of what they said. In this case, see Monroy Mera, "Como llegó el evangelio," 13.

2

THE MONROYS' CURIOSITY

In 1912, following a twelve-year absence of missionaries, a condition that had ended elsewhere in Mexico in 1901[1]—LDS missionaries returned in force to Hidalgo, specifically to San Marcos and its environs, to preach the gospel again.[2] There, as in other areas of Mexico after restoring missionary work, the missionaries were searching for old members and working to reestablish the Church among them. In Hidalgo, they generally sought accommodations in San Marcos or Tula and from there fanned out into the countryside.[3]

In these early recovery efforts, on 15 August 1912, two unnamed and "elegantly dressed" young American missionaries entered the Monroy store in San Marcos, not seeking to convert the attendants or owner but rather to purchase supplies and collect information. They were looking for Jesús Sánchez, whom August Wilcken had baptized in 1881 during Apostle Moses Thatcher's mission to Mexico.[4] How the missionaries knew Sánchez was in San Marcos is lost to time. However, in their pursuit of all the old members throughout central Mexico, the missionaries finally arrived in San Marcos looking for him.

At the Monroy store, the missionaries amply acquired what they sought, as supplies were plentiful. Moreover, astonishingly, the Monroys not only knew Sánchez, but Rafael and at least his sister Guadalupe considered him a friend. (Their mother, Jesusita, eventually came to hold him in great esteem.)[5] Delighted, the missionaries quickly departed for Sánchez's home where they visited, stayed overnight, and returned on numerous occasions before his death the following year.[6] On each visit, they took occasion to stop at the Monroy store.

The next time Jovita and Guadalupe Monroy spoke with Jesús Sánchez, they stippled him with questions:

"Why were the young Americans looking for you?"

"They are missionaries of the Church of Christ."

"What do you mean 'Church of Christ'?"

"Yes, it is the true Church!"

"How is it that the Catholic Church is not the true one?"

With a few follow-up words, Sánchez gave the Monroy women his testimony.[7] If any missionaries were to return to San Marcos, the women asked Sánchez to bring them over to their home for a visit.

Nearly three months after that initial missionary trip to San Marcos, around 13 November 1912, Elders W. Ernest Young and Seth E. Sirrine paid a follow-up visit to San Marcos.[8] They had been to Nopala to call on José Yáñez, who, along with Jesús Sánchez, was also one of the early converts from 1879 to 1881.[9] After their stay with Yáñez, they went on to Tula to see the pre-Columbian ruins there and then to San Marcos to visit Sánchez. Sánchez brought the young men to the Monroy compound, where they found the daughters primed to pepper them with questions.

Jesusita became alarmed at what she interpreted as her daughters' attraction to rudiments of the Mormon message if not to the missionaries themselves. She prayed that the missionaries would cease coming to San Marcos.[10] Rafael's wife, Guadalupe Hernández, also voiced her objections to the missionaries' presence.[11] However, not content with just hearing the missionaries' response, the stubborn Monroy daughters later borrowed Sánchez's Bible (the version of

Cipriano de Valera) and began to study it in light of what the missionaries had told them.

A friend said to them, "Chucho Sánchez's Bible is no good. He is a Protestant. If you want to read a good Bible, Tomás Ángeles has one that used to belong to Father Lino, my uncle."[12]

Tomás Ángeles was also a Monroy family friend, so the daughters went to his house to borrow a proper Catholic Bible (version of Padre Cío San Miguel), so they could make comparisons. They found Sánchez's Cipriano de Valera translation perfectly acceptable. Later, the Monroy daughters' brother, Rafael, also asked Sánchez about his affiliation with a church called "Mormon." Sánchez gave him the same testimonial response he had given to his sisters.

Given Mexico's class structure at the time, it is remarkable that the Monroys had friends among various social strata. As for Sánchez, he was in a subservient social and economic position to the Monroys, yet they had an amicable relationship, and he certainly did not cower when presented with an opportunity to testify of his convictions. Generally, contacts across the classes were not so cordial and good natured and frequently tended toward exploitation and abuse, which is one reason Mexico had its revolution.

One explanation as to why the Monroys could so easily relate across social chasms despite their having deferential servants and employed laborers is that just one generation ago they had toiled daily as members of the rural life themselves. They still remembered "how it was" for them. They had not had time and had certainly exhibited no inclination to develop the social snobbery that so often accompanies the nouveau riche at whatever level. In addition, the Monroys had a large and relatively affectionate extended family, and not all of its members had prospered as had Jesusita and her offspring. Thus, when Sánchez told them of his religious convictions, the Monroy children were not preconditioned to reject his worldview out of hand simply because he was relatively uneducated and came from a less-advantaged social class.

Through Jesús Sánchez, the attractive young men and subsequently their message began to take hold of the Monroys, first with Jovita and Guadalupe; soon thereafter with Rafael; later with their mother, Jesusita, and her married daughter, Natalia;[13] and then with other members of the extended family. Events surrounding the death of Jesús Sánchez seemed to seal the matter. In life, and then in death, Sánchez continued to imprint what he considered the most important part of his life's message.

SÁNCHEZ'S DEATH

W. Ernest Young and various missionary companions had begun to make periodic trips to the Hidalgo region, stopping one time, as already noted, in San Sebastian in January 1913 to visit Lionel Yáñez. Lionel was a grandson of Desideria Quintanar de Yáñez, the first female baptized in central Mexico.[14] Regardless of wherever else they visited, the young missionaries always ended up in San Marcos for more conversations with the Monroy family. The Monroys were a magnet. Usually on these visits, the missionaries stayed overnight or longer in Sánchez's home, but sometimes they also found accommodations in the Monroy home. San Marcos did not have a hotel, boarding house, or overnight rooms for rent. It was a village.

At the same time that the missionaries were making their visits in an attempt to reclaim early members of the Church, Mexico's national political scene reeked of precursors of a full-blown revolution or, more accurately, a civil war (1910–17) that would radically transform Mexican society, culture, and government. Although the clouds of war hung low over the landscape in central Mexico, the missionaries did not yet feel alarmed.

Some have said that almost inevitably every nation will experience its revolution. In the relatively recent past, England, the United States, and France had theirs. Scores of countries followed. In the last two-and-a-half centuries, hardly a geographic place or race or ethnic people have been unscathed. So it is with Mexico and its revolution of 1910–17, a fratricidal conflict of sufficient magnitude that historians call it a civil war. Around a million lives were lost to battle, disease, hunger, and privation. Some of them were Latter-day Saints.

The Latter-day Saints lived in their villages and hamlets in central Mexico and in their various colonies in the northern states of Chihuahua and Sonora. During the revolution, civil disturbances and armed conflicts shifted from locale to locale, eventually affecting all the Saints. The hostilities disrupted homes and families with attendant loss of life. It was a perilous time for all of Mexico's residents, as the country struggled to form a new social identity, a new economy, and a new political system.

As the clouds of war began to hang yet lower in central Mexico, federal troops, impromptu militias, loosely organized guerrilla bands, and opportunistic gangsters roamed the land in search of their enemies or booty, first in the south and the north but ultimately in central Mexico, where nearly all the ethnic Mexican Mormons lived.[15] The federal troops, rebel militias, guerrillas, and gangsters took on various names attached to their principal leaders at any given time. Carrancistas, Maderistas, Villistas, Zapatistas, Huertistas, Obregonistas—these are some of them.[16]

In central Mexico, the whipsawing between federal troops and, in particular, Zapatistas afflicted many Mormon families. Sometimes the Saints could not maintain any appearance of neutrality, which Church authorities had counseled them to do. Sometimes the conflict became a pretext to settle old grudges among neighbors. Sometimes members helping members made the difference between life and death. Remarkably, the Relief Societies throughout central Mexico aided members all during the civil war. Equally remarkable was that many of the branches continued to function, their priesthood leaders doing what they could to protect the Saints and care for those who had been hurt or displaced.

The insurgent Francisco Madero and his allied forces had overthrown the decadent, corrupt, and dysfunctional regime of Porfirio Díaz, whose tortured social philosophy had bathed the entire land in a tsunami of discontent. In turn, Victoriano Huerta secretly plotted with US ambassador Henry Lane Wilson to overthrow Madero and arrange his assassination, an act set in motion when Huerta and his principal coconspirators met at the US embassy to sign the *Pacto de la Embajada*, or the Embassy Pact.[17]

Huerta's sordid and ultimately naked pursuit of personal power at whatever cost caused US president Woodrow Wilson to recall and subsequently cashier his ambassador and to ultimately refuse to recognize Huerta. Unfortunately, the repugnant episode contributed to the US invasion of Veracruz a year later. Among the less-than-privileged classes, anti-American sentiment rose feverously.[18] The American missionaries began to watch their backs carefully.[19]

In this environment, in March 1913, before the revolution finally reached central Mexico, the missionaries received word that Jesús Sánchez had developed a life-threatening illness. Jesusita Monroy, ever the comforter, accommodator, and compassionate service giver, reached out to her family's friend and his loved ones. Sánchez's wife had wanted to bring in the Catholic priest to administer last rites. Sánchez's daughter Felix respected her father's religious persuasion and did not know what to do. Jovita and her friend (a family employee and later her husband, the young Bernabé Parra) came to the house also. The Monroys persuaded Felix to send for the missionaries, who had not been around for a couple of months. This seemed natural, given that Sánchez was a Mormon and the Monroys had learned from both him and the missionaries about sacred healings by the laying on of hands. The literate Monroys could write letters, and they knew the missionaries' address in Tlalpan, so they initiated the invitation.[20] Interestingly, Sánchez's death-invoking illness did not deter his venting outrage at Madero's assassination,[21] perhaps a precursor of how most Mexicans now view the role of the despised alcoholic Huerta in the history of their land.[22]

Responding to the request to return to San Marcos, W. Ernest Young and Willard Huish arrived at the train station in Tula that served the nearby American-owned Tolteca cement factory, with its numerous British and American administrators and technical workers. Unfortunately, the missionaries were unable to walk the nearly three miles to reach Sánchez's home before he died on 29 March 1913. Thus, upon finally arriving several hours following the death, they found Sánchez's family and the Monroys already grieving. The missionaries had reached their destination too late to perform what the Monroys apparently had hoped would be a priesthood healing.

Young and Huish offered to hold a funeral service the following day, to which the Sánchez family gratefully agreed. For the moment, the missionaries extended what comfort they could to the grieving family and then returned to San Miguel, near the train depot, where they sought accommodations at the home of one of the American cement-factory workers, R. V. McVey. McVey and his wife, Natalia, another Monroy daughter, would both join the Church later.

The following day, 30 March, Young and Huish conducted Sánchez's funeral. Afterward, Jesusita invited them to her home for lunch, where they, along with her daughters Guadalupe and Jovita, talked about the restored gospel.[23] Their conversations lingered into the evening. Rafael came by, and everyone stayed up late discussing the funeral, what the elders had said there, and what the Mormon gospel that Sánchez had professed revealed about the meaning of life and the eternal journey of the soul. The Monroy daughters were mesmerized. Rafael was interested. Jesusita was delighted with her guests if not their message.

The following day, the missionaries returned to visit the Sánchez family and "found them very comforted."[24] They stayed on in Hidalgo until 2 April and then took the train back to Mexico City.

A VISIT TO SAN PEDRO MÁRTIR

As demonstrated by the case of the Monroys, the impact of social relations on potential converts' decisions to affiliate with the Church could be substantial. It all happened when the Monroy family was on the cusp of social displacement in San Marcos. The Monroys' association with foreign missionaries, not to mention Natalia's spousal relationship with the American McVey, had begun to create community commentary. By then, the Monroys may have begun to feel a social distancing that later would become intense persecution. Whether for that reason or because of an irresistible desire to see what Mormons in Mexico were doing, they decided to accept an invitation to attend a district conference in San Pedro Mártir, near Mexico City.

The Church's San Pedro Mártir Branch was organized in 1907. Under the aegis of its first president, Agustín Haro,[25] and with the assistance of the Latter-day Saints in nearby Ixtacalco, San Pedro Mártir Branch members would subsequently tutor a growing body of Mormons in San Marcos after the full-time missionaries were withdrawn when insurgency morphed into a full-scale civil war.

In 1912, San Pedro Mártir was an excellent example of several locales in Mexico that were first converted to Protestantism before receiving the restored gospel.[26] There was a certain evangelical enthusiasm there, and Mormons in the area tended to be fervent about their new faith. With what they considered a proper Mormon expression of welcoming visitors—one comfortably ensconced within the rubric of Mexican culture—branch members would affectionately embrace the Monroys.

Ever the enterpriser, in May of 1913, W. Ernest Young invited the Monroys to the San Pedro Mártir conference scheduled for the twenty-fourth to the twenty-sixth of the month. In those days, conferences were multiday affairs that many Saints traveled long distances to attend and for which many sought overnight accommodations, mostly in members' homes. Young was fully aware that the Monroys were acquainted with Mexico City and would have no trouble traveling from San Marcos to attend if they wanted to and no trouble acquiring hotel accommodations while so doing. Young had already alerted the Monroys to the possibility of meeting mission president Rey L. Pratt, by then a legendary figure among Mormons in Mexico and, by all counts, a spellbinding orator. The invitation had the desired effect of initiating a conversation within the Monroy household.

Rafael Monroy's sisters María Guadalupe and Natalia were interested. Thinking the conference would be in English, Rafael was not attracted but changed his mind when he learned otherwise. The trio journeyed to Mexico City, where they arrived at the mission home not only well before the appointed hour but even before the Mexican mail service had delivered their previously sent letter of acceptance! Young had no idea they were coming and was therefore delightfully surprised, a mood slightly dampened by having to inform them that Rey Pratt would not be at the conference. The mission president was busy trying to get some members out of prison in Morelos.[27]

Disappointed, the Monroys nevertheless accompanied the missionaries to the Saturday session of the conference, where, President Pratt's absence notwithstanding, they found the messages in general not mesmerizing but certainly interesting, some even compelling. At the conference's midday pause and before the afternoon session, they were surprised to see the missionaries eating the "humble" food the San Pedro Mártir Mormons had prepared for them and other visitors.[28]

Then there was an electrifying surprise! President Pratt abruptly showed up. Members gathered around him, all smiles. Young introduced the Monroys to him. His gracious and magnetic character was on full display.

Saturday evening the members presented a program of music and dance, with little children participating, they too being important among almost all Mormons. On Sunday, the Monroys witnessed a large number of Mormons and their friends enthusiastically gather for the day's meetings. In his discourses, Pratt was true to his oratorical reputation. Then there were baptisms near Ixtacalco. Members were confirmed, children were blessed, a Priesthood meeting was held, and ordinations and ordinances were performed. Afterward, Pratt invited the Monroys to the mission home, where his wife had overseen the preparation of a regal American meal.[29] The Monroys were startled not

Photo 5. Rey Lucero Pratt, president of the Mexican Mission, 1907-31. Courtesy of Google Images.

only at the humble circumstances of the members who attended the conference but also that the gospel fellowship that united them with the Americans could bridge the obvious social-class divisions. However, there was more: the Monroys' elegant visage notwithstanding, the Saints in San Pedro Mártir had embraced them as if they were family. Not surprisingly, the Monroys not only felt welcome amidst the members' humble conditions, they also felt loved across any earthly boundaries that national and social cultures habitually taught people to reinforce. Thus the Monroys were astonished, but warmly so. In San Marcos, they had also bridged such social and cultural boundaries. Witness, for example, their relationship with Jesús Sánchez and later, as we will see, with Bernabé Parra.

Back in their hotel room in the evening after two days of whirlwind activity, the Monroys began to discuss and "feel" the days' events. Sunday evening they could not sleep until very late. All they had listened to and experienced flooded their minds. After sleep finally came, Rafael even dreamt that he was preaching everything he had heard.

Guadalupe, Natalia, and Rafael arose early Monday to catch the morning train at Buena Vista, and when arriving at the Tolteca station in Hidalgo, they saw everything differently. Family members wondered how they could have spent three days in Mexico City without accomplishing any business for their store. Then, in the ensuing days, there was much correspondence, as the Monroys wrote to Elder Young and to President Pratt and received copious replies from both.[30] Perhaps all this motivated President Pratt to schedule a follow-up stay at San Marcos. He wrote to the Monroys requesting to visit them.[31]

Would the Monroys be interested? They may not yet have found appealing a visit from Agustín Haro, the San Pedro Mártir Branch president of humble means, who later would figure large in their lives. However, a visit from President Rey L. Pratt? In three days? Of course!

BAPTISMS AMIDST CONVIVIALITY

On 10 June 1913, President Rey L. Pratt and Elder W. Ernest Young traveled to San Marcos as promised. Their gospel discussions with the Monroys and others (seventeen attended their evening meeting) appeared to last until the early hours of 11 June. The Spirit was present and the decisions were quick. Rafael and his sisters Jovita and Guadalupe opted for baptism, which Young performed midmorning on the eleventh in a nearby river. Their enthusiasm must have been elevated; they wanted to reenter the water to be baptized for their forebears, not yet realizing that by then, vicarious ordinances for the dead, a unique Mormon practice, were done only in the Church's temples.[32] President

Photo 6. Missionary Ernest W. Young (back row) baptized Rafael Monroy Mera and his sisters Jovita and María Guadalupe, San Marcos, Hidalgo, 11 June 1913. Courtesy of Ernest W. Young.

Pratt probably did the confirmations, performed on the riverbank under the secluded ambience of an enormous cypress tree whose branches pushed out over the water.

However reluctantly, Rafael's wife, Guadalupe Hernández, came to witness these strange events, as did Jesusita herself. Present also were the Monroy children's cousins Isauro Monroy, María Carlota Monroy, and Eulalia Mera Martínez. Eulalia would subsequently become Vicente Morales's wife. Oh, yes, present also was the nineteen-year-old Bernabé Parra, whose larger-than-life role in San Marcos was waiting to unfold.[33] Rafael was thirty-five, Jovita twenty-nine, and Guadalupe twenty-seven. It had been two and a half months since Jesús Sánchez's funeral. The Monroy siblings became the first people baptized in the municipality of Tula in well over a quarter century.[34]

Among Mormon converts of the time, the Monroy family members were unusual because they were comfortably ensconced in a nascent rural middle class that, with a few notable exceptions, characteristically eschewed the restored gospel's message. Abandoning Catholic traditions, or in some instances a community's subsequent Protestant leanings, imperiled a family's social standing. True, such angst was a problem across all social classes, but its gravity increased with prominent social standing.

The three baptized children of Jesusita were educated and cultured. They were acquainted with a few of the literary and philosophical treatises circulating in Mexico at the time and not only enjoyed parlor music, for example, but the young women also demonstrated it on Jesusita's piano. The Monroys frequently traveled to Mexico City and its environs to provision their store and enjoy the lights, sounds, and ambience of a relatively large city. Being well acquainted with Mexico's passenger trains, the family knew how to travel, including which routes and, aside from trains, which lateral conveyances to use. The Monroys had domestic servants; employed laborers on their ranch, El Godo; consorted with foreigners, particularly Americans, one of whom Natalia even married; and were politically well connected.[35]

The Monroys' situation was quite distinct from most rural LDS converts of the time, who frequently were only marginally literate if at all, and who often dressed in the humblest of traditional fashions, females frequently not even wearing shoes, most likely because they could not afford them. Most of these early converts were vulnerable to capricious acts of nature and to political and social abuse as they struggled daily to put bread on the table, sometimes being unsuccessful when disease, the government, or the powerful plowed over their well-being. Like the early Saints in Great Britain,[36] most Mexican Mormon

Photo 7. Monroy family in San Marcos, Hidalgo, ca. 1913. Rafael, his daughter María Concepción, his wife Guadalupe Hernández, his sister Natalia Monroy Mera, his mother Jesusita, and his sisters Jovita Monroy Mera and María Guadalupe Monroy Mera. Courtesy of Church History Library.

converts of the time were what some called the dregs or the "deplorables" of society. But in time, they assembled a surprise. Many converts, including numerous of their descendants, became stalwarts in the Mormon kingdom and boundless contributors to their communities' development.

A week following their baptisms, Jovita and Guadalupe, perhaps in Mexico City conducting business related to their store, showed up unannounced at the mission home for a quick visit. Guadalupe had told her sibling about Sister Pratt and the mission home, and Jovita wanted to see everything for herself.

They found Elder Young there, perhaps doing nonmissionary activities. The civil war was hindering their missionary efforts, he said, and they were often unable to make planned visits and sometimes did not know what to do. In the meantime, he was carrying three suitcases upstairs to President Rey L. Pratt's wife, Mary (May) Stark Pratt, who had begun to pack her family's belongings in the event that the US embassy ordered evacuations from the country.[37]

War concerns notwithstanding, the Fourth of July was about to arrive, and, as usual, American residents in Mexico City planned to celebrate their independence day in Tivoli Park, enhanced this year by a circus at the location. This time, however, American attendance was sparse not only because of the war but also because there was now considerable acrimony between Mexicans and Americans, fostered in large part by US ambassador Henry Lane Wilson's political machinations. Pratt invited the Monroy family to the festivities, and they all showed up, including Natalia's husband, R. V. McVey. Astonishingly, by present-day standards, and despite the drunken rowdies in attendance at the festivities, the missionaries "found some nice girls to dance with."[38] Today it seems strange that they would dance at all.

ENSUING BAPTISMS SPAWN HOSTILITY

In the middle of July, with war increasingly in the news, President Pratt and his family (wife and five children, ranging in age from nine to one) took a ten-day vacation to San Marcos, where they stayed in the Monroy home. For the Monroy family, as well as for their servants and remaining friends, the Pratt family was a major attraction, which included their message about the restored gospel. Within days, Pratt conducted another baptismal service: joining the Church were Jesusita, her niece Eulalia Mera Martínez, and the nineteen-year-old field hand and incipient manager, Bernabé Parra, who had begun to have feelings for Jovita, ten years his senior. Surprisingly, Rafael's wife, Guadalupe Hernández, was also baptized a week later. All of them echoed Jesusita's words: "With happiness I accepted baptism in The Church of Jesus Christ of Latter-day Saints," adding "and my life changed."[39]

Aside from their feelings of joy and happiness for accepting the gospel and its ordinances, which was accompanied by alterations in their worldview and their life expectations, the Monroys saw their relationship with the citizens of San Marcos change. The townspeople began to ramp up their criticisms of the

Monroys, even to the extent of publically praying for them, working their rosaries daily, and making offerings so that the family would return to its Catholic roots and the Mormons, the foreigners, be banished from the land.[40] That effort proving to be a failure, the public shunning and store boycotts were ramped up, a phenomenon that eventually included even members of the extended Monroy family who withdrew their association.[41] Friends ceased to come by and even refused to receive the Monroys in their own homes.

In the meantime, the Monroys, their close relatives, and Bernabé Parra were content and happy "for knowing that they had accepted the true doctrine of Christ and they rejoiced in seeing themselves as true Christians."[42] At the time, they appeared to have little realization that, looming on the war's frontier, their association with Americans would contribute to a catastrophic quandary for them.

While in San Marcos, Pratt became concerned about how to return to Mexico City. The rebels had cut through more rail lines, and transit was being interrupted everywhere except for the line to Veracruz.[43] The war had begun to expand its tentacles even in central Mexico.

ORDERS FOR EVACUATION

Another district conference was scheduled for 9 August 1913, this time in Toluca, in the state of Mexico. Winds of war aside, President Pratt intended to be there and invited Rafael Monroy to accompany him. By this time, Pratt had not only developed a keen social liking for Monroy but also trust and confidence.

Not wanting to travel alone during increasingly perilous times, Monroy took with him his trusted field managers—Bernabé Parra and Monroy's nephew Isauro Monroy. They met up with Pratt and several missionaries at the mission home in Mexico City, and together they all traveled by train to Toluca, arriving in time for the morning conference session.

Unlike the conference in San Pedro Mártir, the Toluca experience was not a happy one. Locals threatened the missionaries with death and harassed members and investigators who came to attend. Rafael no doubt felt alarmed, and he was likely relieved to return quickly to his home in San Marcos.

Two weeks later, Pratt sent letters by trusted couriers to all the branch presidents (and to Monroy as well, who was the "senior male member" in

Photo 8. Isauro Monroy Mera, ca. 1900. First cousin to Rafael Monroy Mera, Isauro played a significant role in caring for the Monroys during difficult times. Although later alienated from the Church for many years, he remained a faithful Mormon. Scores of his descendants are found in the Church today, including Malena Villalobos Monroy, wife of Benjamín Parra Monroy, the Church's first ethnic Mexican mission president. Courtesy of Maclovia Monroy de Montoya.

San Marcos), informing them that the American embassy had issued evacuation orders for all Americans due to President Victoriano Huerta severing diplomatic relations with the United States.[44] Consistent with LDS President Joseph F. Smith's admonition to follow the lead of the American embassy on this issue, Pratt, his family, and all the foreign missionaries were quickly packing and in the afternoon of 29 August would take the 8:15 p.m. train to the port of Veracruz. Pratt's wife, Mary, had fallen ill from so much work and worry, and everyone in the mission home was in a panic to get ready to leave.

Given that Monroy did not receive his letter until the morning of the twenty-ninth, he had little time to do what he felt he must—travel to Mexico City to wish Pratt and the missionaries a safe journey and say goodbye. It was a fateful decision.

MONROY BECOMES BRANCH PRESIDENT

How does a man of good will show up unexpectedly among panicked foreigners who have no time for chitchat and still be able to give them a proper Mexican *despedida*, a culturally appropriate farewell? The record gives no hint. However, it does disclose that Pratt, who was astonished that Monroy could make it to Mexico City so quickly, felt impressed to confer the Melchizedek priesthood upon him, ordain him an elder, and then set him apart as the president of the San Marcos Branch. Otherwise, the members there would have had no institutional leadership.

W. Ernest Young, then the mission secretary, saw it this way:

> We were surprised by our dear Brother Rafael Monroy from San Marcos, Hidalgo, who came to tell us goodbye. He is a fine fellow and has the spirit of the gospel. He came in a good time. Although he had only a short experience in the Church, President Pratt thought it wise to ordain him an elder so that he could baptize and care for the small branch in San Marcos, Tula, Hidalgo. He accepted this call, and I gave him my hymnbook and other items to assist him.[45]

Photo 9. Emiliano Zapata, 1914. A national hero in Mexico, he was famous for popularizing the phrases "Land or Liberty" and "It is better to die on your feet than live your whole life on your knees." One of his militias, in alliance with Villista forces, took the Revolution to San Marcos, Hidalgo, where in 1915 they executed Rafael Monroy and Vicente Morales, president and counselor in the San Marcos Branch presidency. Courtesy of Google Images.

AGUSTÍN HARO TO THE RESCUE

A freshly minted branch president seventy-nine days following his baptism, Rafael Monroy had his Cipriano de Valera Bible,[46] an 1886 translation of the Book of Mormon,[47] and a 1912 Mormon hymnbook containing the texts but no musical scores to twenty-three songs. But it did have cross-references to English hymnals that indicated which music was to accompany the verses.[48] He had a few missionary pamphlets, including Parley P. Pratt's *A Voice of Warning*.[49] He had neither the Doctrine and Covenants nor the Pearl of Great Price, two of the faith's four canonical works, both of which were yet to be translated into Spanish in any form.[50] He had no handbooks on Church administration or policies[51] and no lesson manuals for any auxiliary. He was on his own. And thus it was for two months.

As an evacuee in the United States, Rey Pratt issued copious correspondence to the branch presidents in Mexico. Some of the correspondence arrived at the intended destinations despite the war. It appears that in one letter Pratt asked Agustín Haro, president of the San Pedro Mártir Branch, to look after the members in San Marcos, perhaps suggesting that he involve the Ixtacalco Branch in some form of ad hoc administrative oversight. In any event, after consulting with Ángel Rosales, president of that branch, Haro penned a letter to Monroy, which arrived in San Marcos on 24 October 1913, advising him that he was sending Elder Jesús Flores from his branch and Francisco Rodríguez, a priest from the Ixtacalco Branch, to give Monroy a hand. He asked Monroy, and through him all the members in San Marcos, to receive them kindly. When the visitors arrived the following day, a Saturday, the letter of introduction they presented was from Ángel Rosales.[52]

The next day being Sunday, normal Church meetings would finally take place. They would be the first in San Marcos under the aegis of President Rafael Monroy.[53] However much he had tried to be a shepherd to his new flock of Mormons in the two months since his calling, holding formal Sunday meetings was not on his agenda, likely because he simply did not know what to do. Thus, on Sunday, 26 October 1913, the branch held the first formal meetings under Monroy's presidency. He quickly learned how to do it, held meetings every Sunday thereafter, and faithfully kept the record books of those meetings, the *Book of Acts*, until his execution twenty-one months later on 17 July 1915.

In the meantime, Monroy had his ranch (El Godo) to attend to and field hands to supervise, his family's store to help sustain, a wife and child to support and nurture, a widowed mother and two single sisters to be responsible for, and two nieces and one nephew living in his mother's household, who, to some extent, depended on him. He was a busy man, and all this before the severe persecutions began.

GROWING THE FAITH IN SAN MARCOS

Whether from Rey Pratt's urgings or from Agustín Haro's and Ángel Rosales's independent leadership instincts and commitments, the branches in San Pedro Mártir and Ixtacalco extended consistent alternating assistance and support to the members in San Marcos. For example, merely two weeks after Agustín Haro's visit to get sacrament meetings under way, President Ángel Rosales from Ixtacalco showed up with his priest Francisco Rodríguez to offer assistance and see how things had gone during the intervening time. The previous Sunday, President Monroy had held the meetings as instructed, and he was ready for more counsel and advice.[54]

Aside from the direct visits of Haro and Rosales, Rey Pratt continued to send numerous letters to Monroy; the two carried on a lively correspondence. Additionally, W. Ernest Young and Presidents Haro and Rosales also sent letters of advice and counsel, all intended to fortify Monroy with knowledge and confidence in his leadership and to give spiritual comfort to the San Marcos Saints, reminding them that it is not only for this life that humankind lives.[55] The concepts of *eternity* and *we are not alone* are powerful matters of the heart that help build institutionally solid and personally committed congregations.

By January 1914, twenty-three members and investigators were meeting in San Marcos, President Monroy was always talking up the Church with his friends and acquaintances, and Agustín Haro again made his presence felt, this time in company of Santiago Alquisira. The magnificent chronicler Guadalupe Monroy observed, "These missionaries encouraged the Saints and their faith increased."

Haro and Rosales's visits to San Marcos made them consider calling part-time local missionaries to take up the slack made evident when the full-time missionaries had been evacuated the previous August. Haro assigned his San Pedro Mártir Branch member Vicente Morales to begin missionary visits to San Marcos, usually every two weeks or so. Morales began in January 1914, arriving with various companions over the ensuing months, the first being Juan García, who had lived in the Mormon colonies in Chihuahua and—although a mature man of considerable experience—held only the priesthood office of teacher. Being a musician by profession, García enchanted the Monroy daughters.

Vicente Morales—a deacon who had long been committed to the gospel and ported a powerful testimony but was short on gospel finesse and knowledge and Spanish language ability, Spanish not being his mother tongue—was a representative of the "rustic part" of the Mormon social spectrum that was nevertheless being bonded into a community of Saints. During the next twelve months, his status changed from itinerant part-time missionary to Rafael Monroy's ranch employee at El Godo. On 3 January 1915, he happily entered the Monroy family as the husband of Eulalia Mera Martínez, Jesusita's niece, who had by then been living with the Monroys for at least two years.[56]

Through the visits of Vicente Morales and his companions, knowledge of the Monroy family and its work on behalf of the Church began to circulate in other areas, at least in San Pedro Mártir, Ixtacalco, and Toluca. There, people had become aware that the Monroys were relatively privileged people, which placed them in the customary position of being possible grantors to good causes. Around February 1914, the part-time missionary Francisco Rodríguez, from Ixtacalco, who had visited the Monroys on at least two occasions, sent a letter requesting help in settling some debts he had with Juan Páez, also a member, who was ill and needed assistance. Another member, Amado Pérez, a long-time faithful member, probably from Ixtacalco at the time, asked the Monroys to accept his only daughter into their family because the political situation had become precarious and he feared for her safety.[57] Civil order was breaking down, and not even the high broken-glass and barbed-wire-topped walls of well-to-do family compounds could continue to protect their residents. Other requests would come, some with an attitude of entitlement. It made no difference. The Monroys helped where they could with their money, time, and other resources.

Along the way, instructive spiritual blessings reinforced Rafael Monroy in his ecclesiastical and pastoral work in San Marcos. The branch president's two-year-old daughter, María Concepción, affectionately called Conchita, fell morbidly ill with an undiagnosed, or at least undisclosed, disease that lasted forty days. Neighbors affirmed the illness to be God's punishment for the family changing its religion. They added a prescription: Monroy should repent and pray to the Virgin of Guadalupe to heal his daughter.

Monroy was devastated. Although he may have consulted with the visiting part-time missionaries and perhaps even with Presidents Haro and Rosales, he ultimately wrote to Rey Pratt about his afflictions. In response, Pratt sent several letters of encouragement. (The civil war notwithstanding, the postal system still made deliveries almost everywhere in central Mexico.) In one of the letters, Pratt recommended that Monroy use his priesthood to anoint and bless his daughter and therefore heal her. This may have been the first time that Rafael had experienced an occasion to use his priesthood this way. Pratt gave him specific instructions. Monroy did as instructed, and the child was healed and lived thereafter to a relatively advanced age.[58] Heartened, San Marcos's branch president redoubled his ecclesiastical and pastoral efforts.

Help from afar continued. Ángel Rosales was released as the Ixtacalco branch president, and his former priest, now elder, Francisco Rodríguez, who had been a recipient of the Monroys' humanitarian aid, had become the new branch president there.[59] He wrote frequently to Rafael, giving him instructions, and now seemed to be in the forefront of sending part-time missionaries to San Marcos. Thus, on 27 March 1914, he sent Antonio Páez with Vicente Morales to get the Sunday School set up; in the evening, they held a missionary meeting.

Whether for this visit or other reasons, three days later another baptismal service was held in San Marcos in which Jesusita's daughter, Natalia, and other family members or friends were baptized. Aside from Natalia, these included Daniel Montoya, Taurina Pérez, Juana Mera, Isauro Monroy, and Alberto Tovar. Now, with increased confidence and experience, branch president Rafael Monroy performed the baptisms and confirmations himself.[60]

A week later, Agustín Haro, with companion Teodoro Juárez, arrived and established the pattern of holding Sunday School in the mornings and *cultos*, sacrament meetings, in the afternoons or evenings.[61] Whatever conversations the San Pedro Mártir and Ixtacalco leaders were having with each other and whatever the source of their administrative oversight—whether from competition, autochthonous desires to help, President Pratt's letters, or perhaps district leaders President Pratt was trying to put in place at the time—the new San Marcos Branch, its members, and its branch president were amply being looked after.

Having received much help from others, the San Marcos Saints were now in a position to reciprocate. It happened this way: Around the latter part of April 1914, some of the male members in the San Pedro Mártir and Ixtacalco branches were running the risk of being conscripted into the Twenty-Ninth Battalion of the federal army. President Pratt had counseled members throughout Mexico to remain neutral and not take sides in the war. The San Pedro and Ixtacalco men tried to follow his counsel by fleeing to other parts of central Mexico. However, by so doing they left their home branches bereft of a priesthood base sufficient even to hold meetings. In any event, the men were afraid to be at gatherings of the Saints lest federal troops appear and conscript them on the spot.[62]

President Francisco Rodríguez of Ixtacalco was one who fled. This patriarch of a large family was now left without work to support his loved ones, even to obtain their basic food with which to sustain life. He pled with the San Marcos Saints to impart a few funds to help them. They responded. Then, Trinidad Haro, son of branch president Agustín Haro in San Pedro Mártir, bolted to San Marcos looking for refuge. He found it with Rafael Monroy at El Godo, along with a remunerative job as a ranch hand.[63] Others followed. As the war continued to unfold, San Marcos became, for a while, a place of refuge for a number of Mormons throughout central Mexico, whom the members embraced as fellow Saints.

Rafael had a large project in mind that was perhaps partially underway to aid destitute members who were arriving in San Marcos seeking refuge from the war. The Mormon colonies in Chihuahua and Sonora inspired this project. Through lengthy conversations with Juan García, who had lived in those colonies, Monroy became aware of how the Anglo American Mormons there "helped one another . . . and how all worked together, women and children as well as the men" to advance their communal cause and prospects for survival.[64] Monroy may have seen something like the Mexican *ejido* (communal land) system, which had regained much ideological currency at the time, in these Mormon practices.[65] He raised the matter by letter with President Pratt, who in mid-December 1914 responded enthusiastically to the idea but also laid out a dose of realism on practical problems within the local Mexican culture. At the same time, he extended his counsel on how to work around cultural impediments to such a project. Pratt emphasized the idea of a formal contract. Emboldened, Monroy went to work to secure the lands.[66] In six months, he would be dead, so the project never really got off the ground.

That reality notwithstanding, refugees kept arriving. For example, Casimiro Gutiérrez, along with his wife and numerous children, showed up when no available housing existed in San Marcos, so the McVeys got them settled in

San Miguel, where they helped Casimiro start a business. Gabriel Rosales; his wife, Modesto Gutiérrez; and their son; and President Francisco Rodríguez; his wife, Anacleto; and their sixteen-year-old ward, Ana Páez, all from the Ixtacalco branch, were among those settled with the members in San Marcos and were helped to find ranch and domestic employment.[67] Rosales later joined the Zapatistas.[68]

In June 1914, the San Marcos members celebrated the first anniversary of the first baptisms in their community. As a sign of development and emerging maturity, some of the converts routinely took part in the services, testimony meetings were lively, and the Church gave evidence of becoming institutionalized in the village.[69] This was a good prognosis given that Pratt's only influence in the mission was through his weekly letters, which the San Marcos Branch routinely received, although Pratt apparently did not receive any responses.[70]

Despite the war and even the Carrancista and Villista/Zapatista occupations of San Marcos in 1915, the members continued to grow spiritually, holding their meetings almost every Sunday, enjoying visits from local missionaries from Ixtacalco and San Pedro Mártir, reading and rereading Rey Pratt's letters, conducting baptisms, and seeing their congregation grow to almost forty people.[71] Indeed, for the first branch conference held in San Marcos on 3 January 1915, sixty-three people attended, a number of them guests for the Vicente Morales–Eulalia Mera Martínez wedding that took place the following day.[72]

The war, the newness in the gospel, and the resettlement problems all posed challenges. It was certainly true that the period 1913–15 was difficult for the San Marcos Mormons. However, one central fact remained. The members were studiously engaged in internalizing the Mormon way, which included not only Mormon doctrine, however esoteric, but also a social gospel that embraced member refugees and extended them humanitarian aid. It was a time of growth—spiritual, temporal, experiential—increasingly on their own.

NOTES

1. For a specific discussion, see LaMond Tullis, "La reapertura de la Misión Mexicana en 1901," 15 November 2012, http://www.sud.org.mx/historia-de-la-iglesia-en-mexico/articulos/la-reapertura-de-la-mision-mexicana-en-1901. See also LaMond Tullis, *Mormons in Mexico*, 73–85.

2. The interregnum of twelve years is discussed in LaMond Tullis, "Los colonizadores mormones en Chihuahua y Sonora," 26 September 2012, 14–15, http://www.sud.org.mx/historia-de-la-iglesia-en-mexico/articulos/los-colonizadores-mormones-en-chihuahua-y-sonora.
3. During January 1913, missionary W. Ernest Young twice mentions being in San Marcos. On the eleventh, he stayed with LDS member Jesús Sánchez. On the twenty-eighth, he visited the Monroys "and other friends." He mentions Sánchez as "our only member." On this trip, he, with local missionary Eliseo Jiménez, went to San Sebastian to visit Lionel Yáñez, son of José María Yáñez and grandson of Desideria Quintanar de Yañez, the first woman baptized in central Mexico. For the account of Desideria, see LaMond Tullis, "La primera mujer bautizada en México: Desideria Quintanar de Yánez (1814–1893)," 7 December 2012, http://www.sud.org.mx/historia-de-la-iglesia-en-mexico/pioneros-articulos/una-solitaria-pionera-mexicana; and Clint Christensen, "Solitary Saint in Mexico: Desideria Quintanar Yáñez (1814–1893)," in *Women of Faith in the Latter Days*, vol. 1, *1775–1820*, ed. Richard E. Turley Jr. and Brittany Chapman Nash (Salt Lake City: Deseret Book, 2011).
4. "Martirio en México," 4. W. Ernest Young, in the reflective appendix of his diary (669), says: "During the first years of the Mexican Mission, 1879 to 1889, converts were baptized in San Marcos, a town forty-five miles north of Mexico City. In the year 1881, Elder August Wilcken baptized Jesús Sánchez. It was he that still lived in San Marcos in 1913. He had been visited at times during the intervening years, but proselyting had not been carried there for years until 1913. We had heard of his illness, and on March 29 Elder Willard Huish and I arrived in San Marcos to see him." For a discussion of the mission of Apostle Moses Thatcher, see LaMond Tullis, "La misión del apóstol Moses Thatcher a la Ciudad de México en 1879," 12 October 2012, http://www.sud.org.mx/historia-de-la-iglesia-en-mexico/articulos/la-mision-del-apostol-moses-thatcher-a-la-ciudad-de-mexico-en-1879. Missionaries were also active elsewhere in Hidalgo. In 1880, for example, Helaman Pratt visited Nopala and San Sebastían when the Yáñez family was deciding to join the Church there. See also Grover, "Execution in Mexico," 11.
5. Young, *Diary*, 86–87; Monroy Mera, "Como llegó el evangelio," 1.
6. "Jesús Sánchez was a faithful member of the Church from his baptism 5 July 1881 until his death in San Marcos 29 March 1913. Despite the first missionaries who baptized him having left Mexico, he remained faithful. New missionaries visited him whenever possible even before contacting the Monroy family. Thus, after his

death the formal preaching of the Gospel to the Monroy family began." "Martirio en México," 4.
7. I have reconstructed this conversation from Monroy Mera, "Como llegó el evangelio," 1.
8. Some accounts state that Young and Sirrine were the first to contact the Monroys. Guadalupe Monroy, one of the principals, states that a pair of missionaries—not these two—had approached them two months earlier. Monroy Mera, "Como llegó el evangelio," 1.
9. Tullis, "La primera mujer bautizada en México"; Christensen, "Solitary Saint in Mexico." As for Young's and Sirrene's tour, see Young, *Diary*, 81–82.
10. Monroy Mera, "Como llegó el evangelio," 3. Guadalupe Monroy, who never found a marriage partner, had hoped to marry a missionary or at least fantasized as much. Everyone was urging her simply to take a partner in order to have children, but she could not bring herself to marry outside the Church, and no young, available Mexican Mormon appealed to her. Among the normal, nearly imponderable issues of attraction, social-class differences would have weighed on her. In the waning years of her life, she reminisced: "My youth unfolded. The age for selecting a husband disappeared as flocks of birds fleeing the coming winter in search of a better climate. I ceased trying with the missionaries. All the young Americans were steeped in a racism that forbade their liking Mexican girls" (*Mi juventud se deslizó. La edad para elegir un esposo voló como las aves vuelan cuando el invierno viene, y se van en bandadas a buscar un clima mejor. No traté más con los misioneros. Todos ellos jóvenes Americanos, que el racismo los tenía bien vedados de simpatizar con las mexicanas.*) "Como llegó el evangelio," 110.
11. Monroy Mera, "Como llegó el evangelio," 1.
12. Monroy Mera, "Como llegó el evangelio," 1–2.
13. Natalia was married in May 1912 to the American R. V. McVey, who was in San Marcos as a skilled worker for the American-owned Tolteca cement-manufacturing plant, which symbolized the extent to which the Monroys had taken up with the Americans.
14. Desideria Quintanar de Yañez, baptized 22 April 1880, may not have been the first female baptized in all of Mexico. The missionary journal of Louis Garff, companion of Melitón Trejo on their mission to Sonora, records the following: "Sunday, May 20, 1877, I baptized José Epifanio and Jesús. On Thursday the 24th of May I baptized José Severo Rodríguez, *María la Cruz Pasos*, and José Vicente Parra, in a small settlement

a few leagues from Hermosillo city in the State of Sonora. These five baptisms were the first in all of Mexico in The Church of Jesus Christ of Latter Day Saints."

15. Mormon expatriate colonists in the northern states of Chihuahua and Sonora first felt the scimitar of the Revolution and were driven from their lands back into the United States. This book deals with the Saints in central Mexico. However, interested readers may find this chapter in my book to be useful: "Revolution, Exodus, Chaos," in *Mormons in Mexico: The Dynamics of Faith and Culture* (Logan: Utah State University Press, 1987), 87–108.

16. Some basic works on the Mexican Revolution are noted in endnote 3 of chapter 1.

17. See Horacio Labastida, *Belisario Domínguez y el estado criminal, 1913–1914* (Mexico: Siglo XXI Editores, 2002).

18. A relevant and nearly contemporaneous view is Luis Manuel Rojas, *La culpa de Henry Lane Wilson en el gran desastre de México* (México: Compañía Editora "La Verdad," ca. 1928). Wilson's apologia over the firestorm his service in Mexico created is his *Diplomatic Episodes in Mexico, Belgium and Chile* (Garden City, NY: Doubleday, Page & Company, 1927). Henry Lane Wilson's legacy appears to have outlived his tenure as ambassador to Mexico, which ended with his dismissal on 17 July 1913. The outrage in San Marcos may have been an afterglow from the legacy of Wilson but may have also derived from a rumored US invasion of Veracruz. However many Mexicans lamented the assassination of Francisco Madero (for example, as did the old San Marcos Mormon Jesús Sánchez) and the involvement of Ambassador Wilson in that sordid act, the US position under newly elected US president Woodrow Wilson was decidedly anti–Victoriano Huerta. He cashiered Wilson and appointed a new ambassador, John Lind, a former governor of Minnesota and a member of the US House of Representatives, to whom he gave careful anti-Huerta instructions. Nevertheless, "Lind spoke no Spanish and carried strong Protestant, anti-Catholic prejudices into the overwhelmingly Catholic Mexico. . . . Lind was empowered to negotiate with Mexican officials. [US president] Wilson had instructed Lind to press Huerta's government for 'an immediate cessation of fighting throughout Mexico', an 'early and free election' in which all parties could participate, a promise from Huerta not to be a candidate, and an agreement by all parties to respect the results of the election. In return, the United States promised to recognize the newly elected government. The Huerta regime met with Lind but refused to accede to Wilson's demands." Mark E. Benbow, "All the Brains I Can Borrow: Woodrow Wilson and Intelligence Gathering in Mexico, 1913–1915," *Studies in Intelligence: Journal of the American Intelligence Professional* 51, no. 4 (2007): 1–12. The venomous relations

between Mexican president Victoriano Huerta and US president Woodrow Wilson's new personal representative to Mexico, John Lind, are captured in John Lind, *Mexico in Transition: The Diplomatic Papers of John Lind, 1913–1931*, comp. Dan Elasky (Bethesda, MD: LexisNexis, 2005), microfilm reel 1.

19. The mission even developed a set of precautionary guidelines for missionary conduct during this time. Grover, "Execution in Mexico," 13; Young, *Diary*, 92.
20. Young, *Diary*, 90–91; Monroy Mera, "Como llegó el evangelio," 2; "Martirio en México," 5.
21. Young, *Diary*, 90–91.
22. Frank McLynn, *Villa and Zapata: A History of the Mexican Revolution* (New York: Carroll and Graf, 2000).
23. Young, *Diary*, 90–91.
24. Young, *Diary*, 91. The missionaries never returned thereafter to the Sánchez home. Thus, "with Señor Sánchez's death the missionaries never returned to this brother's house because his family had no interest and they rejected the true religion that their father had professed." Monroy Mera, "Como llegó el evangelio," 2.
25. Sally Johnson Odekirk, "Mexico Unfurled: From Struggle to Strength," *Ensign*, January 2014, 38.
26. María Guadalupe Monroy Mera reflected on this phenomenon in the appendix of her narrative about San Marcos, "Como llegó el evangelio," 108. Apparently, it was a topic of continuing conversation down through the decades. Isaías Juárez, the district president during and following the troubling times that the revolution began, commented about how the first Mormons in San Pedro Mártir also had been the first Protestants.
27. According to María Guadalupe Monroy, the issue was the impressment of Cándido Robles and Regino Reyes into the Zapatista militia. Even by this time, the Monroys had negative views about the insurgent Zapatistas. Monroy Mera, "Como llegó el evangelio," 4. However, several Mormons from Morelos, and those who would become Mormons, were inclined toward the Zapatistas, including Ambrosio de Aquino, who, before joining the Church, became a major in the Zapatista militia. Armando Ceballos and Dina DeHoyos de Ceballos, "Nefi De Aquino Gutiérrez: heredero de una historia de fe en Santiago Xalitzintla, Puebla" (unpublished typescript, ca. 2014); this document is based on an oral history recorded by Anselmo Mata and Luz Mata on 11 August 2013 and submitted to the Church History Library. The more likely event is that Mexican federal troops had picked up the men,

along with other Mormons, and *accused* them of being Zapatistas. Pratt was trying to get the federal forces to release the men. Tullis, *Mormons in Mexico*, 98–100.
28. "We were surprised to see the missionaries eating the really humble food that the members in San Pedro had given them." (*Nos quedamos sorprendidos, de haber visto comer a los misioneros las comidas tan humildes que les habían dado los hermanos de San Pedro.*) Monroy Mera, "Como llegó el evangelio," 4.
29. Monroy Mera, "Como llegó el evangelio," 4.
30. Monroy Mera, "Como llegó el evangelio," 4.
31. The Monroys received the letter on 7 June 1913 and learned that Pratt would be in San Marcos on the tenth. Monroy Mera, "Como llegó el evangelio," 4. Pratt would have sent his letter by the latter part of May, just a few days following the conference. His assistant, W. Ernest Young, must have given him a glowing report about the Monroys in San Marcos.
32. Young, *Diary*, 99. The Monroys' request was not unusual. Immediately following the early Mormons' expulsion from Nauvoo and during their trek across the plains to the Great Basin, they performed vicarious work in the "natural temples" along the way (streams and brooks and secluded groves). The Saints also did these ordinances at Winter Quarters (Nebraska) and in the Council House in Salt Lake City until they completed the Endowment House there in 1855–56. After this time, they confined vicarious work to the Endowment House until the dedication of the St. George Utah Temple in 1877. Thus, the natural inclination the Monroys had was not out of line with LDS temple practices of the time period two or three generations before their own baptisms in 1913. Richard E. Bennett, "'The Upper Room': Latter-day Saint Temple Work during the Exodus and in Early Salt Lake Valley, 1846–1854" (presidential address, Mormon History Association conference, San Antonio, Texas, 7 June 2014). See also Bennett, "'Which Is the Wisest Course?' The Transformation in Mormon Temple Consciousness, 1870–1898," *BYU Studies Quarterly* 52, no. 2 (2013): 5–43; and Bennett, "'Line upon Line, Precept upon Precept': Reflections on the 1877 Commencement of the Performance of Endowments and Sealings of the Dead," *BYU Studies* 44, no. 3 (2005): 39–76.
33. Monroy Mera, "Como llegó el evangelio," 4–5. See also, Young, *Diary*, 106–7; and "Martirio en México," 4.
34. Sánchez was among several that W. Ernest Young mentions as being baptized in the vicinity of San Marcos during 1879–81.
35. As an example, as the family was moving into San Marcos, one politically well-placed family member secured a teaching position for Natalia in the village of Llano, a teaching

position for Jovita in San Marcos, and a position of police commander in Tula for Rafael. "Biografía de Mamá Jesusita Mera narrada por Minerva Montoya Monroy" (unpublished typescript, five pages, copy provided by Hugo Montoya Monroy, 1 March 2014), 2–3.

36. Richard Thomas, in his 3 September 2014 critique of an earlier draft of this book, transcribed his personal audio recording of the following comment from President Gordon B. Hinckley, which he made to new LDS mission presidents on 21 June 2005: "Now I wish to say a word concerning the kind of people with whom our missionaries work. We've never been able to get very far with the highly educated, the wealthy, those whose manner is arrogant or self-centered. Over the years, our message has appealed to those in relatively humble circumstances. The great numbers harvested in England and subsequently in Europe in the early days of the Church were generally people of very modest means. The Perpetual Immigration Fund was established to help them immigrate to Zion when they were powerless to help themselves. But, while they were poor in the goods of the world, they were for the most part people of integrity. They were law-abiding and people of good intellect. Their posterity has added to the luster of the lives of their forbearers through education. They become people of great capacity, of great faith, of great activity and leadership in the Church."

37. Young, *Diary*, 100.

38. Young, *Diary*, 101.

39. "Biografía de Mamá Jesusita Mera narrada por Minerva Montoya Monroy," 3.

40. "With their *novenas* and rosaries [recitation of prayers], which they did daily so that the Monroy family would return to being Catholic." Monroy Mera, "Como llegó el evangelio," 5. In the Roman Catholic Church, *novenas* refers to a recitation of prayers for nine consecutive days for a specific purpose and to induce a sought-after end.

41. During Pratt's visit to the Monroys, one of Rafael's paternal aunts—who loved him, at least by her previous words and actions—came to the Monroy home for a visit, arriving during one of the "cottage meetings" that Pratt was conducting. Offended, she quickly withdrew and alerted other family members regarding the "cult" happenings in the Monroy home. The extended family thereafter pulled away. Monroy Mera, "Como llegó el evangelio," 6.

42. Monroy Mera, "Como llegó el evangelio," 5.

43. Young, *Diary*, 106.

44. Francisco Ramírez was Pratt's courier to San Marcos. Monroy Mera, "Como llegó el evangelio," 6. The war seemed to take international observers by surprise, even the Buffalo Historical Society in New York, which refocused its entire annual volume in 1914 to address the Mexican Revolution. Within the volume's first chapter, the

machinations of Mexico's Victoriano Huerta and the US response are chronicled. See Frank H. Severance, "The Peace Conference at Niagara Falls in 1914," in *Buffalo Historical Society Publications*, vol. 18, ed. Frank H. Severance (Buffalo, NY: Buffalo Historical Society, 1914), 3–75.

45. Young, *Diary*, 110. Guadalupe Monroy records the event as her brother Rafael related it to her. Monroy Mera, "Como llegó el evangelio," 6.

46. Rafael Monroy would have owned either the 1865 or the 1909 version of the Cipriano de Valera Spanish version of the Bible, frequently also known as the Reina-Valera translation, which was prepared for the then-blossoming Protestant movements in Spanish-speaking countries and widely regarded as the Spanish equivalent of the King James Version in English. An informative discussion that places Valera's enormous work in historical context is A. Gordon Kinder, "Religious Literature as an Offensive Weapon: Cipriano de Valera's Part in England's War with Spain," *The Sixteenth Century Journal* 14, no. 2 (Summer 1988): 223–35. Some indication of Valera's far-reaching impact are the over thirty-five thousand entries retrievable from the Internet.

47. The 1886 translation of the Book of Mormon, prepared by Melitón González Trejo and James Z. Stewart, is the first complete published Spanish edition. LaMond Tullis, "El Libro de Mormón en español: la primera traducción y cómo llegó a México," 19 July 2012, http://www.sud.org.mx/el-libro-de-mormon-en-espanol. See also Eduardo Balderas, "How the Scriptures Came to Be Translated into Spanish," *Ensign*, September 1972, 29.

48. At the time, Mexico was the only Spanish-speaking country where missionaries were working, and the effort to create rough-text Spanish hymnals took place entirely there. In 1907, missionaries had produced a twelve-hymn forerunner to the referenced 1912 version. An extensive and heavily documented treatise on this subject is John-Charles Duffy and Hugo Olaiz, "Correlated Praise: The Development of the Spanish Hymnal," *Dialogue: A Journal of Mormon Thought* 35, no. 2 (Summer 2002): 89–113. Analogously, US Mormons had produced many "frontier poets" who wrote their poetry intending it to be set to music scores of established hymns or songs. An example is Mary Brown Henry. LaMond Tullis, *A Search for Place: Eight Generations of Henrys and the Settlement of Utah's Uintah Basin* (Spring City, UT: Piñon Hills Publishing, 2010), 212–13.

49. Sixty-eight English editions have been published of Parley P. Pratt, *A Voice of Warning and Instruction to All People; or, an Introduction to the Faith and Doctrine of the Church of Jesus Christ of Latter-day Saints* (Salt Lake City: Deseret News, 1874). The first Spanish edition was prepared and published in Mexico in 1880. Tullis, "La misión del Apóstol Moses Thatcher," 8, 14n20.

50. Portions of the Doctrine and Covenants were published in Spanish in the early 1930s as *Revelación de los últimos días*. The entire Doctrine and Covenants was not published in Spanish until 1948, the same year that the Pearl of Great Price was also published. Thus, not until the mid-twentieth century did the Church's entire canonical works become available to Spanish-speaking members. See Eduardo Balderas, "How the Scriptures Came to Be Translated into Spanish," *Ensign*, September 1972, 29.
51. By 1939, English speakers had access to John A. Widstoe's authorized work that was revised in 1954 and published as *Priesthood and Church Government in the Church of Jesus Christ of Latter-day Saints* (Salt Lake City: Deseret Book, 1954). It was heavily abridged in 1956 and published in pamphlet form as "Melchizedek Priesthood Handbook." Understandably, as late as 1956, there still were no manuals in Spanish dealing with priesthood administration, and the Doctrine and Covenants had been available only since 1948. In desperation, in preparing leadership-training modules for the Saints in Central America in 1956, LaMond Tullis, then serving as first counselor to Edgar L. Wagner in the Central American Mission presidency, unskillfully translated the Melchizedek Priesthood Handbook, printed a hundred copies on the office mimeograph, and circulated them to priesthood leaders throughout the mission.
52. Monroy Mera, "Como llegó el evangelio," 6.
53. Monroy Mera, "Como llegó el evangelio," 6–7.
54. The Sunday visit took place on 9 November 1913. Monroy Mera, "Como llegó el evangelio," 7.
55. "All of these letters dealt solely with the beautiful knowledge of the Gospel that we had accepted and our hope in a life hereafter." (*Todas estas cartas se relacionaban únicamente al hermoso conocimiento del Evangelio que habíamos aceptado y de la esperanza en la vida venidera.*) Monroy Mera, "Como llegó el evangelio," 7.
56. Monroy Mera, "Como llegó el evangelio," 7. See also Grover, "Execution in Mexico," 16.
57. The Pérez name figures ubiquitously in the Monroy family connections. The records do not disclose whether Amado Pérez was part of the extended family. Monroy Mera, "Como llegó el evangelio," 8.
58. Monroy Mera, "Como llegó el evangelio," 8–9.
59. Monroy Mera, "Como llegó el evangelio," 8–9. It is unclear how these administrative tasks were undertaken and how the administrative structure was working in Mexico at the time. Pratt may have been doing all this by letter from the United States, relying on trusted people such as Isaías Juárez, who later would become the district president, to carry out the tasks under Pratt's direction.
60. Monroy Mera, "Como llegó el evangelio," 10.

61. Monroy Mera, "Como llegó el evangelio," 9.
62. The prospect of conscription (forced enlistment) in the federal army or any of the militias opposing it was terrifying. For most people the actual experience was traumatic. Women were also conscripted as fighting soldiers (and many volunteered, especially for the Zapatista militias). See Francisco Martínez Hoyos, "El Vientre de los Ejercitos," in *Breve Historia de la Revolución Mexicana* (Madrid: Ediciones Nowtilus, S. L., 2015). Rural women in the Yucatán organized themselves into bands to forcefully resist the conscription of their men. See Allen Wells and Gilbert M. Joseph, *Elite Politics and Rural Insurgency in Yucatán, 1876–1915* (Stanford, CA: Stanford University Press, 1996), 242.
63. Monroy Mera, "Como llegó el evangelio," 10. Following advice to stay neutral at such times certainly points out the unintended real-world consequences. At this time, except perhaps in the state of Morelos, most Church members appear to have been in favor of the government (the Carrancistas) in whatever permutation rather than preferring the Zapatistas or Villistas, whether in coalition with each other at any given moment or not. An uncharitable observation would be that the presidents of Ixtacalco and San Pedro Mártir saw Rafael Monroy less as a man who had a slow learning curve and who needed considerable help than one who could perhaps offer a place of refuge to them, their families, and perhaps other members if they struck up a relationship with him. However, there is no direct evidence to support this position. Later, Monroy would try to set up a colonization effort for such people, following the earlier pattern that Anglo members had undertaken in the states of Chihuahua and Sonora.
64. Monroy Mera, "Como llegó el evangelio," 12–14. For a treatise on what Monroy was trying to replicate, see LaMond Tullis, "Los colonizadores mormones en Chihuahua y Sonora."
65. The enduring strength of this ideology is reviewed by Nora Haenn, "The Changing and Enduring *Ejido*: A State and Regional Examination of Mexico's Land Tenure Counter-Reforms," *Land Use Policy* 23 (2006): 136–46.
66. Monroy Mera, "Como llegó el evangelio," 14.
67. Monroy Mera, "Como llegó el evangelio," 13–14.
68. Monroy Mera, "Como llegó el evangelio," 24.
69. Monroy Mera, "Como llegó el evangelio," 11.
70. Monroy Mera, "Como llegó el evangelio," 11.
71. Grover, "Executions in Mexico," 14.
72. Monroy Mera, "Como llegó el evangelio," 12.

3

PRELUDE TO THE MARTYRDOMS

The Monroys' new religion was a startling viral introduction into the settled Catholic ambience of San Marcos, disturbing the village's "homeostatic equilibrium"[1] and threatening to undo age-old patterns of social relations and political arrangements that ordered not only who got what but also who gave the orders and who obeyed and for what reasons. Unlike in San Pedro Mártir—and perhaps Ixtacalco and several of the villages nesting at the base of the massive, picturesque, and anciently symbolic volcano Popocatépetl in central Mexico (where Mormonism took early root in the late nineteenth century)—Protestant versions of Christianity had not made a significant impact in San Marcos, had not, in a sense, "prepared the way."[2] Thus, in San Marcos, Mormonism presented itself not only as a social irritant but also as a first, startling nonindigenous doctrinal competitor to Catholicism. In time, some of the village folk considered it a cancer they had to excise in order to avoid God's calamitous judgment on the land. How else to do it but force the sinners to repent or, failing that, push them out? Or even kill them?

Thus, Mormonism's presence in San Marcos and the increasing numbers of people embracing it merited "persecution." These two factors—the new religion and persecution—not only isolated the early members socially but also made them vulnerable within Mexico's frequently ad hoc arrangements for maintaining social order.

Four additional factors that contributed to the martyrdoms and their aftermath are also worthy of note: (1) The early members' association with foreigners, especially Americans, such as the missionaries and the Tolteca cement factory's expatriate worker team, further raised suspicions about whether the members were loyal to Mexico during the upheaval of the civil war. (2) Fueled by rampant rumormongering, the excesses of the civil war itself strained the boundaries of social restraint in San Marcos. (3) The conspicuous position of the Monroys as a relatively well-off family invited Zapatista antipathy. (4) One rabid pro-Catholic Zapatista officer commanded soldiers to assemble a firing squad that putatively legitimized a malevolent deed.

These six factors—the new religion, subsequent persecution, association with Americans, the civil war, the Monroy's economic position, a Zapatista commander's decision—largely explain the martyrdoms in San Marcos.[3]

THE VOLCANIC PERSECUTION BEGINS

Why do people habitually dislike, if not hate and abhor, one another across boundaries of race, ethnicity, nationality, region, clan, tribe, families, religion, politics, and many other social affiliations? Is the human genome hardwired this way? On the other hand, do opinion makers simply ignite us, and we then respond to their rumormongering? By demeaning another, do we embrace the attendant revulsion and fear that play on our insecurities, inferiorities, or objective conditions of vulnerability to make us feel better if not more protected? Does "whipping up hysteria" serve to enhance a negative solidarity of a people, for whatever reason?

Christ certainly railed against these age-old problems. Most Christian faiths at least pay lip service to his teachings on love, tolerance, and a prescribed goodwill of humankind.[4] The enduring problem is that many steeped-in-the-mire bigots emboldened by ignorance and prejudice who self-attest to their own religiosity may attend church for a lifetime but never internalize a Christian or any other like-minded religious sermon. Mobocracy is one result. It has produced millennia of social heartaches.[5]

The Saints in San Marcos gradually began to feel a sadness of loss from prejudice and persecution, ultimately punctuated by the martyrdoms. Yet, in Jesusita's defiant words, most of the members firmly staked out their position: "Our trials have been great, but so also has our faith and we will not become faint hearted."[6]

At first, the early members thought they could have both their new faith and their old friends and certainly retain the loving embrace of their nonmember extended families. For a while, it worked that way. For example, the Monroy daughters liked to host parties, and in early March 1914, nine months following their baptisms, they invited a number of friends to their store to plan a big splash for the village's social scene. At their planning session they chatted about music, drama, and organizing a literary soirée for later in the month that would honor the culturally significant "Name Day" (*onomástico*)[7] of Benito Juárez, the *Benemérito de las Américas*. Juárez was Mexico's only indigenous and arguably best president (1861–72) and was one for whom in the mid-1880s the LDS Church's crown colony in Chihuahua and in 1964 its then-flagship school in Mexico City were named.[8]

Faithful to their plans, on 21 March the planners held a lively public party in the Monroy compound that attracted the participation of numerous young people and even some of their educational mentors. Perhaps the attendees were among the village's rebellious souls. Traditional, established opinion makers were annoyed, if not jealous, and even spoke of having the participants arrested.

Under this social pressure, little by little even the presumably rebellious youth who fraternized with the Monroys gradually withdrew, leaving

Photo 10. Benito Juárez, president of Mexico from 1861 to 1872. Of Zapotec origin in Oaxaca, Juárez was arguably Mexico's best president and certainly its most beloved. Courtesy of Google Images.

the family isolated from its friends.⁹ Then persecution became severe.¹⁰ Several people, including Jesusita, warned Rafael to get out of San Marcos to save his life, because of the venomous language in the village and the death threats coming his way. He declined, saying, "Why would anyone kill me if I have done no harm to them? However, if God desires, then let it be done according to Him who is all powerful."¹¹

Some of the Mormon civil-war refugees arriving in San Marcos for resettlement posed a problem. It was hard to abandon what once were relatively stable circumstances for the rigors of starting life over as refugees, even in a safe environment. For some of the evacuees, the severities and uncertainties posed serious psychological and emotional adjustments. For a few, it exceeded their capacity to cope. Among other things, some of the women were not accustomed to hand grinding their own corn into meal for tortillas, as was then required in San Marcos, and some of the men could not stand up to the rigors of the manual-labor employment that Monroy had offered them on his ranch.¹² The male Rodríguez adults—Ixtacalco branch president Francisco Rodríguez and his family—soon left for what they thought would be paid employment as musicians with the progovernment Carrancista army then in control of Tula. As of April 1915, no one among the Mormons in San Marcos had heard from them again. This "Mormon connection" with the Carrancistas and the resulting implied affiliation with the Americans prompted some anti-Carrancista opinion makers in Tula to further spread scandalous views about the Mormons, which became a serious issue when within three months the fanatically pro-Catholic Zapatistas took over the region by military force.

After the martyrdoms, Jesusita was desperate to leave San Marcos and remove her family from the prejudice and persecution that had fallen upon them. She prayed fervently to the Lord for guidance on how "to leave these ungrateful people who [have] rejected the divine light."¹³

ANTI-AMERICAN HYSTERIA

Americans had a bad reputation in Mexico. Mexican president Porfirio Díaz and his close-knit advisors, the *científicos*, had sold out the country to them and other foreigners, a fact that for years fueled a prevalent hatred for Americans, particularly among the Zapatistas. One analysis showed that "U.S. citizens had controlling interest in 75 percent of the mines, 72 percent of the metallurgy industry, 68 percent of the rubber companies, and 58 percent of the petroleum industry. Combined foreign interests controlled 80 percent of all major Mexican industries."[14] Mexico had lost Texas to the Americans in 1836.[15] They had seen present-day California, New Mexico, Nevada, and Utah ripped off in 1848 at the Treaty of Guadalupe Hidalgo[16] and had, by believable rumor and concrete fact, experienced the nearly constant meddling of the United States in its internal affairs, particularly during 1910–13 under US ambassador Henry Lane Wilson.[17]

In the latter part of April 1914, a rumor, unfortunately founded on verifiable facts, quickly reached San Marcos and flashed through the village: the Americans were tinkering with Mexico's internal politics—again—and this time at the level of the presidency itself. The "negative solidarity" this created brought people of all political stripes together in one cause, which was to defend their country against foreign meddling, whether French, American, British, or German, in its corporate and military guises. Tula's chief political officer and finance administrator gathered a large crowd from the municipal capital, San Marcos, and other surrounding towns and led a march on the American-owned Tolteca cement factory. He had admonished the demonstrators to arm themselves with sticks and stones. The emotions were so high that even women and children demonstrated against Americans living in Mexico, fearing they would be a "fifth column" of advance spies to guide another invading US army into their country. The mob had come to lynch the British superintendent, who had wisely left the place the day before.[18]

At the time, the United States had indeed planned an imminent invasion of Mexico at Veracruz, which the US Marines ultimately occupied in late April 1914.[19] The invasion was a strike against Victoriano Huerta, the insurgent who, with the collusion of the cashiered US ambassador Henry Lane Wilson, had overthrown Francisco Madero, ordered his assassination, and taken the Mexican presidency illegitimately for himself.

The US presidency had just transitioned from Howard Taft to Woodrow Wilson. Wilson was appalled at what Taft's administration had been up to in Mexico and sought to undo it by supporting Venustiano Carranza's constitutionalist army at Veracruz. Everything was complicated. Although most Mexicans grew to hate Huerta, they hated the meddling Americans more.[20] An oft-quoted phrase from the dictator Porfirio Díaz gained additional traction:

"Poor Mexico, so far from God, so close to the United States" (*Pobre México, tan lejos de Dios, tan cerca a los Estados Unidos*).

The general hysteria and the protest at the Tolteca cement factory mobilized the local police, who were easily politicized by one thing or another. The mob had failed to get the superintendent but decided to ambush Roy Van McVey, a member of the factory's foreign-worker team, at his home in nearby San Miguel. However, the American McVey, who was married to Jesusita's daughter Natalia, had also fortunately fled the previous day, abandoning his house to the care of his Mexican wife and his store to Casimiro Gutiérrez, the recent Mormon refugee from Toluca.[21]

The police predictably came, ransacked the house and store, found a rifle that McVey had for personal protection, and made the usual threats. Small wonder that Natalia, with her home and store in shambles, fled to find her husband, probably by then somewhere in Mexico City at a place they had agreed upon, and on 20 May 1914, the two departed for Veracruz.[22] After a couple of months, Jesusita traveled to the port city to retrieve her unhappy daughter, leaving McVey in place for a while "until political matters improved in the country."[23] They did not mend, particularly for Americans. Sometime later, McVey returned to his haunts in the United States and did not see his wife again for many months until she went to be with him in Texas for a time. Later, traveling separately, they both eventually returned to Mexico.

In the meantime, the citizens of San Miguel who not only hated Americans but also the Mexican Mormons who fraternized with them threatened Casimiro's

Photo 11. Henry Lane Wilson, US ambassador to Mexico from 1909 to 1913. Courtesy of Google Images.

life. He fled with his family to Tepeji, which left the McVey compound without any occupants. Once in control of the area, the Zapatistas immediately sacked the place again and carted off anything left of value they could find.[24]

Hate born of fear is a powerful motivator of evil causes. Everything for an attack on the Mormons was in place in the municipality of Tula, Hidalgo, needing only the breakdown of civil order and an execution command from a drunken, and perhaps otherwise psychologically unstable, rabidly Catholic Zapatista military commander.

THE REVOLUTION REACHES SAN MARCOS

Soon the revolution's calamity, with its accompanying breakdown of traditional social and political order, fell upon San Marcos and the Monroy family. As elsewhere in Mexico, during this fratricidal conflict, cities, towns, and villages frequently became dueling grounds, as warring factions alternated control while each sought retribution from enemies, real or alleged. Opportunists took advantage of the anarchy to settle personal, political, and religious scores; repudiate debts; sack stores and homes; and sometimes dishonor their female occupants. It was a sad time everywhere in Mexico.

Zapatistas were at war with wealthy landowners and even Mexico's small middle class. Emerging out of the state of Morelos after sundry alliances to help topple the old dictator Porfirio Díaz, they found their pursuit of land reform and freedom denied under the new regime of Francisco Madero, with whom they had been in an anti-Díaz alliance. In a dizzying array of subsequent temporary alliances, the Zapatistas returned to the battlefield to seek a place for Mexico's rural poor in what they hoped would become a fair and justly renovated state.

Emiliano Zapata, the founder of the Zapatista movement, eventually codified his demands in the *Plan de Ayala*. The fifteen terse main points denounced former ally Francisco Madero for his betrayal of the Zapatistas as soon as he became president and demanded immediate implementation of the land reform for which they had fought Díaz and his aristocrats. In sum, the *Plan* insisted on the restoration to their respective communities of all communal indigenous lands stolen by fraud or outright thievery under the old dictator. Beyond, one-third of the area of large plantations that a single individual or family owned was subject to nationalization and thereafter distribution to poor farmers. Those resisting would have the other two-thirds of their land confiscated as well.²⁵ Large-scale foreign and national landowners' initial irascibility quickly morphed into terror.

The Zapatistas were radically Catholic and fiercely xenophobic, despising foreigners for their sometimes-gratuitous attacks on their church as well as the social and economic injustices that fueled their rebellion. They detested any Mexican who associated with outsiders, and they radically opposed anyone preaching an alien religion.²⁶ Small wonder the Americans feared the revolutionary Zapatistas as, indeed, apparently did most Mexican Mormons in Hidalgo (but not in Morelos), who were anxious about their religious liberties.²⁷ Unfortunately for Mormons, in 1915, San Marcos briefly came under Zapatista military control.²⁸

Just prior to the Villista-Zapatista victory in Tula and their troops' occupation of San Marcos, the Carrancistas had been in control there. As an occupying force, they had given appropriate guarantees to the civilian population. Nevertheless, they had made a rabid anti-Catholic statement by shelling some of the religious buildings, setting up their officers' quarters in habitations commandeered from the local clergy, and taking prisoner many Catholic priests.²⁹ The Zapatistas found all this to be both morally and mortally offensive,³⁰ and they and their partisans would spare no Carrancista, no matter the cost. No wonder the Carrancista troops had retreated in terror in the face of the Villista-Zapatista alliance that was overwhelming them in Tula Hidalgo and its environs. Fittingly, many Carrancista partisans from the area bolted into the mountains.

Andrés Reyes, a neighbor and one of San Marcos's Zapatista partisans, informed the Zapatistas that Monroy routinely provisioned the Carrancista soldiers who previously had occupied the town and whom every Zapatista was sworn to kill. He also spread a profoundly false and damaging accusation that Monroy was a Carrancista officer and had a secret arms cache in his mother's store.³¹ Later, some people thought this malicious blathering was retribution for the Monroys having become Mormons.³² The religious question was never far from people's minds.

The accusation that Monroy was a Carrancista officer was nothing more than grist circulating in the anti-Mormon rumor mill in San Marcos at the time, perhaps resulting from a few times when Monroy did indeed fraternize with Carrancista officers. However, the accusation that he was an armed combatant was patently false. There is no evidence to support such a charge and, beyond, Monroy—being a dyed-in-the-wool Mormon leader—would have assiduously followed President Rey L. Pratt's dictum: "Remain neutral. Do not take sides in the Revolution." Moreover, had Monroy been a Carrancista officer, it is unlikely that a weeping, grieving mother whose six sons the Carrancistas had killed would have come to him seeking solace and spiritual comfort.[33] On this pastoral count, it is much more likely that a few villagers viewed Monroy as an approachable religious figure during times when a traditional Catholic priest may not have been.

The Monroys did have a store well stocked with basic provisions. No matter how much the family may have preferred the Carrancistas to the Zapatistas in the fight to rule Mexico, at a local level they were in a difficult situation. Whichever faction "controlled the plaza" obviously had its privileges, in particular because the Carrancistas and Villistas (and therefore the Zapatistas when in an alliance) had their own printed currency, otherwise worthless except at the barrel of a gun or the fear of confronting one.

Not accepting an occupying army's uniquely designed currency as legal tender was tantamount to declaring oneself a partisan of the opposing side (with all the attendant consequences).[34] As long as the Carrancistas "held the plaza" in Tula and the surrounding areas, like San Marcos, the Monroys accepted their currency, however reluctantly. They had no choice. They sold them food, for which they received payment in proprietary currency that would be worthless the second the troops left town. Following ancient traditions and necessities, proprietary currency was a thinly disguised way for an invading army to loot the land. It went further. A number of people hurried to the Monroy store to pay their accounts in worthless currency.[35] Many people were looking for whatever advantage they could get.

There was one perhaps avoidable fraternizing excess. Rafael entertained Carrancista officers in his family's compound, providing meals for them on several occasions.[36] Did he in some way feel forced to extend that social courtesy? Was he obligated, or just found it socially useful, to be visibly friendly, as was the whole Monroy family, with the Carrancista captain Pedro González? Was Monroy simply a closet partisan, hoping that the Carrancistas would prevail in the civil war?[37] Was there some other extenuating circumstance? We do not know.

People held Monroy's fraternizing with Carrancista officers against him, which also occasioned the arrest of his sister Guadalupe, who had returned to San Miguel to try to retrieve some gold coins that her sibling Natalia had securely hidden in her now-sacked home and store. Zapatistas held Guadalupe prisoner for three days.[38] "Guilt by association" is an ancient ploy justifying all kinds of heinous acts.

Additionally, for three months Rafael and his workers had not been able to carry out any ranching activities at El Godo. It was too dangerous even though Rafael had given to both Carrancista and Zapatista forces "help yourself" signals for his livestock.[39] All the Monroys and some of their employees had taken refuge in the central Monroy compound in San Marcos. While there, someone invited Rafael to join the Zapatistas, thereby offering him a way to get out of a difficult situation. He declined, which seemed to mark him[40] and ultimately foreshadowed his execution, as we shall see in the next chapter.

NOTES

1. The early benchmark that solidified the biological concept of *homeostasis* to social systems, now subsumed in cybernetics subfields, is Chalmers Johnson, *Revolutionary Change*, 2nd ed. (Stanford, CA: Stanford University Press, 1982), especially 55–60.
2. Monroy Mera, "Como llegó el evangelio," 108.
3. In his superb study of the executions, Mark Grover, "Executions in Mexico," 8, summarizes five factors: (1) Rafael Monroy and Vicente Morales rejected Catholicism at a time when Zapatistas were rabidly pro-Catholic; (2) Monroy's middle-class status when Zapatistas were preaching "Liberty or Death"; (3) Rafael's consorting with Americans (members and nonmembers); (4) Rafael's imputed support of the Carrancistas; and (5) the fact that Zapatistas took out their wrath indiscriminately on medium-scale merchants.
4. As for The Church of Jesus Christ of Latter-day Saints, one impressive statement is from then-Apostle and later–Church president Howard W. Hunter in his address in the October 1991 general conference of the Church, just after the Cold War had ended. President Hunter stated, "This is a message of life and love that strikes squarely against all stifling traditions based on race, language, economic or political standing, educational rank, or cultural background, for we are all of the same spiritual descent.... We have a divine pedigree; every person is a spiritual child of God." A decade and a half earlier Brigham Young University sponsored a symposium on internationalizing the Church and the need for such a philosophy. See F. LaMond Tullis, ed., *Mormonism: A Faith for All Cultures* (Provo, UT: Brigham Young University Press, 1978).
5. Nearly 2.5 million works treating the causes, consequences, and applications of persecution emerge from a simple search on the Internet. One in particular, a seminal treatise laying out the wretched consequences of denying religious freedom through official proscription as well as societal prejudice, is Brian J. Grim, *The Price of Freedom*

Denied: Religious Persecution and Conflict in the Twenty-first Century (New York: Cambridge University Press, 2011).
6. "Carta de Jesús M. Vda. de Monroy," 8–9, with commentary by Hugo Montoya Monroy, https://sites.google.com/site/linajemonroy/rafael-monroy-mera/carta-de-jesus-m-vda-de-monroy. (*Grandes han sido las tribulaciones pero también grande es nuestra fe y no desmayamos.*)
7. Name days originated in lists of holidays set aside to celebrate saints and martyrs as established by the Catholic Church. It has been a tradition in Catholic countries since the Middle Ages. Various countries have differing lists. See *Wikipedia*, s.v. "Name Day," https://en.wikipedia.org/wiki/Name_day.
8. Monroy Mera, "Como llegó el evangelio," 9. Benito Juárez's presidency and his *Reforma* represented a temporary pause in the power of traditional forces that supported centralized autocracy and economic exploitation of the lower class. Juárez was a founder of Free Masonry in Mexico and as such held strong anticlerical, antitheocratic views that riled the Catholic Church. It is unclear if the party planners, in choosing to celebrate his patron-saint day, were deliberately sticking a spine in the eyes of local clerics and their most rabid supporters. Today, Mexicans generally view Juárez as a national hero. A succinct summary is "Benito Juárez," *Encyclopedia of World Biography*, 2nd ed. (Detroit: Gale Group, 2004).
9. Monroy Mera, "Como llegó el evangelio," 9. (*Aún así muchos de estos jóvenes se fueron retirando poco a poco y la familia quedó más aislada de sus amistades.*)
10. From the perspective of Jesusita and her daughters, the persecution became widespread and unremitting. A later family member considered that among the poor and middling people in San Marcos and the administrators of the cement factory, the Monroys always had friends. Three or four influential families in their extended numbers were behind all the malice. (*Los Monroy tenían muchas amistades entre la gente pobre y de mediana clase y del gerente de la fábrica de cemento. Pero hubo tres o cuatro familias influyentes que declararon cargos en contra de Monroy.*) Daniel Montoya Gutiérrez in "Martirio en México," 6. However, given the configuration of power and prestige in San Marcos, these families' influence would have far exceeded the relative strength of their numbers, which accounts for the pervasiveness of the persecution that the Monroys felt.
11. Monroy Mera, "Como llegó el evangelio," 32.
12. Monroy Mera, "Como llegó el evangelio," 13–14.
13. Monroy Mera, "Como llegó el evangelio," 28. (*Y con todo el fervor de nuestro ser rogábamos [al Señor] iluminara nuestra mente para salir de este pueblo ingrata que rechazaba la luz divina.*)

14. Ramón Eduardo Ruíz, *The Great Rebellion: Mexico, 1905–1924* (New York: W. W. Norton, 1980), 103.
15. For differing perspectives, some from the participants themselves, see the following: Richard G. Santos, *Santa Anna's Campaign against Texas, 1835–1836*, rev. 2nd ed. (Salisbury, NC: Documentary Publications, 1981), which features the field commands issued to Major General Vicente Filisola; Antonio López de Santa Anna, *The Mexican Side of the Texas Revolution, 1836*, trans. with notes by Carlos E. Castañeda and illustrations by Carol Rogers and Jim Box (Austin, TX: Graphic Ideas, 1970); and Alwyn Barr, *Texans in Revolt: The Battle for San Antonio, 1835* (Austin: University of Texas Press, 1990). Spanish readers will capture the poignancy of Mexicans' feelings about this war in Francisco Martín Moreno, *México mutilado* (México City: Editorial Santillana, 2004).
16. The treaty was officially entitled the *Treaty of Peace, Friendship, Limits and Settlement between the United States of America and the Mexican Republic*. A good discussion is by Richard Griswold del Castillo, *The Treaty of Guadalupe Hidalgo: A Legacy of Conflict* (Norman: University of Oklahoma Press, 1990). Spanish readers who are interested in seeing how the war played out in Mexico's northeast in and around Tamaulipas should read Leticia Dunay García Martínez, "Una guerra inevitable: el noreste de Tamaulipas frente a los Estados Unidos, 1840–1849" (master's thesis, El Colegio de San Luis, A. C., 2013).
17. See the discussion about Henry Lane Wilson in note 18, chapter 2.
18. Monroy Mera, "Como llegó el evangelio," 10.
19. Jack Sweetman, *The Landing at Veracruz: 1914* (Annapolis, MD: Naval Institute Press, 1968). See also the various articles by Mexican authors in *La invasion a Veracruz de 1914: enfoques multidisciplinarios* (Mexico City: Secretaría de Marina-Armada de México, Secretaría de Educación Pública, Instituto Nacional de Estudios Históricos de las Revoluciones de México, 2015).
20. Rey L. Pratt, "Un mártir de los últimos días," 2, the Monroy family's translation of Pratt's "A Latter-Day Martyr," *Improvement Era* (June 1918), 720–26, https://sites.google.com/site/linaje monroy/rafael-monroy-mera/un-martir-de-los-ultimos-dias.
21. "Carta de Jesús M. Vda. de Monroy," 4.
22. Rafael Monroy in San Marcos to Elder W. Ernest Young in Tucson, Arizona, ca. June 2015, read by José Luis Montoya Monroy at a Monroy descendants' reunion in Salt Lake City, 28 December 2006.
23. Monroy Mera, "Como llegó el evangelio," 11 (*mientras mejoraban las cosas políticas del país*).

24. "Carta de Jesús M. Vda. de Monroy," 8. Hugo Montoya Monroy adds the following: "Natalia and her husband had hidden a large amount of their incomes in the house in the form of several gold coins. In that time, the gold coins—*hidalgos*—were issued by the National Bank in commemoration of the 100th anniversary of Mexican Independence [from Spain]. Guadalupe made a courageous decision to go to San Miguel in order to retrieve this treasure. She was imprisoned by the Zapatistas. When she was released she recovered the hidden treasure for her sister."
25. Christopher Minster, "Emiliano Zapata and The Plan of Ayala," Thought Co., http://latinamericanhistory.about.com/od/thehistoryofmexico/p/planofayala.htm. Also, Frank McLynn, *Villa and Zapata: A History of the Mexican Revolution* (New York: Carroll and Graf, 2000); and Pito Ulloa Ortiz, "La lucha armada" in *Historia general de México*, ed. Daniel Cosío Villegas et al. (Mexico City: El Colegio de México, 1976), 757–821. As indicated earlier, the "gold standard" on this subject is still John Womak, *Zapata and the Mexican Revolution*.
26. In addition to John Womak, *Zapata and the Mexican Revolution*, cited previously, helpful interpretations may also be found in Michael J. Gonzales, *The Mexican Revolution: 1910–1940* (Albuquerque: University of New Mexico Press, 2002); Andrés Reséndez Fuentes, "Battleground Women: Soldaderas and Female Soldiers in the Mexican Revolution," *Americas* 51, no. 4 (April 1995); and Frank McLynn, *Villa and Zapata: A History of the Mexican Revolution* (New York: Carroll and Graf, 2000).
27. Moroni Spencer Hernández de Olarte links some members of the LDS Church, if not the Church itself, with the Zapatista movement in the state of Morelos. Bradley Hill brought this to my attention in a critique of an earlier version of this monograph.
28. Monroy Mera, "Como llegó el evangelio," 24. We do not know the motivation for the Zapatistas' being in Hidalgo, outside their normal field of operations, specifically in the municipality of Tula and thereafter in San Marcos. This apparent departure may have been related to their temporary alliance with Pancho Villa's forces that were operating in the area and the Zapatistas' reciprocating in some kind of tit-for-tat military cooperation. In any event, during this period, local observers noted the fierce battles occurring between the Carrancistas and Villistas, with Zapatista troops probably loosely organized under the Villista command structure.
29. The anti-Catholic policies of the Carrancistas were felt elsewhere in Mexico also. Reynaldo Rojo Mendoza, "The Church-State Conflict in Mexico from the Mexican Revolution to the Cristero Rebellion," *Proceedings of the Pacific Coast Council on Latin American Studies* 23 (2006): 76–96.
30. Monroy Mera, "Como llegó el evangelio," 19.

31. Grover, "Execution in Mexico," 15.
32. One of the best treatments of the episodes during Monroy's last week of life is Grover's "Execution in Mexico," 6–30. I have drawn from his study for this section of the paper.
33. Monroy Mera, "Como llegó el evangelio," 23.
34. There were two types of money used alternatingly in San Marcos, one issued by the Carrancistas, the other by the Villistas. Food, especially corn (maize), was scarce, and people did not want to sell what they had but, in any event, were loath to have one faction's currency on hand when another "took the plaza." Monroy Mera, "Como llegó el evangelio," 30. Seven pictures of currency in use during the revolution, issued by various bands and putative legal entities, may be seen at "Currency of the Mexican Revolution," Latin American Studies, http://www.latinamericanstudies.org/revolutionary-currency.htm. A catalog with over two hundred entries, many with pictures, is available at "Mexico Banknotes of Revolution 1910–1917," World Paper Money Catalog and History, http://www.atsnotes.com/catalog/banknotes/mexico-revolution.html.
35. Monroy Mera, "Como llegó el evangelio," 30–31.
36. Mark L. Grover cites Daniel Montoya Gutiérrez, who worked for Rafael Monroy, as indicating that Carrancista officers "had eaten at the Monroy home several times and it was this familiarity with the Carrancistas that attracted the attention of the town and resulted in the accusation." See Grover, "Execution in Mexico," 2.
37. Before and during the Carrancista occupation of Tula, Rafael Monroy appears to have been an accorded municipal authority of some kind, perhaps continuing his service in the development of water irrigation systems in the region or even from his earlier appointment as a commander in the Tula police force. In any event, he was a weekly participant in municipal council meetings. The incessant association with the Carrancista occupiers in this and related activities would have turned the rumor-mongering gristmill against the Monroys. That, coupled with Rafael's "betrayal" by joining the Mormons, would have accelerated it. Monroy Mera, "Como llegó el evangelio," 23–24.
38. Monroy Mera, "Como llegó el evangelio," 21–22.
39. Monroy Mera, "Como llegó el evangelio," 23.
40. Monroy Mera, "Como llegó el evangelio," 32.

4

THE EXECUTIONS

The Zapatistas justified the executions by taking Reyes's rumormongering as established fact. "Rumor equaling fact" is an ancient ploy of the human mind and is even used today for partisans' advantage. The Zapatistas needed weapons, particularly ammunition. Reyes and other locals who wished the Monroys harm told stories that resonated well. Certainly, the Monroys' economic condition presented evidence of their being able to afford a cache, had they wanted one. Besides, they had been fraternizing with the Carrancistas and the Americans who were supporting them, and both had the wherewithal to pay for a hidden cache. The task was to extract a confession or, failing that, to dismantle the store and find the cache anyway.

Vicente Morales had been building an adobe-block partition in the store. Being more specific about his accusation, Andrés Reyes suggested the weapons cache was there, somehow hidden by the partition. Zapatista soldiers extracted Monroy from his family compound and questioned him vigorously. He and Morales denied the accusation, and Guadalupe stoutly defended both, telling the soldiers to tear the store down block by block if they did not believe her.[1] They partially obliged, ransacking the store, not finding their target but hauling off whatever they could conveniently carry.

ARRESTS AND TORTURE

Shortly thereafter, Zapatista soldiers detained Morales, Monroy, and Monroy's three sisters, Natalia, Jovita, and Guadalupe. Along with others of San Marcos's more well-to-do citizens, the soldiers held them in detention in a local home commandeered as an improvised prison. The high security walls, topped with broken glass embedded in concrete, that economically secure people characteristically constructed to keep out hooligans and thugs could also keep people in.

Despite dismantling the Monroy store and finding nothing, the Zapatistas were so convinced that the hidden arms cache existed somewhere that they pulled Monroy out of their makeshift prison and further pressured him into disclosing the whereabouts of his secreted munitions. The Zapatistas were on the cusp of desperation, it appears, because they were running short of ammunition. Force evolved into torture. Monroy could truthfully say only that he knew of no arms. Unlike his brother-in-law McVey, he did not even possess a rifle for personal protection or for use on his ranch.

To stop the torture, as so many others wracked with unbearable pain in similar situations have done, Monroy could have tendered a false confession. However, its falsity would quickly be verified and his personal condition thereby made worse. In misery and anguish, he brought up his sacred texts, telling the soldiers again that the only arms he had were his Bible and Book of Mormon and offered to give copies to them. The soldiers were rabid but mostly ignorant defenders of traditional Catholicism whom the Carrancistas had acutely offended by violating their churches. With many Zapatista combatants not blessed with even an ability to read or write, Monroy's offer, at best, went unnoticed. At worst, it inflamed the soldiers more. They returned Rafael to their makeshift prison and rethought their options.[2]

FURTHER DEPREDATIONS

Unconvinced that Monroy was being truthful, Zapatista officers sent a new contingent of soldiers armed with sledgehammers to the Monroy store. The soldiers again ransacked the place, this time even knocking down partitions. They also further availed themselves of whatever they had not already destroyed or confiscated. Again finding no weapons, they moved their search to the Monroy home where a terrified Jesusita was secluded, the Zapatistas not allowing her to see her children or present evidence and witnesses (only one was willing) to counter the accusations.

The Zapatista commander, General Reyes Molina, and some of his soldiers entered the Monroy home three times before the killings and searched every room and every piece of furniture.[3] They wanted food from the kitchen as well as the arms, the ammunition, and papers proving that Rafael was a Carrancista colonel.[4] They found nothing. They told Jesusita that unless they received these things by 9:00 p.m. that very day, they would shoot Rafael.[5] Jesusita was apoplectic and consumed with anxiety and fear.

MONROY, AN INFLAMMATORY CHALLENGE TO THE ZAPATISTAS

Rafael presented an inflammatory challenge to the Zapatistas. Their methods so far had been unsuccessful in obtaining a confession or in finding the weapons through their own searches. They would try something else. From their makeshift prison, they force-marched Rafael and Vicente to a nearby large tree where they hung them to unconsciousness several times, loosening their nooses long enough each time to revive them and enquire if they were ready to confess.[6] The alleged secret cache yet remaining elusive and the day drawing on, the soldiers apparently returned Vicente to his confinement quarters but questioned and beat Rafael several more times. Frustrated in their failure to extract the information they were certain resided in the inner yet secret reaches of Rafael's mind, they abruptly returned him to be with his incarcerated siblings and their friend Vicente in the Zapatista "House of Confinement."[7]

In the early evening of 17 July 1915, Jesusita tried once more to gain access to the prison house as she brought an evening meal to Vicente and her children. Without someone to bring meals, the prisoners did not eat—at least not often. As she passed by a kitchen window, Rafael and Guadalupe happened to be looking out. Guadalupe called out to her in a sobbing voice: "Mother! You are as a feather in the wind, alone, dragged along by your pain. All of your children are prisoners."[8] Not permitted to enter, Jesusita left the food and returned to her home.

Rafael was distraught, perhaps realizing that his end was near. Usually serene in the confidence of his innocence but now perhaps feeling that the Lord would not extricate him from this predicament, he pulled a handkerchief from his pocket and wiped the tears from his eyes. Still, he refused to be angry, refused to curse his tormentors, and refused to relinquish the firm foundation of his faith.[9] He had told the mother whose six sons the Carrancistas had murdered that she would eventually see justice but that it might well have to await the next life. Rafael Monroy was a firm believer in justice and in the next life.

Before finishing their meal, the Monroys and Vicente heard the movement of soldiers and weapons outside, followed shortly by an order for Rafael and Vicente to appear at the door and accompany them. On leaving the room, Rafael called out, "Nata, come with me." Natalia stood and was going to follow him, but the guards pushed her back.[10]

THE FIRING SQUAD

Presumably on orders of the local Zapatista commandant, the "sanguinary" General Reyes Molina, the soldiers marched Rafael and Vicente a short distance away, not out of earshot, probably to the hanging tree, and lined them up to be executed by gunfire. No family members were present—the sisters were still detained, and Jesusita and perhaps Eulalia as well were back in the Monroy compound.

Later that evening, Rafael's sister Guadalupe heard a soldier say that the men were offered clemency if they would repudiate their alien religion and cease to pervert the land with its ideas. Rafael and Vicente had explained that their testimony would not allow them to deny their faith. Rafael reportedly said, "Gentlemen, I cannot renounce my religion because I know that I have made covenants and have accepted the gospel of Jesus Christ."[11] They asked to pray, a request that the executioners surprisingly allowed. The men pled with the Lord to have compassion upon their families, their unborn descendants, and even the soldiers who they said had no idea what they were doing. Afterward, Rafael stood up, folded his arms and said, "Gentlemen, I am at your service." The shots rang out. It was 17 July 1915. The civil war raged on.[12]

That even in the face of mortal consequences Monroy and Morales refused to deny their faith and repudiate their testimonies sealed their distinction as martyrs. Rafael Monroy's grave remains a hallowed place where six generations of his descendants and others, including the author, have paused to pay immense respects for the strength of character and conviction that these martyrs presented at such a dreadful moment in their short lives.

News of the executions quickly circulated among the Zapatista soldiers who were temporarily bivouacked in San Marcos but not involved in the slayings: "What did they find in the Monroy house?" "Why did they kill the bricklayer?"

The questions highlight the social-class nature of the civil war. It was hard for ordinary Zapatista soldiers to think of Rafael and Vicente as being equally worthy of execution. Rafael was relatively well educated and economically prosperous, part of an emergent rural middle class in Hidalgo—that butchery they could understand. Vicente was a bricklayer, a servant, only marginally literate, speaking rough Spanish as a second language to his native Otomí, part of Mexico's economic underclass that included more than half the population—the soldiers had trouble comprehending such a wanton killing of someone like him. The Zapatistas were fighting *for* the Vicentes of Mexico by directing their fury against the *porfiriato*, that national and international cabal that had ruled Mexico for nearly three decades and which the Zapatistas quite correctly viewed as contributing to their oppression and economic impoverishment.[13] Why execute the intended beneficiaries of Zapatista sacrifices? The soldiers wondered. Some even marveled.

Beyond speculating on the reasons for the executions, the soldiers had trouble embracing the idea that men of such disparate social standing could equally yoke themselves in a religious brotherhood the Zapatistas ill understood, if not loathed, for its foreign origins. They understood the two men to be shepherds of an emergent flock of Mormons in Hidalgo. The belief "better to put an end to this while we can" has justified martyrdoms throughout the ages, including those of Joseph and Hyrum Smith, two of Mormonism's principal founders.

The rebels' leading light, Emiliano Zapata from the state of Morelos, today a veritable national icon in Mexico, had popularized the phrases, "Land or Liberty," and "Better to die on your feet than live your whole life on your knees." All that notwithstanding, had Zapata been on the scene, he may have seen the error about to be committed in San Marcos and might have countermanded the executions that his remote commander had authorized.[14]

THE ZAPATISTA ENIGMA

However many factors a social scientist or a historian may marshal to try to account for an historical event such as martyrdom, in the end, even in mob violence, the matter usually depends on a leader's decision somewhere along the line. "Spontaneous violence" is indeed violent but hardly ever spontaneous. It can have a host of underlying causes, as we have pointed out. However, there is almost always a simple decision. Shoot or do not shoot. Marshal a mob or do not marshal a mob. Spread a rumor and inflame a population or try to calm the waters. Some identifiable individual usually makes such decisions.

San Marcos observers have posited that the executions were simply the product of a rogue firing squad devoid of significant leadership. This is likely not the case. Zapatista General Reyes Molina was definitely on the scene, and he unquestionably was giving the orders for everything else, so presumptively, he also gave orders for the executions.

How, then, can one definitively explain the decision of one man? Without a psychiatric examination, that would be quite difficult, and even with one it would perhaps be improbable. Nevertheless, the historical evidence we have suggests two important psychological ingredients tormenting Reyes Molina—unbridled anger and vindictive revenge. These two psychological factors, and perhaps others, exploded on the principal underlying disputes: the irritation that the new Mormon religion had sparked; the subsequent persecution of the new members, complete with the unremitting gossip directed against them; the Monroys' economic well-being and their association with the hated Americans; and the excesses of the civil war itself. Rampant rage and vindictive revenge were likely the triggers in Reyes Molina's tormented mind that ignited his decision to order the executions.

Aside from indigenous groups like the Tarahumaras or Rarámuris in the Copper Canyon area of northwestern Mexico,[15] the Zapatistas as a social class were among the most harmed in pre-Revolutionary Mexico. Poor, marginalized, deprived, exploited, robbed, dispossessed, suppressed, all in the name of industrialization and colossal theft under the *porfiriato*, the Zapatistas arose in Morelos and attempted to throw off their yoke. In the withering gunfire of the civil war, they gave as much as they got, and both they and their enemies suffered.

In their fury at having been denied the munitions they sought, the Zapatistas went to Monroy's ranch, El Godo, just before the executions and ran off or killed all Rafael's remaining livestock and further sacked his store there. They confiscated his bedding, his wife's treasures, and all that the couple had.[16] The following day when Jesusita, her daughters, her daughter-in-law, and her niece were trying to get their dead buried, the Zapatistas returned and ransacked the Monroy compound again—twice—searching for the cache of arms and munitions they had not yet found.[17]

If they weren't troubled at possibly having made a mistake and thinking to exonerate themselves by finding evidence to justify the executions, then the Zapatistas were frantically looking to address the scarcities in their war matèriel. In any event, they remained convinced that the cache existed. There was some urgency. Within weeks, fortified Carrancistas returned from their Pachuca stronghold and in a rout flushed out the Zapatistas from Tula and its environs.

THE EXECUTIONS

No matter the forces in control at any given moment, atrocities, injustices, and violations occurred in every town and village where the war impinged. At the national level, and in retrospect, Mexicans see the Zapatistas—particularly Emiliano Zapata—as national heroes. They sacrificed to restructure Mexico's society, economy, and, ultimately, politics to permit a strong, vibrant, and more just nation to emerge.

At Emiliano Zapata's tomb in the center of Cuautla Morelos stands an enormous and heroic statue of the rebel. With a large Mexican hat, a cape, a bandolier of cartridges strung over his shoulder, and a rifle propped in his left hand, he holds in his right hand the scroll of the *plan de ayala*. It is the plan that set forth many of Zapata's goals for his people. Zapata was one of the greatest idealists in Mexican history, and at least a few of his principles are now partially realized in a modernizing state. Overall, the nation is better for it. Tragically, along the highway of conquest, individual Zapatista commanders made decisions that snuffed out the lives of innocent people and devastated their loved ones. Rafael Monroy and Vicente Morales and their families were among them.

NOTES

1. Monroy Mera, "Como llegó el evangelio," 26.
2. Guadalupe Monroy recounts the dramatic events in Monroy Mera, "Como llegó el evangelio," 25–27.
3. Monroy Mera, "Como llegó el evangelio," 26.
4. Monroy Mera, "Como llegó el evangelio," 26.
5. Monroy Mera, "Como llegó el evangelio," 26.
6. Monroy Mera, "Como llegó el evangelio," 27.
7. We have no idea how the owners of the house were dealing with this confiscatory issue. The prisoners were pretty much confined to the kitchen, which may have reduced their being involved in any potential damage to the house. Some of the Zapatista soldiers were apparently quartered in the house, temporarily enjoying accommodations beyond their wildest dreams. The soldiers were not known for exercising restraint when they commandeered other people's property. On the kitchen issue, see Monroy Mera, "Como llegó el evangelio," 26.
8. Monroy Mera, "Como llegó el evangelio," 26. Guadalupe's anguished expression in the elegance of her own tongue: "¡*Madre mía! Vas como pluma en al aire, sola, arrastrada por tu dolor, pues todos tus hijos están presos!*"

9. Monroy Mera, "Como llegó el evangelio," 27.
10. Monroy Mera, "Como llegó el evangelio," 27.
11. "Martirio en México," 3.
12. All information about what actually went on at the killing site is derived from secondary sources, thus explaining some of the variations. Mark Grover has Rafael repeating Christ's words, "Father, forgive them, for they know not what they do" (Grover, "Execution in Mexico," 20). Rey L. Pratt concurs in this imagery (Rey L. Pratt, "A Latter-day Martyr," 723). A new history video in the Church's visitors' center in Mexico City has Rafael saying, as he raises his hands holding his scriptures, "These are the only arms I have, the arms of truth against error" (email from Hugo Montoya, 3 March 2014, 2–3). Elsewhere, Pratt quotes Monroy as saying, "I love my religion more than life itself and I cannot abandon it" ("Un mártir de los últmos días," 8.) According to the Monroy family, Rafael's words were, "Gentlemen, I cannot abandon my religion because I know that I have made covenants and accepted the Gospel of Jesus Christ" ("Martirio en México," 3).
13. Daniel Cosío Villegas, *Historia Moderna de México: El Porfiriato—Vida Económica* (México DF: Editorial Hermes, 1994; winner of the Clarence H. Haring Prize, 1996). See also Friedrich Katz, *El Porfiriato y la Revolución en la historia de México: una conversación* (México DF: ERA, 2011).
14. The "Liberation Army of the South" (*Ejército Libertador del Sur*), commonly known as the Zapatistas, had a loose command structure and was organized into small units, quite independent one from the other, rarely numbering more than one hundred men and women (females were also combatants and held command posts), each headed by a jefe or minigeneral. The unifying element was the charismatic Emiliano Zapata, who, while giving overall direction, did not issue field-level commands in small forays such as occurred in San Marcos. However, at the time of the executions the Zapatista San Marcos occupiers were in alliance with the Villista Tula occupiers, who may have issued the command.
15. The substantial literature on the Tarahumaras, ranging from *National Geographic* to university press publications, is skewed toward studies of their religion, their culture, and their phenomenal prowess as maxi-long-distance runners. An interesting introduction into their philosophy and religion is María Elena Orozco H., *Tarahumara: una antigua sociedad futura* (Chihuahua: Subcomité Especial de Cultura de COPLADE del Gobierno del Estado de Chihuahua, 1992). A university press publication from the period is Wendell Clark Bennett, *The Tarahumara, an Indian Tribe of Northern Mexico* (Chicago: University of Chicago Press, 1935), updated with the collaboration of Robert M. Zingg and published in 1976 by the Rio Grande Press in Glorietta, New Mexico.
16. Monroy Mera, "Como llegó el evangelio," 27.
17. Monroy Mera, "Como llegó el evangelio," 28.

5

THE AFTERMATH

Early on the morning of 18 July 1915, following the executions, Zapatista guards released the Monroy daughters from detention. Tearfully, they approached the execution site where numerous townspeople had already gathered to gawk at Vicente's and Rafael's prostrate bodies. As the women struggled to retrieve the cadavers to take them to the Monroy compound, none of the onlookers offered to help.

Upon arriving at their home, the women found a number of their humble sisters from the San Marcos Branch weeping and commiserating with the hysterical Jesusita.

Amidst panic-stricken anguish, Rafael's mother and the women she harbored and loved confronted the finality of the previous evening's events. It was a frightening time. Most of the men in the faith had gone into hiding, leaving the women and children nearly alone in their grief and fear.

JESUSITA REBUKES THE ZAPATISTAS

Someone suggested the women kneel in prayer to seek solace in and guidance from the Lord and to petition him for help. What to do? Where to turn? Should they flee to the United States (a thought Jesusita had entertained for some time)? How could they deal with their grief and shock? Who could or would help them? How could they protect themselves from enemies who seemed not only to be everywhere but who also had the support of a factional wing of a rebel army?

One anti-Mormon gossipmonger who had goaded the Zapatistas to violence toward the Mormons over the fictive arms cache made it seem like the community's reaction to the new religion was part of the members' ordeal—the shunning, the persecution, the sacking of Jesusita's store and Rafael's ranch, the violation of the Monroy compound, the executions, and then the new threats. Having fervently adopted a new faith, the Mormon Saints had lost the local social connections that might have moderated the Zapatistas. In addition, circumstances dictated that neither the illusory arms cache nor the Saints' faith could fade from center stage. The arms cache had become an existential commitment for the Zapatistas. Their commander presumably did not want to be wrong about the matter.

Just as the women ended their prayer for God's guidance, they heard the butt of a rifle stock beating on the thick wooden door to the Monroy compound. The women, jolted once again by an unrestrained assault on their privacy if not their safety, shrieked in alarm, rightly suspecting that the racket was not heralding a messenger from the Lord in answer to their just-uttered supplication.

A new contingent of Zapatista soldiers presented an order to search the house again—for the third and not the last time. Marching to rumormongering extremes, more locals had added to the story that the Monroys had a munitions dump in their house by accusing them of storing Carrancista uniforms and currency. (They may have been right on the currency because Jesusita's store was obligated to conduct transactions in that currency when the Carrancistas held the plaza.) Had they been denied permission to enter, the soldiers, according to their orders, said they would be obligated to imprison the occupants and enter by force.

Jesusita and her sister members appeared to believe that the soldiers had come to dishonor and perhaps kill them. However, the combatants seemed almost apologetic, courteously taking off their sombreros when entering the salon where the cadavers were laid out.[1] Jesusita reproved them. "We have nothing to give you! You have unjustly killed my son and you have refused to believe that we are not Carrancistas! The hate among the people [that you are listening to] is because we are not Catholics. We believe in the true doctrine of our Savior Jesus Christ and this is the principal cause of this libelous slander."[2]

Jesusita was on dangerous ground. Criticizing Zapatistas who held the plaza might not be forgivable. Nevertheless, her resolve was absolute as she declared that she cherished her religion more than life itself. Her fury was unrestrained.

The soldiers respectfully listened, then explored the compound—once more, they found nothing that matched the rumors giving foundation to their general's article of faith about the cache. They were beyond frustrated, perhaps fearing a dressing down from their *comandante*. The women went back to preparing the bodies and dealing with how to get them buried.

CASIMIRO GUTIÉRREZ ASSUMES LEADERSHIP

Around three in the afternoon, Casimiro Gutiérrez, one of the few brothers who had not gone into hiding (although he was keeping a low profile), appeared at the Monroy home. No doubt he was attempting to fill the leadership vacuum occasioned by the execution of the two members of the San Marcos Branch presidency. Months before, Rafael had ordained him an elder, and he may have been serving as Monroy's second counselor. He arranged for funeral services. First, however, someone had to make the caskets quickly because in those days cadavers were not embalmed. Who would make the caskets?

Regular carpenters throughout the municipality of Tula were either among those inclined to cast aspersions on the Mormon Monroys and their friends or were fearful of pitting themselves against the area's pro-Zapatista power brokers. Would the Zapatistas kill the carpenters, too? They declined all entreaties to make the coffins.[3]

Why not purchase a coffin at the mortuary? There were neither mortuaries nor ready-made, off-the-shelf coffins in the area. People took care of their own dead, which made it even more difficult to bid goodbye to loved ones without any way to bury them properly. But there was respite for the Monroys. Margarito Sánchez Villalobos, a Mormon from San Marcos who elected to stand with the women during their ordeal, and a young Mormon lad, Bernardo Villalobos, possibly Margarito's nephew, came to the rescue. They did their best to make suitable coffins for Rafael and Vicente.[4]

Despite threats circulating that people would kill any Mormon man on sight, more help soon came. Gabriel Rosales, formerly of Ixtacalco prior to the Monroys' having received his family and him in San Marcos as war refugees, came out of hiding, perhaps for the express purpose of attending the funeral. The Monroys had welcomed his family to San Marcos as war refugees when they fled from Ixtacalco. He and Casimiro Gutiérrez did the "heavy lifting" to move the bodies to the burial site over a mile away in Tula.[5] On the way to the cemetery, a few townsfolk taunted, "You knew the people hated you. Why didn't you just leave?"[6]

Despite all, Isauro Monroy went to the Tula recorder's office to register the deaths,[7] and Gabriel Rosales dedicated the grave without any interference. Except for Casimiro Gutiérrez, Gabriel Rosales, a youthful Daniel Montoya Gutiérrez, Isauro Monroy, and the coffin makers Margarito Sánchez Villalobos and Bernardo Villalobos, it appears that other male members in San Marcos stayed in hiding for the duration of the Zapatista occupation. Even then, Daniel Montoya was the only member who stayed on hand twenty-four hours a day to help the Monroy and Morales women.[8]

Threats against the men's lives were credible. Indeed, during one of the subsequent "many times" that the Zapatistas came to search the Monroy home, the women hid Montoya in their chicken coop, where, out of fright, he thereafter took up a fitful temporary "residence." "Our hearts were racing and legs quaking as we tried to prevent Daniel from being killed. By divine intervention those soldiers left and Daniel's life was spared."[9]

ZAPATISTAS ON THE DEFENSIVE

By late July 1915 (certainly before the twenty-fifth, when seventeen members, including at least five men who had come out of hiding, met once again in a sacrament meeting[10]), the Carrancistas returned in force from their stronghold in Pachuca and routed the Zapatistas. Now the tables were turned. The

Mormon antagonists were on the run, obsequiously reversing their affiliations or reconsidering whom they should fear. They had good reason. The Carrancista captain, Pedro González, thought of Rafael as a friend. Military intelligence had informed the Carrancistas of the slaughter in San Marcos. González told the Monroy women that his forces would now take revenge on the gossipmonger ultimately culpable for the executions. "We know who he is."[11]

Expecting the women to cheer him on, González was surprised to hear Rafael's widow, Guadalupe Hernández, say, "Sir! No! I do not want another unfortunate woman to have to cry in her loneliness as do I. Let it go. God will bring justice in his own time."[12] The record does not disclose whether González proceeded on his stated task, the widow's protest notwithstanding.

Bernabé Parra Gutiérrez, who had left San Marcos more than a year earlier to find work near Santiago Tezontlale in his hometown of Guerrero, Hidalgo,[13] returned to San Marcos shortly after the Carrancista reoccupation. People informed him of all that had happened. He listened in astonishment. The military had fast-spreading intelligence, but the larger population frequently was left in the dark—no newspapers, no radio, only a plethora of rumors on the human gossip chain. News or even gossip of the executions had not reached Bernabé in Guerrero.

Parra immediately went to the Monroy home to see his friend Jovita, Jesusita's daughter. Learning about his cousin Daniel Montoya Gutiérrez, Parra pulled him from his hiding place in the chicken coop where he had taken up a semipermanent abode. He no longer needed to be afraid for his life because "now the Carrancistas are retaking the plazas [in the municipality of Tula]."[14]

PEACE, TRANQUILITY, TURMOIL

With the Carrancistas back in town, a welcome modicum of tranquility returned to San Marcos members' homes. Safety and security—for these they were grateful and perhaps for some they were enough. However, members of the Monroy household had the economic and experiential wherewithal to think of their sadness expansively, in part because they did not see a continuing place for themselves in San Marcos whether or not it was safe and secure. "The ignorance and fanaticism of our Mexican people continued to pursue us."[15] Where to turn, where to go?

Jesusita was now desperate to leave San Marcos and go anywhere—if not the United States, then somewhere else in Mexico. As her daughter Guadalupe expressed, "To live under oppression among this people [in San Marcos] would not be possible. To leave the Gospel to be able to live in peace with our people would be more impossible. No, no, we would prefer to die, as did my brother, rather than deny the testimony we had received."[16]

Five weeks after the executions, Jesusita wrote to the Mexicans' beloved friend, President Rey L. Pratt, still in administrative exile in the United States, to ask his opinion.[17] In addition, she expressed her anger at her son-in-law Roy Van McVey, advising Pratt that neither she nor her daughter, McVey's wife Natalia, could bear to write to him because they held him responsible for Rafael's execution (he was a friend of the Carrancistas and had business dealings with them). In their torment, they seemed to wish that it had been McVey rather than Rafael who had faced the firing squad. Jesusita nevertheless asked Pratt to inform McVey, who was biding his time in Texas, about the executions.

Amidst the odious sentiments burning in their hearts, Jesusita offered an opening. "I know full well that we have a second commandment and it is to pardon our enemies. We will do this, my good brother, and we are working to blot out every kind of hate, and when this sentiment leaves us, we will write [to McVey]."[18] It would take some time for this family rift to heal.

As if reasserting her defiance to the whole community, Jesusita closed her letter to Pratt saying, "Our sorrows have been grievous, but our faith is strong, and we will never forsake this religion."[19] The Monroys' enemies in Tula would not win in this contest of wills.

In the meantime, McVey, who had been writing letters to his wife that she had not received, had asked Pratt, whose correspondence was getting through, please to inform Natalia of an opportunity. McVey had contacted one of his friends who, with the reappearance of the Carrancistas, had returned to the Tolteca cement factory to assess the damages from the Zapatista occupation. McVey's friend told Jesusita that he would take them all to McVey in Texas. He spoke of San Antonio, where many Mexicans lived and Spanish was widely spoken.[20] A boiling cauldron of unrequited disappointment and lost hope fired Jesusita's evanescent decision to flee the flames of hatred. Fortunately, her mind did not stay fixed on it long enough to make it happen. The Monroys stayed in San Marcos and became bedrock for the expansion of the Church there.

The community's objection to the Mormon Monroys and their friends remained, although with the Carrancistas now holding the plaza in Tula and environs, people judiciously attenuated their persecution. The Carrancistas were quite secularized and perhaps still held to the pluralistic promise of Benito Juárez's *La Reforma*,[21] which national and international politics had wiped out more than a quarter century before. For this or alternative reasons, Carrancista officers had high esteem for the Mormons they knew. Reflecting on this, more and more Saints in San Marcos came to believe that their religion was at the root of all they had suffered. They had become Mormons, which was a negation of Catholicism, which started the gossiping about consorting with foreigners, which led to allied accusations such as the Monroy's having an arms cache, which led to Rafael's and Vicente's executions, which legitimized the continuing persecution.[22] All this notwithstanding, numerous members stoutly joined Jesusita's sentiments: "We will never forsake this religion."

Less than a week following the execution squad's performance, and now under the protection of the Carrancistas, these faithful Saints held Church services on Wednesday, 25 July 1915, unable even to wait until Sunday. Casimiro Gutiérrez, the newly self-appointed leader of the Mormons in San Marcos, conducted the services. He had stepped forward at great personal risk to organize the funeral and help to bury the deceased. President Rey Pratt could not have been involved in Casimiro's self-selection; he had yet to hear of the executions.[23] Casimiro was simply assuring a modicum of leadership continuity. Who else could?

Many of the men in hiding came forth, and following Sunday school services, some spoke in the subsequent sacrament meeting: Gabriel Rosales, a teacher; Isauro Monroy, a deacon; Casimiro himself, an elder; and Bernabé Parra and Maclovio Sánchez Villalobos, whose priesthood offices the record did not disclose.[24] The Saints met to commiserate their losses, to reinforce one another's gospel sentiments, to thank the Lord for their lives, to reflect affectionately and graciously on the departed, and to petition God to bless every member to be able to carry on and resolutely face whatever was yet to come.

It was in each other that most of the San Marcos Mormons found their strength. However, for the Monroys, who had been accustomed to a more expansive lifestyle than had the others, the downfall was onerous. Devoid of associations from their accustomed social class, old friends, or even their extended family to reassure and succor them in their grief, it was a wretched time. Although some people may have felt sorry for them, many who continued their shunning no doubt remained terrified of the social condemnation waiting to resurface with vigor as soon as the Carrancistas either vacated or surrendered the plazas of the municipality of Tula. Non-Mormons did not want to accept this vulnerability.[25]

There were additional stresses, perhaps presaging the interplay of the Mormons' personal failings with additional cataclysmic times that were yet to descend upon them. For example, within weeks of the Wednesday sacrament meeting of 25 July, a few of the Saints who considered their losses greater than even the Monroys' began to admonish Rafael's sisters to share more of their remaining goods with them. Occasionally, they used church meetings to call attention to the economic discrepancies they felt were not in accordance with the gospel.[26]

Jesusita judged that these feelings and the executions put Rafael's sister Jovita Monroy into a downward health spiral that left her crippled for years and, despite months of medical treatment in Mexico City, nearly took her life.[27] Nevertheless, trying to rise above these tensions, the Monroy daughters and Rafael's widow, Guadalupe Hernández, articulated their testimonies on the first Sunday in August 1915, affirming that despite the executions, the calamities of the war, and the divisions lurking beneath the community of the Saints, the gospel was true and their faith was unwavering.[28] They and others were working firmly to find a new way forward from the morass of their misery. It would be hard slogging for all the Saints. Dislocations of mind and spirit when the body is under extreme stress are quite common. Some people rise to the occasion and face life with a renewed resoluteness. Others lose all hope and simply expire either in mind, spirit, or body—or sometimes, all three.

NOTES

1. Monroy Mera, "Como llegó el evangelio," 28–29.
2. Monroy Mera, "Como llegó el evangelio," 29–30.
3. Monroy Mera, "Como llegó el evangelio," 29.
4. Bradley Lunt Hill to LaMond Tullis, email, 21 February 2014, sent from Mexico City. Leopoldo Portillo of the village of Vicente Guerrero in Hidalgo stated that a former landlord in Mexico City from the mid-1980s, Bernardo Villalobos, told him

he was the one who made the two coffins for the martyrs since the other carpenters were afraid of the consequences for helping the Monroys in any way. Guadalupe Monroy claims that an unidentified neighbor in San Marcos made one and the other was made by a member of the Church, Margarito Sánchez Villalobos, with the help of one of his sons, most likely a nephew. See Monroy Mera, "Como llegó el evangelio," 29.

5. See Monroy Mera, "Como llegó el evangelio," 29–30.
6. See Monroy Mera, "Como llegó el evangelio," 29.
7. The records are *Acta 233* and *Acta 234*, which register the deaths of Rafael Monroy and Vicente Morales with the municipal, or county, recorder. Facsimiles provided by Minerva Montoya Monroy were attached to her email of 21 September 2016.
8. Guadalupe claims that Daniel Montoya was the only one who stood by them, which clearly is not correct. I interpret that she meant he stood by them for the entire time of the Zapatista occupation rather than darting in and out, as one does when coming in and out of hiding. See Monroy Mera, "Como llegó el evangelio," 29–30.
9. Monroy Mera, "Como llegó el evangelio," 30.
10. Monroy Mera, "Como llegó el evangelio," 32.
11. Monroy Mera, "Como llegó el evangelio," 31.
12. Monroy Mera, "Como llegó el evangelio," 31.
13. Bernabé Parra left for Guerrero in the state of Hidalgo around April of 1914. Monroy Mera, "Como llegó el evangelio," 9.
14. Monroy Mera, "Como llegó el evangelio," 31.
15. Monroy Mera, "Como llegó el evangelio," 32.
16. Monroy Mera, "Como llegó el evangelio," 32.
17. "Carta de Jesús M. Vda. de Monroy," 9. Guadalupe Monroy also discusses this. See Monroy Mera, "Como llegó el evangelio," 28.
18. "Carta de Jesús M. Vda. de Monroy," 9.
19. Young, *Diary*, 121. Elsewhere, the phrase is rendered, "Aunque grandes han sido las tribulaciones pero también es grande nuestra fe y no desmayamos." See "Carta de Jesús M. Vda. de Monroy," 8–9. See also Grover, "Execution in Mexico," 20.
20. Monroy Mera, "Como llegó el evangelio," 32.
21. La Reforma ripped political control from the Catholic clergy and its conservative allies and instituted a period of social, political, and economic reform in Mexico, 1856–75. Jan Bazant, *Alienation of Church Wealth in Mexico: Social and Economic Aspects of the Liberal Revolution 1856–1875* (New York: Cambridge University Press, 2008).

22. Monroy Mera, "Como llegó el evangelio," 30.
23. Unusual leadership arrangements persist even in present-day Mexico. In 2012, a bishop was suddenly released from service in the Lomas de Chapúltepec Ward, yet his counselors continued to run affairs for more than six months before the stake president called a new bishop. This author was a member of the ward.
24. Monroy Mera, "Como llegó el evangelio," 32.
25. Monroy Mera, "Como llegó el evangelio," 33.
26. Monroy Mera, "Como llegó el evangelio," 33. Inequality and its practical or simply emotive consequences have always been a problem for utopian religious communities. Among Mormons in the United States attempting to live the united order, the struggle came front and center in Orderville, Utah. See Mark A. Pendleton, "The Orderville United Order of Zion," *Utah Historical Quarterly* 7, no. 4 (October 1939), 141–59.
27. "Reseña de la vida de Jovita Monroy Mera" (typescript, 4 pages, n.d.), copy provided by Hugo Montoya Monroy, 1 March 2014, 1. One wonders about posttraumatic stress disorder (PTSD) and associated autoimmune reactions associated with hyperstress. A sample objective affirmation is Ljudmila Stojanovich and Dragomir Marisavljevich, "Stress as a Trigger of Autoimmune Disease," *Autoimmunity Reviews* 7, no. 3 (January 2008), 209–13, doi:10.1016.
28. "Reseña de la vida de Jovita Monroy Mera," 2.

PART 2

MATURING THE FAITH IN A MEXICAN VILLAGE

6

INSTITUTIONALIZING THE CHURCH IN SAN MARCOS AND ENVIRONS

In San Marcos, the Church's institutionalization took time. When the Church is institutionalized in any area, its doctrines, mission, policies, vision, action guidelines, codes of conduct, central values, and eschatology associated with the restoration of the gospel become integrated into the culture of its leaders and members and sustained through time by its organizational structure. Even under the best of conditions, institutionalization is a lengthy temporal and spiritual process for a new faith.[1] The social, political, and economic upheavals affecting the early Church in Kirtland, Ohio; Nauvoo, Illinois; and Utah Territory from 1833 to around 1915 certainly illustrate the conundrum.

During the Church's early years in San Marcos, optimal conditions for institutionalization did not exist. The cultural changes required of a people of God were slow in coming to some of its leaders and members. The drag of traditional Mexican culture was at times robust and resilient. Unsettled political conditions, including the civil war, thwarted necessary attention from Church headquarters. Leaders' self-education in gospel and Church governance matters was thwarted by a lack of Church literature, including a complete

Spanish translation of the Doctrine and Covenants (not available until 1948)[2]. In the early days until 1919, when they dedicated their first self-built chapel, the San Marcos members had no adequate facilities in which to meet. Aside from that, people's testimonies, no matter how deeply embedded in the sentiments of their souls, could not replace the members' need to have more than just basic knowledge about their new faith. The Saints needed taproot information about what they should be doing to draw nearer to God within the fabric of a gospel culture that incorporated the faith's doctrines of salvation.

Despite all these impediments, a century later in 2015, San Marcos has two vibrantly functioning LDS wards attached to the Tula Mexico Stake.[3] Two more wards are in the outskirts of the municipal seat of Tula,[4] and there is one ward in nearby San Miguel,[5] plus an additional four wards and two branches in the larger municipality.[6]

Along the way toward developing an institutionalized church in San Marcos, members have made impressive accomplishments. Early on, they launched an innovative chapel-building program to meet their worship needs. They pioneered a member-sponsored educational endeavor that became the prototype for the Church's 1964–2013 educational system in Mexico.[7] They successfully resisted the overtures of Mormon dissidents and schismatics such as Margarito Bautista and his New Jerusalem, and Abel Páez and his Third Convention.[8] They have produced a large number of local and regional Church leaders. Its members have been financial contributors; temple attenders; missionaries; teachers; mission presidents; temple presidents; and local, regional, and general authorities. Some of its families have accomplished a difficult-to-replicate conservation of knowledge of their history.[9]

In the here and now, no community of Saints can perhaps ever completely embrace a gospel culture (that of the City of Enoch and the Nephite period following Christ's visit to the Americas, as Mormons note, being exceptions). However, the members in San Marcos have moved a considerable distance in the transition toward such a culture. It has not been easy.

The turbulent journey the Mormons traveled from 1912 when the Church cemented its roots in San Marcos to as late as the mid-1970s was stormy from time to time. A number of factors threatened institutionalization. First among them, of course, was the civil war and its wholesale assault on normal life that also occasioned the martyrdom of two members of the San Marcos Branch presidency and produced an uncertain outcome in leadership succession. Further complicating everything was the inexperience of the faith's leaders who were isolated from mission president Rey L. Pratt by nearly two thousand miles of inhospitable terrain and hampered by an only partially working mail system. Leaders from San Pedro Mártir and Ixtacalco helped fill the void, but they, too, were unseasoned and very isolated. They nevertheless pursued every avenue open to them to help the Saints in San Marcos as well as other LDS congregations in Hidalgo.

Aside from these structural issues, the personal failings of some of San Marcos's successor leaders not only sapped their spiritual vitality but, for a time, also set a poor example for instilling a gospel culture among the Saints. Afterward, the lure of schismatic breakaway movements caused pause, something that had to be resolved to cement the Saints' faith in their convictions. Of course, the development of faith and conviction is something that has to happen in every new generation. In San Marcos, although there were hiccups along the way, this institutionalization began to transpire as well.

To illustrate the transformative process and point out the enormous chasms the San Marcos Saints have bridged (and perhaps even to suggest some of the necessary conditions for institutionalizing the Church among a new people, including progressive efforts to adopt a gospel culture), we look at the following: leadership succession, education, cultural change, membership core, and institutional support. We take up leadership succession in this chapter, and the balance in chapter 7.

LEADERSHIP SUCCESSION

By example in word and deed, personally ministering to the Saints in their needs, Church leaders strive to teach Christ's expectations not only about faith but also about behavioral and other standards—social conduct, ethics, and an understanding of what it means to be informed by a gospel culture. Most of the time, good examples reign supreme over the other kind. However, sometimes the exceptions are spectacular.

Ordinarily, at the local level a branch presidency or ward bishopric dissolves when its president or bishop is unable to continue serving. Ecclesiastical authorities (e.g., stake presidents, mission presidents, Seventies, Area Presidents, or Apostles, depending on the level of the vacancy) take counsel and decide on a replacement. Thus, periodically, a nearly seamless transition occurs as qualified leaders take lay-leadership positions in a church that, at local and regional levels, has no paid clergy. Usually, such people have received training through a number of years to be able to step in whenever a need arises. Sometimes there are disappointments—immorality, lack of dedication, insufficient knowledge, politicization of a religious office, embezzlement—and on occasion, sooner-than-expected releases occur. However, overall, leadership transitions are accepted and the Church moves on.

In San Marcos, the need for a new branch president arrived when Rafael Monroy was executed. As no ecclesiastical authority was around to effect a replacement,[10] the succession, if there was to be one, would require someone's impromptu decision. Who was that someone?

CASIMIRO GUTIÉRREZ

Casimiro Gutiérrez stepped forward. After Rafael's death, Gutiérrez was the only one in San Marcos who held the Melchizedek Priesthood. During the civil war, he and his family had arrived from Toluca as member refugees. Rafael took note of his commitment to the Church and ordained him an elder, later perhaps inviting him to serve as second counselor in his presidency.

Casimiro conducted Rafael and Vicente Morales's funeral. Barely a week later, as soon as it was safe, he conducted Sunday School and sacrament services for the Saints—on a Wednesday! For many months thereafter, he faithfully shepherded these weekly meetings in the Monroy home. He tried to reconstitute the presidency by bringing on as assistants Gabriel Rosales, a teacher, and Isauro Monroy, a deacon.[11]

It appears that as soon as Rey Pratt became informed of events, he ratified Casimiro's leadership status even though no one was around who could set him apart as the new branch president. In due course, Pratt began to write letters to Casimiro not only giving him counsel and advice but also reproving him for some of his actions that someone had reported.[12]

THE MISCUES

What were Casimiro's actions, omissions, and miscues? Whatever they were, Church members perceived them from the vantage of the social and psychological fright that had just savaged their lives. That, together with the absence of their beloved Rey Pratt, made it difficult for the new leader to achieve an accorded authority that would legitimize his leadership.[13] As some opined, he was well intentioned, but his actions undermined him.

Casimiro carried a lot of hurtful cultural baggage—authoritarianism, caudillo mentality (a way of viewing leadership as controlling people through vigilance and patronage rather than leading with trust and fraternal love), reluctance to accept counsel, propagation of female subservience, and consumption of alcohol as a stress reliever. All these were attitudes and behaviors embedded in traditional Mexican culture of the time but quite antithetical to the principles of a hoped-for gospel ethos.

Casimiro's best intentions and efforts notwithstanding, in quick order he began to offend people. Members in San Miguel were among the first to push back by ceasing their attendance at Church meetings. Others felt shoved away. Some of the younger members, including Bernabé Parra, began to admonish a few of the older ones about their drunkenness and adulteries, which further created a generational divide. Sensitivities to class divisions within the membership arose, and gossiping became ferocious. Those with weak testimonies and those who became severely offended simply stopped attending church.

All these problems aside, week after week Casimiro continued to conduct Church meetings for all who would come. Many branch members gave talks and taught lessons, including the unordained Bernabé Parra, who appeared to be working hard to calm people down, urging them to reconsider the larger issues that had brought them together.[14]

By mid-year 1916, Ángel Rosales from Ixtacalco had returned to San Marcos, as he would yet do several times, to preside over the meetings.[15] Perhaps he was trying to take stock of the seriousness of the leadership turmoil. It is likely that he made a report to mission president Rey L. Pratt.

BREAKDOWN

Casimiro's personal disappointment about these events joined his cultural baggage to foster domestic issues with his wife and children, which again turned him to alcohol and infidelity. Yet, even as an addicted alcoholic and a breaker of the law of chastity, he continued as branch president, holding meetings and carrying on with his duties. However, by early 1917, his dissonance became greater than his will, and even he ceased attending church. Oddly, rather than Gabriel Rosales or

Isauro Monroy, the president's "assistants," it was Daniel Montoya, a teacher, who conducted some of the services in Casimiro's absence. The branch presidency, if there was a branch presidency, had evaporated. Apparently, the members simply gathered and on a weekly basis voted on someone to lead their services. One time, they even selected the newly ordained deacon Bernabé Parra.[16]

For four months, the nominal president of the San Marcos Branch was absent from Church services. Somehow, others carried on, focusing principally on Sunday School, sacrament meeting, and a branch social or two. Upon returning to church the first Sunday in May of 1917, Casimiro took the opportunity at fast and testimony meeting to complain that someone had been writing to President Pratt giving false information about him, which had occasioned his withdrawing from the Church meetings. Characteristically, *caudillos* fail to accept personal accountability for at least some of their problems. Leadership maturity would yet be some time in coming to the Church in San Marcos. The Church's institutionalization was somewhere in the future.

Two months later, Casimiro decided to pick up his role as branch president again by initiating a memorial service (*culto fúnebre*) for Rafael and Vicente.[17] Astonishingly by today's standards, he was able to do this simply because the members had forgiven him his sins. However, his wife had not. She took her turn at the subsequent fast and testimony meeting to denounce her husband.[18]

All this was too much for everyone, certainly for President Rey L. Pratt. In a move that localized district oversight for San Marcos in the Church's leadership at Ixtacalco, by letter Pratt instructed Dimas Jiménez of that branch, whom he personally had ordained to the Melchizedek Priesthood, to "renovate" the San Marcos Branch presidency.[19] Along with others from Ixtacalco, Jiménez appeared at the Sunday services of 13 August 1917 with Pratt's letter in hand, which instructed him to release Casimiro, which he did.

Some people live an exemplary life when life is easy, some when it is hard. Casimiro Gutiérrez, a good man in many ways, fell in between. The cultural circumstances of his life, the structural conditions under which he lived, and the turbulence of a civil war imposed burdens beyond his ability to cope. All his efforts notwithstanding, and accepting at face value the goodness of his intentions, he was unable to adopt some of the essential elements of the gospel culture he aspired to embrace. Someone needed to make a new effort to reclaim the disenchanted Saints and bring them back to the community of the faithful.

BERNABÉ PARRA GUTIÉRREZ

Pratt's letter instructed Dimas Jiménez to advance the youthful and unmarried Bernabé Parra from deacon to elder in the priesthood and to set him apart as the new branch president. In his acceptance remarks, Parra expressed appreciation for the much good that Casimiro had accomplished while also lamenting his periodic withdrawals from the Church.

This top-down leadership change was all new to the Saints in San Marcos. They appropriately wondered if Bernabé Parra would be any more successful than Casimiro as branch president, nevertheless acknowledging the comforting role Casimiro had played in many of their lives as he strove to find and do the will of the Lord for them. In varied levels of sophistication, whether Bernabé would be successful appeared to be the question on most people's minds even as some of them wondered who this Dimas Jiménez was, anyway, and by what right was he making these changes, Pratt's letter notwithstanding. Was the communication really from Pratt?

At least by age eighteen or so (ca. 1912), Bernabé Parra had begun his work for Rafael Monroy as a field hand at his El Godo ranch, later working up to an administrator. Parra had little if any formal schooling but, admirably, worked hard on his own to overcome this deficit. To improve his life he had come to San Marcos from Colonia Guerrero in the village of Tecomatlán, approximately eighteen miles away. His quick mind and ingratiating and loyal spirit soon endeared him to Rafael, his sisters, and their mother, Jesusita, and, eventually, nearly all the San Marcos members.

Jesusita and her daughters had taken Bernabé with them to Jesus Sánchez's home to comfort that ancient-of-days member who was dying. Parra had accompanied the Monroys to their baptism in June of 1913[20] and within a few weeks had joined them as a baptized member of the Church.[21] A few weeks later Rafael had taken Bernabé as a traveling companion to a district conference in Toluca.[22] Rafael completely trusted Bernabé and quickly gave him administrative responsibilities and opportunities at his ranch.

Sometimes the civil war made it impossible for Monroy to be at El Godo for months on end. In 1913 his ability to pay his employees catastrophically declined, which in April of 1914 prompted Bernabé to return to Tecomatlán where he could take refuge with his extended family and perhaps find a remunerating job.

Political disturbances in San Marcos over the American-owned Toluca cement factory, prejudices against foreigners in general, and the persecution of the fifty San Marcos Mormons in particular[23] may also have figured in Parra's decision to leave. Within a month following his exit, Natalia Monroy and her husband, Roy Van McVey, fled, deciding on the relative safety (for foreigners) of the port city of Veracruz.[24] At the same time, refugee members from Toluca and Mexico City were arriving in San Marcos. Everything was in flux, and members' individual circumstances were highly varied.

Unaware of the executions until returning to San Marcos in July of 1915, less than a week after the horrific event, a shocked Bernabé Parra quickly checked on the Monroy family. On 25 July 1915, he took advantage of the first resumed Church meeting to make an impromptu oration. Such a young man, still he was able to fortify the Saints. In the ensuing weeks, he was decisively active as he helped members by assuming a strong leadership role in the branch without actually holding a leadership position. After a period, he returned to Tecomatlán, but in May of 1917, nearly a year later, he returned to San Marcos as a permanent resident.[25]

JOVITA

Bright, energetic, fully committed and spiritually strong, Parra seemed confident he could revitalize the branch as its new president. However, he was young (age twenty-three), unmarried, and in love with Jovita Monroy, ten years his senior. One might think these were enough obstacles. There was more. How would Bernabé handle this?

Against the uncertainty of disease, the logic of actuarial statistics that separated their life spans by a decade, the disapproval of Jovita's family because of the age differences, and the educational chasm that separated them, Bernabé and Jovita nevertheless shared their hearts and hopes for a life of togetherness in the gospel of Jesus Christ. In truth, there were not many options for the Monroy girls if they wanted to marry in the Church. Jovita and Bernabé set a date for their wedding, which would have happened ten days or so before Parra's sudden call to be branch president. Elders Cándido Robles and Dimas Jiménez from Ixtacalco had arrived to marry them, and Jovita's family, despite the reservations, had planned a joyous celebration. However, Jovita suffered from a crippling, perhaps autoimmune, disease triggered shortly after her brother's execution two years earlier. Because of joint pain, she required crutches just to get around. Shortly before she was to be wed, Jovita's condition suddenly worsened. Jesusita whisked her daughter to a hospital in Mexico City. With Jovita's condition suddenly worsening, the wedding was shelved, at least temporarily. The young woman remained in Mexico City for three months, unimproved, and nearly died.

Bernabé was devastated. At the sacrament meeting a week before his call, the young man's cousin, Daniel Montoya, who was directing the branch that week, took occasion to "comfort the young Bernabé Parra, citing the scriptures and saying, 'When trials occur it is because God is closer to us and perhaps they may be God's test of our faith.'"[26]

As Bernabé assumed the mantle of leadership of the San Marcos Branch, his heart was vicariously in Mexico City at the bedside of his intended wife, whose ailment, he feared, would not only leave her crippled for life but might even cut it short. Thus, Bernabé took on his new Church calling carrying a heavy emotional burden, comforted somewhat in knowing that the Ixtacalco leaders were making frequent visits to the hospital to give blessings and encouragement to his intended and her mother and sisters.[27] Jovita did not return to San Marcos until December, three months after the date set for their anticipated and now halted wedding. If Bernabé was depressed, he had ample reason.

PRATT RETURNS TO MEXICO

By the beginning of 1917, civil war disruptions had largely ceased in the municipality of Tula and elsewhere in central Mexico, replaced in part by sporadic banditry in the countryside and unbridled lawlessness in the cities as successive governments strove to reestablish civic order. Nevertheless, by September of that year, life was sufficiently secure that mission president Rey L. Pratt could return to Mexico briefly with a group of foreign missionaries to try to revive the Church in central Mexico. Pratt also called local full-time missionaries to assist him. Of course, all of them were interested in San Marcos.

President Pratt and a contingent of missionaries visited San Marcos in December of 1917, arriving just in time to celebrate the baptisms of Trinidad Hernández of Santiago Tezontlale and Dolores Martínez de Estrada, Bernabé Parra's foster mother of nearby Guerrero. While living in Tecomatlán, Bernabé had worked to bring these and other everlastingly influential souls into the

Church.[28] Despite Parra's youthful age, he clearly had wide-ranging influence within and outside his extended family and had no hesitation in being an unofficial emissary of the restored gospel.

In San Marcos, mission president Pratt made a curious decision. Thinking he needed to further legitimize Parra's leadership and concretely demonstrate his approval of Elder Dimas Jiménez's role in ordaining him and setting him apart, Pratt ordained Parra an elder *again*, and *again* set him apart as the branch president, doing so in front of the congregation. No doubt, he also did some public explanation and perhaps some remonstration. Several members had complained that Jiménez did not have the "real" authority to establish a new branch president in San Marcos.[29] However, in attempting to address these perceptions, Pratt's choice of means could do nothing other than undercut Jiménez's authority as his emissary. Institutionalization of the Church in San Marcos would yet take time.

A SPIRIT OF CONTENTION

A spirit of contention had taken hold of some of the members in San Marcos, even tearing a few member families apart. Aside from the issue of the new branch president, Jesusita's sister Juana Mera and her son Isauro Monroy Mera, baptized in March of 1914, were upset that Bernabé, as a prospective Monroy in-law, had been given an economic advantage at El Godo, which they felt should have gone to Isauro. Isauro was particularly distressed because Jesusita had replaced him with Bernabé as the ranch steward (*mayordomo*). After a period of acrimony, in 1918, Juana renounced her sister and left the Church.[30] Isauro Monroy tried to repress his offense, but when ex-President Casimiro Gutiérrez took to the pulpit to accuse him of "certain sins" and publicly reprimand him, he also withdrew from the Saints and did not return until advanced in age.[31]

Casimiro was still struggling with repairing his own life, apparently concluding that one way was to remonstrate others as they had done him. Some were offended and stopped attending the meetings. Other members stopped attending Sunday services because they had grievances with the Monroy family, and Church services were being held in the Monroy home. Never mind that it was the only available place of sufficient size to accommodate the members. Where was Christ in their lives? Some San Marcos Saints were constantly toiling to remember.

Alarmed at the loss of members in San Marcos, more local missionaries showed up to fortify the Saints, including Juan Mairet and Tomasa Lozada. Daniel Montoya and Bernardino Villalobos joined Bernabé Parra as counselors in the branch presidency and worked tirelessly to hold many of the members together in a community of the faithful. After 1921, foreign missionaries helped in the branch again as well—at least until 1926 when, once again, they were forced to leave the country (due to the Cristero rebellion).

Newly minted Bernabé Parra could not repair fractured relations among all the members, but he could deal with the building issue. In January of 1919, someone made a proposal that if holding meetings in the Monroy home was objectionable, then they should build a chapel. Parra agreed and began to organize the project. Within several years, aside from erecting the building with little help from Salt Lake City, the members also made their own furniture. In the process of working together, they drowned many sorrows and complaints and strove more diligently toward a gospel culture that embodies Christ's teachings for the behavior of His people.[32]

Photo 12. Making furniture for the first chapel in San Marcos, ca. 1930. Left to right: Bernabé Parra, Benito Villalobos, Othón Espinoza, and Roy Van McVey. Note that Parra is holding a handsaw used in the difficult task of ripping boards for the benches. Courtesy of Church History Library. Copied from the original that was in possession of María Concepción Monroy de Villalobos, San Marcos, Hidalgo, Mexico.

PARRA STUMBLES

Bernabé Parra was still single, and his once-intended Jovita was still unable to walk without crutches. The ardor of their love had not completely cooled, but circumstances had dampened it. Parra was twenty-five or twenty-six; Jovita, thirty-five.

With nearly all the members in San Marcos without remunerative work and scratching whatever they could from the soil or wherever else to sustain life, Bernabé decided he should temporally leave the community again to search for employment elsewhere, which would take him away from the branch for a period. Thus, after a year of ecclesiastical labor as branch president, he wrote to mission president Rey L. Pratt about the difficult economic matters he and others were facing and informed Pratt of his desperate need. Although the record does not enlighten us, it is probable that he had Jovita edit his letter before sending it. The Mexican postal service had resumed normal operations in central Mexico, and in due course Pratt received Bernabé's communication.

Because of Parra's leadership skills and forthright dedication for a year as branch president, because Parra would be returning—perhaps soon—and because Pratt had no information regarding an adequate replacement, the mission president felt it unwise to release Parra outright. Pratt opted to appoint Daniel Montoya Gutiérrez, then a teacher, to preside during Parra's absence. On occasion, Montoya had conducted Sunday services at the election of the congregation when the Casimiro Gutiérrez presidency was not functioning, so he had some administrative experience.

Pratt instructed elders Cándido Robles and Juan Haro from Ixtacalco and San Pedro Mártir to make the change in branch leadership, apparently not advising them to ordain Montoya an elder, a move that would have facilitated his interim presiding. In those days, advancements in the priesthood were generally slow in being made, and then only after much deliberation and a demonstration of substantial need. In San Marcos, the leadership transition—without advancement in the priesthood—occurred 16 February 1919.[33]

Over the next several months, many local missionaries traveled to San Marcos to help.[34] In August, Agustín Haro returned, this time in the company of Isaías Juárez. They showed up ostensibly to assess how well the branch was functioning. Juárez, a man of substantial Church experience and a natural leader who later would lead the Church in central Mexico during troubling times, made a titanic impression on the San Marcos Saints. "No one slept during his powerful oration."[35]

In the meantime, Bernabé had successfully obtained a remunerative position, which resolved one aspect of his life but left him, quite naturally, pining for love and an association with the Saints. No doubt, he also missed his role as the San Marcos Branch president. Did he miss Jovita, too? Were they writing to each other? We have no answers.

Jesusita had a reconciliation of sorts with a few of her deceased husband's sisters living in Arenal. Coincidentally, her daughter Jovita was anxious to "get out of the house" and decided that with the help of Eulalia, Vicente Morales's widow, she could make a trip to see her paternal aunts and renew some aspect of the family's former solidarity. Her aunts could assist her in exercising her joints, thereby improving her mobility. Jovita and Eulalia were gone about three months (from around late August to late November 1919).[36]

Bernabé Parra's new work placed him near Arenal. Would this be a time to reconnect with Jovita while she was visiting her aunts? Did he and his once-intended continue to have feelings for each other? Did they still have any prospects for a marriage?

If he or she tried, a sufficient rekindling of their affection did not occur. What did occur was a furtive union between Bernabé and Eulalia. Amidst the heartache of the times, Parra's youth and desperate loneliness, Eulalia's tender age in widowhood, Jovita's illness, and the prevailing culture that hardly registered disapproval, Eulalia and the otherwise Mormon stalwart Bernabé Parra produced an out-of-wedlock child whom Eulalia named Elena Parra Mera.[37]

Surely, it must have been a hard time for Parra and Eulalia. Parra appeared to have returned to San Marcos about the time that Jovita and her domestic helper did, perhaps not yet knowing that Eulalia was pregnant. In the meantime, as expected, he resumed his position as the branch president.

The culture of the times notwithstanding, as soon as the pregnancy became visible and the event in Arenal no longer deniable, Jesusita was furious.[38] The Church was, too. No doubt in consultation with Rey L. Pratt, Bernabé's priesthood was suspended and his position as branch president terminated.

Despite Jesusita's fury at Eulalia and Bernabé, and notwithstanding Jovita's tragic jolt into considering her own future, illness or not, Parra reconciled himself with both mother and daughter. Jesusita, who seemed to have stood in the way of

Photo 13. Wedding of Jovita Monroy Mera and Bernabé Parra Gutiérrez, San Marcos, Hidalgo, 13 November 1920. Courtesy of Maclovia Monroy de Montoya.

a marriage, now relinquished her opposition. Jovita, Eulalia's pregnancy notwithstanding, now decided to accept Bernabé's renewed marriage proposal. Bernabé had many good qualities—he was a natural leader, Church worker, believer in the Restoration, avoider of alcohol, advocate for the needs of others, and a good prospect to become the family's permanent manager (*mayordomo*) at El Godo. She could absorb both his sexual relations with Eulalia and his illegitimate child.

The nuptials, accompanied by a large celebration that many outside visitors attended, occurred on 19 November 1920. Elder Cándido Robles returned—again—to perform the marriage, successfully this time.

Five months later, Eulalia gave birth to Elena Parra Mera. Thereafter, Eulalia continued in Jesusita's protective care along with the new baby and her and Vicente's daughter Raquel. Generations in the Church trace their genealogy to Eulalia through her daughters Raquel and Elena.

Parra worked to rehabilitate himself. Eventually the Church pardoned him, and in June of 1921, six months after his marriage to Jovita,[39] restored his priesthood office. However, institutionalization of the Church in San Marcos would yet require time as the members struggled to live lives more consonant with a gospel culture. The many laudable features of the then Mexican culture notwithstanding,[40] San Marcos Mormons needed to distance themselves from some parts of their national ethos in which they and their forebears had been embedded for centuries. The Church's teaching on chastity and sexual morality was a good place to start.

In the meantime, who among the Saints in San Marcos would be capable, if not willing, to take on the office of branch president?

DANIEL MONTOYA GUTIÉRREZ

On 8 December 1920, and in the wake of revelations about President Bernabé Parra and Eulalia Mera Martínez viuda de Morales's fornication, Daniel Montoya was ordained an elder and set apart as the branch president in his cousin Bernabé's stead.[41] Montoya's prior interim appointment as acting branch president and his fierce dedication to the Church had given him some preparation.[42] However, his educational deficits were as pronounced as Parra's had once been, and his reserved, guarded, almost withdrawn personality, complicated his life as a Church leader. Nevertheless, embedded faithfully in the Church's teachings, as he understood them, Montoya stepped forth cautiously in this, his new appointment, to do what he could to help the San Marcos Saints progress and develop.

As did others of the period, Montoya had direct links to the increasingly revered Rafael Monroy, whose accorded stature in death sometimes exceeded the reality of his life. Nevertheless, Daniel could point to Rafael's having baptized and confirmed him.[43] He had significant knowledge of Rafael's positive relationships with members and nonmembers[44] and was one of the few male members who dared to stand with the Monroy women after the martyrdom even though he had spent some of the time in the Monroy's chicken coop hiding from rebel Zapatistas.[45] All this gave him credibility with the Saints.

MONTOYA OVERCOMES SOME DEFICITS

Still, the deficits were substantial for a young man in this position, married though he was. Having spent his entire life since childhood working in the fields as a *campesino*, he had come to San Marcos as an unschooled and illiterate adult, a condition he had not significantly altered by the time of his appointment as the new branch president. However, with the calling came a ferocious desire to throw off his mantle of ignorance and learn directly from the sacred texts. In time, he learned to read the scriptures haltingly so that he could teach others, many of whom were even less literate than he.

The local missionaries from San Pedro Mártir and Ixtacalco alternatingly paid monthly visits to give instructions, advice, cautions, and even reprimands based on the scriptures. In addition, from time to time other missionaries came, some of whom continued to make smashing impressions on the Saints in San Marcos. Among these were Abel Páez and Margarito Bautista, two who later would figure prominently in dissident movements resulting in their excommunications from the Church.[46]

All these eventual circumstances notwithstanding, during Montoya's presidency the branch seemed to march along in a steady way.[47]

A NEW CHAPEL AND A REGIONAL CONFERENCE

Because contentiousness about having to meet in the Monroy home for Church services, in 1919 under the presidency of Bernabé Parra the Saints had decided to build themselves a modest chapel (*casa de oración*). They had laid the foundation and started construction on the walls amid concerns about how they could provide enough volunteers and raise enough money. Their principal expense would be the roof because they were making the walls out of adobe bricks by using centuries-old effective and affordable building techniques.

New branch president Daniel Montoya thought they could do it. He continued to give the project encouragement and direction despite its not being his original idea. Bernabé Parra, the old branch president, thought they could do it. Although defrocked, he continued to help finance the construction through his own resources and those of the Monroy family. Jesusita and other opinion makers in the branch thought so. They contributed not only their wherewithal financially but also the enthusiasm of their hearts and the labor of their hands. Charismatic visitors such as Margarito Bautista and Abel Páez thought so. They gave stirring, eloquent orations in support. President Rey L. Pratt sent funds to purchase sheet metal for the roof.

All redoubled their efforts when President Rey Pratt scheduled a regional conference for San Marcos for August 1921, barely two years after the idea of a building had first surfaced.[48] The excitement and almost feverish construction labor aside, the members were not able to get the windows installed in their new building in time for the conference. Nevertheless, they had everything else ready, and the conference unfolded with considerable satisfaction and good feelings.

Jesusita and her daughters remembered the conference they had attended in San Pedro Mártir and how it had helped them decide to become members of the Church. The Monroys, and all others who could, worked busily to receive the many visitors from afar who came to attend. They arranged for food and overnight accommodations, just as in the other regional conferences that members had attended.

The most anticipated event was the scheduled appearance of President Rey L. Pratt. The entire Mormon community was excited that he would be at the conference. Mexican Mormons had a profound affection for Pratt, which the president reciprocated with love, unbridled service, and much personal sacrifice on their behalf.

Jesusita had her piano hauled to the new building for the services so that her daughter Guadalupe could play it for the hymns, which was important since the hymnals themselves had no music staffs, only text, and, in any event, no one outside the Monroy family could read music. In the afternoon session, the clerk read from the pulpit the names of members who had donated to the building fund and the amounts of their contributions, certainly an unusual occurrence in a Mormon congregation.[49]

As usual, Pratt's preaching captured everyone's attention. The uninstalled windows notwithstanding, he also gave a stirring dedicatory prayer. In the evening, he conducted a "very animated" testimony meeting. The Saints loved testimony meetings, which they held at every conceivable opportunity. The following Monday, thirteen more people were baptized.[50]

For his part, branch president Daniel Montoya conducted the proceedings of 27 August 1921 with dignity and grace and with a level of confidence that bespoke well of his growing maturity in the administration and conducting of Church affairs. Overall, the conference, the arrangements, the chapel dedication, the orations, the presence of Pratt, the testimony meeting, and the baptisms were a superb success. If excitement about being in a new cause and building a conviction to sustain it is a prerequisite for institutionalization, the Saints in San Marcos were on their way—that is, were it not for another round of chaotic events.

CHAOS

Personal failings alien to a gospel culture soon dampened the lingering conference enthusiasm and pleasure of having their chapel dedicated. President Montoya's first wife, María Manuela Cruz Corona,[51] had an affair with a nonmember, a matter that traumatized the branch president and sent him to the municipal (county) seat of Tula to sue for divorce. Before the 1914 reforms in the civil code, divorce in Mexico was extremely difficult, if not impossible, for the poorer classes, which was one alleged reason why poor people tended to have common-law unions rather than marry in the first place.[52] (The baptisms of many of the first adult members had to await the formalities of moving their *concubinato* [common-law] unions[53] to a married state blessed by civil authority.)

The snail-pace divorce proceedings became acrimonious. Branch members developed opinions as to who was at fault, which of itself fueled considerable gossipmongering.[54] At a dispassionate level, some wondered if it was Daniel Montoya's sacrifice of time and personal resources for the community of Saints that had caused his wife to consider his service a cost beyond either her willingness or capability to endure. Nevertheless, Montoya carried on alone for a while until revelations emerged that he and his estranged wife, María Manuela, had also been unchaste before their marriage.

With these disclosures and for perhaps other reasons, Montoya was released as branch president. The divorce process was fraught with public shaming, as the Saints resorted to punitive enforcement before they learned how to live a gospel culture that embraced loving discipline. Institutionalization would yet take time. Not until 1925 were Daniel Montoya and his new wife, Margarita Gutiérrez Sánchez, allowed to partake of the sacrament again and become fully reintegrated into the community of the faithful.[55] Nevertheless, both continued to attend Church meetings and contribute financially to the San Marcos Branch. The depths of their eventually complete repentance sustained them during the opprobrium and shunning and kept them and large numbers of their descendants in the Church.

Margarito Bautista visited the branch again, specifically to warn the Saints to have charity with fallen brothers and sisters given that everyone is weak and prone to sin. He admonished the members to always ask God to fortify them in their faith that they might remain faithful.[56] As usual, Bautista had a charismatic aura about him.

Loose attention to the law of chastity had undone three of San Marcos's four branch presidents. However, little by little the Church's teachings made behavioral inroads into the lives of the Saints, not the least of which was the principle of repentance. People fall. They make terrible mistakes. However, with sincere intent and repentant hearts reaching for the heavens, the Savior more quickly reaches out to sinners than do their neighbors. From their mistakes, the fallen can learn to live a better life. With the Savior's love, the repentant can develop a conviction to live what they have learned. So the members learned, and so it was. For most of them.

In the meantime, San Marcos needed another branch president. Benito Villalobos Sánchez, the branch's fifth, was set apart on 1 September 1923. With a new building, however modest by present standards, and with many new members learning the gospel (and new and old members trying to live it), would Benito be able to provide the careful guidance that might lead the Saints into a discovery of how to live gospel-centered lives more adequately? Would the Church become more institutionalized on his watch?

BENITO VILLALOBOS SÁNCHEZ

Benito Villalobos Sánchez got off to a rocky start when, the week following his appointment as branch president, he failed to show up for the meetings. A priest, Othón Espinoza, a recent immigrant and one who would later figure prominently in the dissident Third Convention movement as an assistant to Abel Páez, presided over the meetings, he being one of President Villalobos's counselors.[57] Nevertheless, Benito soon got the time constraints on his life squared away and thereafter presided over the branch until about 1926.

As with previous branch presidents, intense learning characterized Villalobos's tenure, not only in regards to conducting meetings but also in some of the finer points of Church doctrine. He started out young and timid but in less than three years grew in maturity and self-confidence. This served him well, given that during his presidency, contrarian voices entered the Church's proceedings, principally in the person of Margarito Bautista.

THE CHALLENGE OF MARGARITO BAUTISTA

In the three months following Benito Villalobos's setting apart as branch president, Margarito Bautista showed up on numerous occasions to preach his stimulating, nationalist-flavored version of the Book of Mormon and the Restoration, apparently even after his release as a full-time missionary.[58] Other full-time missionaries began to take an increasing role in branch administration to help President Villalobos address this challenge. The matter grew to sufficient concern that in December of 1923, President Pratt showed up to preach a gentle sermon that some interpreted as being "anti-Bautista."[59]

In the ensuing months, Bautista's influence only grew. Through his frequent visits to San Marcos, Bautista was making inroads there (and elsewhere) that Pratt did not like. In March of 1925 at a newly called regional conference in San Marcos, an infuriated mission president addressed his ideas without attacking Bautista personally. Surprised, members listened intently to an uncharacteristically angry Pratt preach a robust and tough sermon against ideas alien to the gospel of Jesus Christ.[60] Members wondered what had caused the outburst and what his sermon meant to them personally. San Marcos appeared to become

Photo 14. Margarito Bautista, 1933.

the whirlpool of one of the fights that eventually exasperated the Church and eventually led to Bautista's excommunication.

Bautista, who had spent much time teaching about temple work and organizing local genealogical societies complete with administrative personnel whom he encouraged to have full-bodied nationalist sentiments (e.g., the eventual religious triumph of Mexicans over their Anglo overlords), had already left for a lengthy stay in the United States, where he would further embellish his thinking before returning again to Mexico. Before, he had been a dedicated and effective missionary. Now he was pursuing his own gospel and confusing people about some aspects of Church doctrine and administration.[61] However, he did have a legacy achievement. He increased people's interest in their genealogy.[62]

DEVELOPMENTAL TRANSFORMATIONS

It was not all stress and distress for branch president Villalobos. People were returning to San Marcos following the civil war's dislocations. Along with other members whom the war had further immiserated, by 1925 (perhaps 1928), Roy Van McVey and his wife, Natalia, had returned to Mexico where McVey picked up his employment at the Tolteca cement factory. They were living in a handsome home the company had provided.[63] McVey and Natalia had spent several years "exiled" in Texas, where McVey joined the Church and he and Natalia, Jesusita's daughter, had traveled to a temple to be sealed.[64] Both were a strong support to the Church in San Marcos.

Aside from displaced members returning to San Marcos, the Saints frequently held baptismal services for young eight-year-olds born to members in addition to the customary convert baptisms, which sometimes included entire families. Some people who had been displaced and uprooted and had seen their life's expectations torn asunder were available for new value commitments. The Church of Jesus Christ of Latter-day Saints appealed to some of them on a variety of fronts.

In his stirring, stunning, aggressively forceful oration at the March 1925 regional conference in San Marcos, Pratt had mentioned that the chapel the Saints had constructed was not large enough. During some meetings, would-be attendees listened to the proceedings from outside the building's windowless, framed portals. It would be a while before the Saints could respond to Pratt's observation, but the idea germinated in their minds. By 1926, they were holding fund-raisers in order to enlarge their meeting house as Pratt had recommended.[65]

Apostle Richard R. Lyman was enthralled with the Saints in San Marcos, whom he visited in August of 1925—the first Apostle ever to do so.[66] Aside from fledgling foreign missionaries, his visit may have been the first time the San Marcos Saints had ever heard a discourse through an interpreter.

INSTITUTIONALIZING THE CHURCH

Photo 15. Photo taken adjacent to the first San Marcos chapel during the visit of Apostle Richard R. Lyman, August 1925. Front row, left to right: María Guadalupe Monroy, Jovita Monroy de Parra, Jesusita Mera de Monroy, Guadalupe Hernández de Monroy. Middle row: María Concepción Monroy, Amalia Monroy. Back row: Bernabé Parra, unidentified man, Apostle Richard R. Lyman, President Rey L. Pratt. Man standing by the cornfield unidentified. Man at right is Amando Pérez. Copied from the original that was in the possession of María Concepción Monroy de Villalobos, San Marcos, Hidalgo, Mexico.

An interpreted message from an Apostle was enough for some. Others, such as branch presidency counselor Othón Espinoza, were "disgusted" at having to listen to such a high-ranking General Authority speak thusly. "The Spirit of the Lord should give him the gift of tongues."[67] There was a lot of institutionalization that yet needed to occur in San Marcos. In the meantime, Bernabé Parra and Jovita Monroy received Apostle Lyman in their home.

The two positions—acceptance and rejection of the linguistic limitations of an Apostle—mirrored a gnawing concern about whether the Mexicans would have "their" church or whether they would always be beholden to Anglo-Americans for their tutoring, and that through an interpreter. After a flurry of discussions, most San Marcos members settled on remaining loyal to Rey Pratt and the leaders in Salt Lake City. A few would later drift away, but not many.

From time to time, the troubling issue of the Church's prior practice of plural marriage (polygamy) stirred people's sentiments, distressing the San Marcos Saints greatly because it gave the Catholics another opening through which to attack them.[68] However, the difficulty with this doctrine was even more complicated. When around 1925 President Benito Villalobos heard of a clandestine plural marriage having been performed "up north," well past the time when such practices should have officially ceased in the Church, he was upset beyond an ability to cope and could not carry on further as branch president.[69] His neighbors' taunting made the doctrinal confusion intense, which, for him, became unbearable and led to his resignation as branch president.

Fortunately, Villalobos's decision did not take him away from the Church for long, because he knew that the gospel's underlying doctrines were true and far outweighed human-caused aberrations or imponderable doctrines at whatever level. His enduring testimony has bequeathed the Church at least five generations of faithful members, now scattered throughout Mexico and beyond.

With President Benito Villalobos gone, now who would lead the branch through its growth epochs as well as troubling times? The Church again tapped the ever-present, ever-ready, ever-willing, and now-rehabilitated Bernabé Parra. Beginning his adulthood as a quasi-illiterate man of the soil (*campesino*), he had risen to become a powerful force in the Church and in the community of San Marcos generally, his personal flaws notwithstanding.

THE RETURN OF BERNABÉ

Bernabé Parra was among the second wave of people to join the Church in San Marcos. He had been with the Monroys from the beginning of their commitments. He had been to regional conferences, had received personal instruction from mission president Rey L. Pratt, and had acquired experience during his first tenure as branch president. Moreover, he had been instrumental in getting a building project under way. Beyond those accomplishments, he had left his work as a field laborer during some of his absences from San Marcos to become an accomplished technical wage earner in electricity as the country's rural electrification projects had gotten under way. This, in addition to his enthusiasm for the gospel, made him a man to admire, his affair with Eulalia Mera aside. Indeed, branch members saw that he had repented and rehabilitated himself during the previous six years, which seemed to make him all the more attractive as their leader. He understood *their* travails. Here was a man, now the de facto head of the Monroy family, whom they could admire and seek to emulate in his repentant state, happily receiving his counsel and following him as their leader.

The records available to us do not disclose whom Parra selected as his counselors in the new branch presidency. However, he, and no doubt his counselors, too, went right to work to heal wounds and to bring a welcomed, assertive commitment to the branch through vigorous, purposeful direction.

Aside from members' commitments to the faith's principles and values, the Church's institutionalization in any given area requires leaders who can help others internalize value commitments and followers who are willing to accept guidance through life's pathways. San Marcos had come a long way from the early days of tender testimonies, martyrdom, jealousy, leadership failings, and the chaos of a civil war. There would still be problems, but if not fewer, they were certainly less intense.

The weekly sermons at sacrament meetings, the Sunday School lessons, the impromptu testimony meetings held in diverse locations, the personal visits to members' homes—all were designed to enhance the Saints commitment to the Church and to show them how to live their lives in accordance with gospel teachings. In short, Parra designed his whole operation to help members learn a gospel culture and incorporate it into their lives. For some it was a long journey. Nevertheless, it is remarkable that so many engaged in the effort and indeed made considerable progress.

A NEW BUILDING PROJECT AND LOCAL LEADERSHIP DEVELOPMENT

By 1926, the San Marcos Mormons had engaged their building project again with an intensity that matched branch President Parra's enthusiasm, holding more fund-raisers and formulating plans for a significant addition to their meetinghouse.[70] Slowly, with more civil disturbances during a Catholic (Cristero) rebellion against the government (1926–29) notwithstanding, they proceeded, even to the point that Parra commissioned a large mural of the Salt Lake Temple to adorn the stage behind the pulpit.[71]

The effort to establish local leaders, such as Parra, throughout the Church in central Mexico had been vigorously underway since 1924. Mission president Pratt had learned that he would soon leave for Argentina to help introduce the

Photo 16. Interior of the second chapel at San Marcos, Hidalgo, that the members constructed. Bernabé Parra commissioned the mural of the Salt Lake Temple. This building has now been replaced. Photo from the Amalia Monroy de Parra Collection.

gospel there.[72] Thus, prior to his departure in 1925, Pratt gave enormous attention to developing a leadership corps throughout central Mexico. Observers reported that the Mexican leaders he appointed functioned so well that the American missionaries could spend all their time proselyting new members rather than also trying to administer the branches.[73] Branch president Bernabé Parra was certainly among President Pratt's success stories.

After Pratt's return from Argentina, he went one step further in his local leadership development efforts by establishing a district presidency to give guidance with suprabranch authority to the Church in Mexico. The man he picked as district president was the grandest orator of them all, Isaías Juárez, with counselors Bernabé Parra and the still-in-the-fold Abel Páez, himself a man of considerable talent, skill, testimony, and willingness to serve.[74]

In some sense, appointing Bernabé Parra as branch president for a second time and then as a counselor in the newly formed district presidency was useful to the organizational structure not only of the Church in San Marcos but later also of the Church in the entirety of central Mexico. In 1926, the Mexican

Photo 18. Abel Páez and Isaías Juárez, district counselor and president in central Mexico, with US ambassador to Mexico J. Reuben Clark Jr., ca. 1931.

The Calles legislation outlawed religious orders, deprived churches of property rights, and stripped their clergy of civil liberties, including a right to trial by jury in cases involving anticlerical laws and the right to vote. Further, the new laws allowed the government to seize church property; close religious schools,

Photo 17. President Rey L. Pratt with Isaías Juárez (seated) and other members of the Church (David Juárez, Benito Panuaya, Narciso Sandoval, and Tomás Sandoval), San Gabriel Ometoxtla, ca. 1931. Man with hat is unidentified.

government under Plutarco Elías Calles—an "anti-Catholic Free Mason atheist," his enemies called him—enacted anticlerical legislation (in response to attempts by the Catholic clergy to undermine his government) known as the Law Reforming the Penal Code or, more crisply, as "the Calles Law."

convents, and monasteries; and expel all foreign priests.⁷⁵ In the municipality of Tula, and therefore in San Marcos, it being a constituent part of that municipality, authorities ordered foreign missionaries and clerics—Catholic, Protestant, Mormon, and whomever else—to leave the country on pain of imprisonment. The government gave them twenty-four hours' notice.⁷⁶

In the absence of the foreign missionaries, the local leaders Rey Pratt had prepared generally distinguished themselves well. The district presidency went into high gear to keep the branches well administered and to make it possible for the Church to carry on during this, the third time that Anglo missionaries had been forced to abandon their Mexican flocks.⁷⁷

Bernabé Parra continued to distinguish himself on behalf of the Saints. Even during and after difficult times that later would befall him, he was remembered with great affection in San Marcos for his critical, influential, and effective work on behalf of the Church there.

BERNABÉ'S RELEASE AND SUBSEQUENT FALL

Bernabé Parra was released as San Marcos's branch president in order to join the newly formed district presidency and thereby serve with President Isaías Juárez and Juárez's other counselor, Abel Páez, as suprabranch authorities. Parra's successor in San Marcos, Maclovio Sánchez Villalobos, who became the seventh president of the San Marcos Branch, was then set apart. Thereafter, quite routinely, Agrícol Lozano Bravo, Sabino Lozano, and Marcelino

Photo 19. Bernabé Parra preaching in the San Marcos chapel, 1966. Amalia Monroy de Parra Collection.

Cerón followed as branch presidents, which provided functioning presidencies in San Marcos through 1952.[78]

Agrícol Lozano Bravo, Sabino Lozano, Marcelino Cerón, and the Saints in their charge continued their work to institutionalize the Church in San Marcos and encourage the development of a gospel culture among the people who joined it. Sometimes the pathway continued to be not only serpentine but also rocky. Nevertheless, during these administrations the Mormons began to more closely understand the cultural, behavioral, doctrinal, and faith requirements of an institutionalized church—their church.

For Bernabé, there were setbacks following his appointment as a counselor in the district presidency. Around 1935, some nine years after his selection, Parra commenced an illicit union with Amalia Monroy that within three years produced two children.[79] Parra was once again defrocked—this time excommunicated[80]—losing his position in the district presidency, his membership in the Church, and all his priesthood blessings. All Parra's great accomplishments notwithstanding, the drag of traditional mores was more powerful than Parra's partially acquired inhibitions and commitments as a Church leader. It would take him a decade to reclaim his membership and receive his priesthood blessings again.

Parra's scorching desire for more children of his own that Jovita could not give him, coupled with the powerful temptations that had taken him down once before,[81] undid him anew. However, in his own mind, and in the minds of the Saints in the municipality of Tula whom he continued to support and defend all during the interregnum of his excommunication, Parra never ceased being a Mormon in spirit and desire.[82] Yet he knew he had to be held accountable for his personal failings.

Bernabé, his wife, Jovita, and his mistress, Amalia, coexisted until about 1945.[83] One of Amalia's children speaks of Jovita as his loving second mother (*mamá Jovita*),[84] which suggests an affectionate and ongoing relationship over the years consistent with Mexicans' love of children, even under these circumstances.

During the April 1946 reunification-of-the-Church meetings in Mexico that Church President George Albert Smith attended, including in the branch of San Marcos, mission president Arwell L. Pierce rebaptized Bernabé, and President Smith restored his priesthood blessings. Given that Bernabé and

Photo 20. María Guadalupe Monroy Mera, María de Jesús Mera Vda. de Monroy, and Amalia Monroy, 1933. Courtesy of Maclovia Monroy de Montoya.

Jovita never divorced and that she lived until 1960, domestic arrangements that separated Amalia and Bernabé had occurred so that, once again, he would have been living a repentant life consistent with a gospel culture. What were those arrangements? For one, around 1945, Bernabé and Amalia stopped living together, convinced that, for them, this was the Lord's will, their children

Photo 21. Bernabé Parra Gutiérrez, with his sons Bernabé Parra Monroy (left) and Benjamín Parra Monroy (right), ca. 1944. Courtesy of Maclovia Monroy de Montoya.

notwithstanding (considering this was the only way that Bernabé could become rebaptized, a matter that had nearly consumed him since his excommunication ten years earlier).[85] Parra continued to interact with his sons, both of whom had great affection and respect for their father.[86] Parra supported them financially with living expenses, his youngest son's mission costs, his oldest son's university studies, and both sons through their middle school and high school (*secundaria* and *preparatoria*) education. He also may have contributed to Amalia's household expenses for fifteen years before Jovita died, and Bernabé and Amalia subsequently chose in 1960 to reconnect with a legitimate marriage.[87] Whatever and how often one's transgressions, the Lord, and the Church, are usually quick to respond to a contrite penitent, especially one whose testimony of the restored gospel never faltered even though his personal life did not yet fully embrace a gospel culture.

Another arrangement that reflected honorably on a contrite and repentant Parra and further sealed his sons' affections for him occurred in 1947. In that year, Amalia left San Marcos for Mexico City, ostensibly to enroll her two children in a postprimary educational experience superior to what San Marcos could offer. The move also geographically disconnected Bernabé and Amalia and publically attested to the separation they had already decided upon. Parra nevertheless kept contact with his sons and financially supported them.

Both Amalia and Bernabé thrived on learning, turning every opportunity to provide their children a good education. Earlier, Bernabé's educational thirst had become the Monroy family's improvement project. Amalia, of course, raised in the Monroy household since she was eleven or twelve, acquired at an early age the family's blistering desire to better itself educationally.

Amalia not only took her two sons, ages eleven and thirteen, with her to Mexico City but also the children's cousin Enrique Montoya and their friend Efraín Villalobos.[88] She cared for them while they pursued their educational desires. Her sons and Efraín Villalobos, and most likely Enrique Montoya too, excelled in their studies. Afterward, at least three of them lent their prodigious energies and educational preparation to the benefit of the Church.[89]

Notwithstanding Bernabé Parra and Amalia Monroy's domestic arrangements initially being contrary to the teachings of the gospel, these parents raised their two children in households of faith. Their service, as that of their children and grandchildren, has blessed untold numbers of people. The twice-defrocked

Photo 22. President George Albert Smith visited San Marcos for a "reunification conference," April 1946. Left to right: Mary Brentnall Done Pierce, mission matron; Arwell L. Pierce, president of the Mexican Mission; Joseph Anderson; María Guadalupe Monroy Mera; President George Albert Smith; Jovita Monroy Mera de Parra; Bernabé Parra Gutiérrez; Roy Van McVey. On this occasion, Parra was rebaptized and his priesthood blessings were restored. Collection of Amalia Monroy, courtesy of LaMond Tullis archives.

Bernabé rose repeatedly to assist members in San Marcos, even facilitating in 1946 the formation of a private school (the "Church School" later named Héroes de Chapúltepec) to educate his own and others' offspring, who otherwise would probably have fallen below a level of literacy and moral persuasion that Parra felt appropriate for the Saints. A most unusual feat for a man who never went to school.

Although Bernabé and Amalia fell into a pattern that was entrenched in traditional Mexican culture, and although Parra was anxious to have heirs that his wife, Jovita, could not give him, having these heirs with Amalia was nevertheless a profound departure from the long trek that adopting a gospel culture entails, especially for a leader of his stature. A national or regional culture antithetical to a strived-for gospel ethos is sufficiently hard to break that even the very elect may fall, as did, for example, Apostle Richard R. Lyman (who in 1925 had visited San Marcos) under analogous circumstances.[90]

LEADERSHIP AND INSTITUTIONALIZATION

Clearly, the impact of leaders is consequential in the Church's transformation from ephemeral implant to an integral part of a community's life. The process by which the Church's doctrines, mission, policies, vision, action guidelines, codes of conduct, central values, and Restoration eschatology become integrated into the culture of its leaders and members and that its organizational structure is able to sustain through time is neither easy nor assured.

In San Marcos, the strength of most early leaders' testimonies and convictions trumped their immense personal shortcomings to, on balance, leave among most members a positive introspection into their own lives:

> Our leaders were as human as we—some with their alcohol, some with their women, some with their backbiting, some with their quick judgments that hurt others, and some with their spousal and parenting problems. Yet, together, we learned not only the doctrinal tenants of the gospel of Jesus Christ but also something of the culture in which it must be embedded. We still have our struggles, but we are a better people than we were. Our children, generally speaking, are an improvement upon us. Is this not the promise of progress that the scriptures and the prophets have foretold for those who, despite sometimes massive personal weaknesses, inadequacies, limitations, and failings, strive to find God and to serve him and, in so doing, make the world a better place in which to live?[91]

NOTES

1. The difficulty is illustrated at, for example, the sectorial level of ethics in any organization. See Ronald Sims, "The Institutionalization of Organizational Ethics," *Journal of Business Ethics* 10, no. 7 (1991): 493–506.
2. Eduardo Balderas, "How the Scriptures Came to Be Translated into Spanish," 29.
3. San Marcos First Ward and San Marcos Second Ward.
4. The wards are Tula and El Huerto.
5. Jasso Ward.
6. San Lucas Ward, Iturbe Ward, El Carmen Ward, Atitalaquía Ward, Bominthza Branch, and Tlahuelilpan Branch.
7. Clark V. Johnson, "Mormon Education in Mexico: The Rise of the Sociedad Educativa y Cultural" (PhD diss., Brigham Young University, 1977), 64–77; Barbara E. Morgan, "Benemérito de las Américas: The Beginning of a Unique Church School in Mexico," *BYU Studies Quarterly* 52, no. 4 (2013): 89–95. The elementary schools were eventually phased out as improvements in Mexico's public education system came on board. The flagship school, *Centro Escolar Benemérito de las Americas* (a high school), was closed in 2013 and transformed into a missionary training center. Barbara E. Morgan, "The Impact of Centro Escolar Benemérito de las Américas, a Church School in Mexico," *Religious Educator* 15, no. 1 (2014): 145–67.
8. Basic information on Bautista and Páez may be found in Tullis, *Mormons in Mexico*, chs. 5–6.
9. As an example, I list the Monroy family's website, https://sites.google.com/site/linajemonroy/home.
10. Agustín Haro may have been functioning as an ad hoc "district president" in conjunction with his role as branch president in San Pedro Mártir. However, in the wake of the dissolution of the San Marcos Branch presidency it was not he who appeared on the scene but rather Gabriel Rosales, one of the refugees in San Marcos who came out of hiding long enough to be of assistance. Gabriel Rosales's only apparent connection with ecclesiastical authority was through Ángel Rosales, president of the Ixtacalco Branch.
11. On the priesthood offices, see Monroy Mera, "Como llegó el evangelio," 32; on reconstituting a presidency of sorts, see "Carta de Jesús M. Vda. de Monroy," 8.
12. One such letter that arrived in May 1916 admonished Casimiro about his treatment of branch members that had pushed some of them from the Church. Monroy Mera, "Como llegó el evangelio," 37.

13. Guadalupe Monroy noted much discord between branch members and Casimiro as they struggled over their losses and insecurities. The stresses were horrendous and some families were falling apart. Monroy Mera, "Como llegó el evangelio," 36.
14. Monroy Mera, "Como llegó el evangelio," 37, 39–40. In January 1917, Bernabé Parra was nominated to be ordained a deacon.
15. Rosales presided over the Sunday meetings of 23 July 1916 and 14 January 1917 and probably others. Monroy Mera, "Como llegó el evangelio," 38.
16. Monroy Mera, "Como llegó el evangelio," 42. The congregation selected Parra to lead the services of 4 August 1917.
17. Monroy Mera, "Como llegó el evangelio," 38, 40, 42. The service was for 17 July 1917.
18. Monroy Mera, "Como llegó el evangelio," 38, 40, 42. The personal attack occurred at the fast and testimony meeting of 4 August 1917.
19. Monroy Mera, "Como llegó el evangelio," 43.
20. Monroy Mera, "Como llegó el evangelio," 2, 4–5.
21. Sanders Morales to LaMond Tullis, 11 February 2014; and Monroy Mera, "Como llegó el evangelio," 5. Bernabé Parra was baptized 28 July 1913. "Referencias del diario de W. Ernest Young," *Linaje Monroy en el estado de Hidalgo, México*, 17, https://sites.google.com/site/linajemonroy/rafael-monroy-mera/el-diarioo-de-w-ernest-young/referencias-del-diario-de-ernest-young.
22. Young, "Diary," 107.
23. Rey L. Pratt, "A Latter-day Martyr."
24. Monroy Mera, "Como llegó el evangelio," 9, 11.
25. Guadalupe Monroy records Parra's return to San Marcos as being 20 May 1917. Monroy Mera, "Como llegó el evangelio," 41.
26. "Reseña de la vida de Jovita Monroy Mera" (typescript, 4 pages, n.d.), copy provided by Hugo Montoya Monroy, 1 March 2014, 2. Also, Monroy Mera, "Como llegó el evangelio," 42. (*Consuela al joven Bernabé Parra citando las escrituras y diciendo, "Cuando hay tribulaciones es que Dios está más cerca de nosotros y quizá sea una prueba de Dios para nuestra fe."*)
27. Monroy Mera, "Como llegó el evangelio," 43.
28. LaMond Tullis recounts the story of Trinidad Hernández in three sources, two of which are *Mormons in Mexico*, 110, 176–77; and "Los Primeros: Mexico's Pioneer Saints," *Ensign*, July 1997, 46–51. The third, "Cómo llegó el evangelio y el Libro de Mormón a México," is the first in a series of lessons on the history of the Church in Mexico published at *http://lds.org.mx/historia-de-la-Iglesia-en-México/colección-de-clases-de-historia*. However, as of this writing, the web page's platform

is being changed and the article is temporarily not available. Also, see Monroy Mera, "Como llegó el evangelio," 44. As for Dolores Martínez de Estrada, Parra's foster mother, Minerva Montoya Monroy (email to LaMond Tullis, 21 September 2016) informs us that this foster mother and her husband, Asención Estrada ["Don Chon"], were "the parents who reared [Minerva's] uncle Bernabé given that his biological mother (María Guadalupe Gutiérrez Martínez) died when he was born. Thus when [Parra] went to Guerrero to teach his family, both Dolores and Don Chon accepted the gospel and later, says my father (Abel Montoya), Don Chon also became the foreman [*mayordomo*] of El Godo."

29. Monroy Mera, "Como llegó el evangelio," 45. The desire to discount the authority of one of their own seems strange given that in the next generation many of the members in Mexico would be arguing that only their kind should be doing the ordinances and heading the administration of the Church, which would give rise to the separatist Third Convention movement. Tullis, *Mormons in Mexico*, chaps. 5–6.
30. Monroy Mera, "Como llegó el evangelio," 46.
31. Guadalupe Monroy (Monroy Mera, "Como llegó el evangelio," 46) notes that as of 1942, Isauro had not returned to the Church. However, Maclovia Monroy de Montoya and her daughter Minerva appended a note to Guadalupe's record stating that "Isauro Monroy returned to the Church following the death of his last wife. While yet alive he attended the temple and remained faithful up to his death." (*Isauro Monroy volvió a la Iglesia después que su última esposa mueriera. En vida asistió al Templo y se mantuvo fiel hasta su muerte*).
32. Monroy Mera, "Como llegó el evangelio," 45–46.
33. Monroy Mera, "Como llegó el evangelio," 46.
34. Guadalupe Monroy lists the names of Juan Haro, Encarnación González, Amado Pérez Cano, Dimas Jiménez, Cándido Robles, Juan Mairet, Agustín Haro, Isaías Juárez, and Jesús Flores. Monroy Mera, "Como llegó el evangelio," 47.
35. *Nadie se durmió en el tiempo que estuvo predicando*. Monroy Mera, "Como llegó el evangelio," 46–47. A short biographical sketch of Isaías Juárez may be found in Tullis, "Los Primeros: Mexico's Pioneer Saints," 46; and, in Spanish, Tullis, "Cómo llegó el evangelio."
36. Monroy Mera, "Como llegó el evangelio," 47.
37. Elena Parra Mera's birth occurred in San Marcos in April 1921. Saunders Morales to LaMond Tullis, 11 February 2014. She grew up in the Monroy compound and enjoyed the educational advantages afforded all the Monroy and Mera children who had lived there. At age twenty-four (1945), she became the secretary-treasurer of

the "Monroy school" that Bernabé Parra and Amalia Monroy had founded in San Marcos the previous year (Johnson, "Mormon Education in Mexico," 67). Eulalia Mera, Elena's mother, later married Felipe Peña de Santiago Hidalgo, with whom she had several children. She died 10 May 1985 in Santiago Tezontlale (Monroy Mera, "Como llegó el evangelio," 47), a place, like San Marcos, that continues with a resolute congregation of Mormons.

38. Monroy Mera, "Como llegó el evangelio," 47.
39. Monroy Mera, "Como llegó el evangelio," 51.
40. As an example, consider the intense generational bonding that comes naturally for Mexicans but that for Anglo-Americans seems to require their presence in holy temples or preparing to be there. A symposium at Brigham Young University in 1977 addressed this and related issues associated with the expanding Church. See, in particular, the discussion on Latin America previewed by LaMond Tullis and addressed by Harold Brown, Orlando Rivera, Efraín Villalobos Vásquez, and Enrique Rittscher in *Mormonism: A Faith for All Cultures*, ed. F. LaMond Tullis (Provo, UT: Brigham Young University Press, 1978), 85–150.
41. Monroy Mera, "Como llegó el evangelio," 47–48.
42. Guadalupe Monroy states that in 1918 the men who attempted most diligently to keep the Church functioning in San Marcos and the gospel alive in people's homes were Bernabé Parra (the branch president), Daniel Montoya, and Bernardino Villalobos. Monroy Mera, "Como llegó el evangelio," 45.
43. Monroy Mera, "Como llegó el evangelio," 10.
44. Daniel Montoya Gutiérrez, oral history, interview by Gordon Irving, 1974, typescript, James Moyle Oral History Program, Church History Library, 2.
45. Monroy Mera, "Como llegó el evangelio," 29–31.
46. After a ten-year hiatus (1936–46), Páez was reconciled and returned with most of his flock of Third Conventionists to the Church. Bautista was never reconciled, fleeing to Ozumba where he founded his New Jerusalem settlement, which still functions long after his death. The Third Convention drama is reviewed in LaMond Tullis, "A Shepherd to Mexico's Saints: Arwell L. Pierce and the Third Convention," *BYU Studies* 37, no. 1 (1997–98): 127–57.
47. Monroy Mera, "Como llegó el evangelio," 47–48.
48. Monroy Mera, "Como llegó el evangelio," 53.
49. Monroy Mera, "Como llegó el evangelio," 53.
50. Monroy Mera, "Como llegó el evangelio," 53.

51. Name provided by Minerva Montoya Monroy, email to LaMond Tullis, 21 September 2016.
52. Lionel M. Summers, "The Divorce Laws of Mexico," *Journal of Law and Contemporary Problems*, 310–11, http://scholarship.law.duke.edu/cgi/viewcontent.cgi?article=1759&context=lcp.
53. *Concubinato* is discussed by Flavio Galván Rivera, "El concubinato actual en México," https://revistas-colaboracion.juridicas.unam.mx/index.php/rev-facultad-derecho-mx/article/view/30097/27172.
54. Monroy Mera, "Como llegó el evangelio," 52.
55. Monroy Mera, "Como llegó el evangelio," 100. In time, Jesusita Monroy and her daughters urged Daniel to consider courting their employee, Margarita Gutiérrez Sánchez, who also had accepted the restored gospel. Daniel and Margarita soon developed a *concubinato* relationship unblessed by marriage until several children had been born. For this reason Daniel remained an excommunicated member for some time. Minerva Montoya Monroy, email to LaMond Tullis, 21 September 2016.
56. Monroy Mera, "Como llegó el evangelio," 77.
57. Monroy Mera, "Como llegó el evangelio," 80.
58. Margarito Bautista was already formulating his ideas that he would later publish in his book *La evolución de México: sus verdaderos progenitores y su origin; el destino de América y Europa* (México: Talleres Gráficos Laguna, 1935).
59. Monroy Mera, "Como llegó el evangelio," 78–79.
60. Monroy Mera, "Como llegó el evangelio," 83–84.
61. Disparate, sometimes ahistorical perspectives on Bautista are from Thomas Murphy, "'Stronger than Ever,' Remnants of the Third Convention," *Restoration: The Journal of Latter-day Saint History* 10, no. 1 (1998): 8–11; and Fernando Gómez, *La Iglesia de Jesucristo de los Santos de los Últimos Días y las convenciones lamanitas: de lo oscuridad a la luz* (México: Museo de la Historia del Mormonismo en México, 2004). See also Fernando Gómez, "The Myth about Margarito Bautista's 1935 Book" (paper, Forty-Ninth Annual Conference of the Mormon History Association, San Antonio, 7 June 2014).
62. The Mexico Area Records Preservation Center has acquired one of Bautista's "librotes" from the 1923 Genealogical Society campaign in the Atlatlahuca Branch. Bradley Hill, personal communication to LaMond Tullis, 18 August 2014.
63. Monroy Mera, "Como llegó el evangelio," 85, gives the 1925 date. Ezequiel Montoya Cruz gives the date as 1928, when he, as a young boy living with the McVeys in El Paso, Texas, was returned to San Marcos, followed in about six months by the McVeys.

Ezequiel Montoya Cruz, oral history, interview by Gordon Irving, 1974, typescript, Church History Library, 5–6.

64. Monroy Mera, "Como llegó el evangelio," 92.
65. Monroy Mera, "Como llegó el evangelio," 105.
66. Monroy Mera, "Como llegó el evangelio," 96. In "Reseña de la vida de Jovita Monroy Mera" (typescript, 4 pages, n.d.), copy provided by Hugo Montoya Monroy, 1 March 2014, 2, the date is listed as 1929 rather than 1925. The 1929 date is most probably not correct.
67. Monroy Mera, "Como llegó el evangelio," 90
68. Monroy Mera, "Como llegó el evangelio," 89.
69. Monroy Mera, "Como llegó el evangelio," 110–11.
70. Monroy Mera, "Como llegó el evangelio," 105.
71. At the time, such murals appeared from time to time in Church edifices elsewhere. Indeed, as late as 1950 an amateur paleontologist/artist painted a mural to adorn the back wall of the rostrum of the Uintah Stake Tabernacle in Utah (constructed 1899–1907) depicting creation scenes that included dinosaurs! The renovated building, without the mural, is now the Vernal Utah Temple. As for the Cristero rebellion, which pitched Catholic leaders' attempts to retrieve control over the Mexican political system from its secular leaders, see David C. Bailey, *Viva Cristo Rey: The Cristero Rebellion and the Church-State Conflict in Mexico* (Austin: University of Texas Press, 1974); and Jean Meyer, *La Cristiada* (México City: Fondo de Cultura Económica, 2006).
72. Rey L. Pratt, "Diary," vol. 8. Also, Dale F. Beecher, "Rey L. Pratt and the Mexican Mission," *BYU Studies* 15 (Spring 1975): 305.
73. William Walser, oral history, interview by Gordon Irving, James Moyle Oral History Program, Church History Library, 1976, 23.
74. Tullis, *Mormons in Mexico*, ch. 6 passim.
75. The chronology, for Mormons, is outlined by Sally Johnson Odekirk, "Mexico Unfurled: From Struggle to Strength," *Ensign*, January 2014. Also, Tullis, *Mormons in Mexico*, 111. The best and most comprehensive treatment of the Cristero period is found in Jean Meyer's two monumental works, *The Cristero Rebellion: The Mexican People between Church and State, 1926–1929* (Cambridge: Cambridge University Press, 1976); and *La Cristiada: The Mexican People's War for Religious Liberty* (Garden City Park, NY: Square One Publishers, 2013). Fondo de Cultura Económica (Mexico) has published a Spanish language edition of *La Cristiada*. An important and perceptive regional analysis is Jim Tuck's *The Holy War in Los Altos: A Regional*

Analysis of Mexico's Cristero Rebellion (Tucson: University of Arizona Press, 1982). An additional well-focused regional study is José Díaz and Ramón Rodríguez, *El movimiento cristero: sociedad y conflicto en los Altos de Jalisco* (México City: Editorial Progreso, 2002). The tenacity of the clerics and fundamentalist Catholics—both peaceful and armed—in the Cristero rebellion is noted in David C. Bailey, *Viva Cristo Rey!: The Cristero Rebellion and the Church-State Conflict in Mexico* (Austin: University of Texas Press, 1974). One of the emotive ingredients in their rebellion was the "Battle Hymn of the Cristeros," penned by Juan Gutiérrez and based on the music of the Spanish-language song "Marcha Real." *La Virgen María es nuestra protectora y nuestra defensora cuando hay que temer / Vencerá a todo el demonio gritando "¡Viva Cristo Rey!" (x2) / Soldados de Cristo: ¡Sigamos la bandera, que la cruz enseña el ejército de Dios! / Sigamos la bandera gritando, "¡Viva Cristo Rey!"* English: "The Virgin Mary is our protector and defender when there is something to be feared / She will vanquish all demons at the cry of 'Long live Christ the King!' (x2) / Soldiers of Christ: Let's follow the flag, for the cross points to the army of God! / Let's follow the flag at the cry of 'Long live Christ the King!'" *Wikipedia*, s.v. "Cristero War," wikipedia.org/wiki/Cristero_war.

76. Monroy Mera, "Como llegó el evangelio," 106.
77. The first, from 1889 to 1901, was caused by the US government's assault on Utah Territory; the second, from 1912 to 1921 was due to the Mexican civil war; the third, from 1926 to 1929 derived from the Cristero rebellion.
78. Monroy Mera, "Como llegó el evangelio," 110–11. Agrícol Lozano Bravo has offered his own insights in his oral history, interview by Gordon Irving, Mexico City, 1974, typescript, Church History Library, OH 389.
79. Bernabé Parra Monroy (b. 4 December 1936) and Benjamín Parra Monroy (b. 4 October 1938). Amalia Monroy was the niece of Bernabé Parra's wife Jovita. She was the orphaned granddaughter through Rafael Monroy whom Jesusita had taken into her home when she was eleven or twelve. Family lore says that "Aunt Jovita agreed to this," that is, to Bernabé's having children by Amalia. Minerva Montoya Monroy, email to LaMond Tullis, 21 September 2016.
80. Bernabé Parra Monroy, together with his wife Irma Soto Ledezma de Parra, oral history, interview by Stephen G. Boyden, Kirk Henrichsen, and Clinton Christensen, 3 October 2008, typescript, LDS Church History Library, OH 4221, 18–20.
81. The only other child that appears in the records we have seen is Elena Parra Mera, conceived in Parra's union with Eulalia Mera Vda. de Morales, which resulted in the Church's defrocking him the first time. "Elena Parra also lived with Jovita and

always called her 'mama Jovita.'" Minerva Montoya Monroy, email to LaMond Tullis, 21 September 2016.

82. Cross-cultural issues on this point confronted the Church from the beginning. Brigham Young's son, Brigham Morris Young, when serving a mission in the Hawaiian Islands, was appalled at the widespread casual sexual encounters he noted there and wrote to his father about the matter. How, he thought, could the Church function in such an environment? President Young's advice: "The immoral habits of many of the natives will doubtless impress you very unfavorably, still you must bear in mind that their practices are apt to be as they are traditionated, just as the rest of mankind are in theirs, and we have to deal with people as they are, and by giving them the gospel and showing them a good example, strive to make them better." Brigham Young, "Letter to Elder B. Morris Young, Honolulu, Hawaiian Islands, 23 October 1873," *Letters of Brigham Young to His Sons*, edited and introduced by Dean C. Jessee with a foreword by J. H. Adamson (Salt Lake City: Deseret Book in Collaboration with the Historical Department of The Church of Jesus Christ of Latter-day Saints, 1974). President Young held the "long view" on this matter, which precisely was George Albert Smith's position when he restored Parra's priesthood blessings.

83. Monroy Mera, "Como llegó el evangelio," 113.

84. Bernabé Parra Monroy, oral history, 27.

85. No mention is made in the records we have seen regarding the membership status of Amalia, given that she, too, was "living in sin."

86. Bernabé Parra Monroy, oral history, 18–20.

87. Monroy Mera, "Como llegó el evangelio," 113.

88. Bernabé Parra Monroy, oral history, typescript, 18–20.

89. Benjamín Parra Monroy became a mission president and raised five sons and one daughter. Bernabé Jr. raised a family of six daughters well embedded in the Church in addition to his serving the Church in various capacities. Efraín Villalobos became an educational administrator for the Church school system, although in his later years his ardor cooled; of his former self, see his "Church Schools in Mexico," in Tullis, *Mormonism: A Faith for All Cultures*, 126–35.

90. Apostle Richard Roswell Lyman was excommunicated from the Church in 1943 for adultery for a polygamous relationship he had entered in 1925 and kept secret for nearly two decades. In 1954, he was rebaptized into the Church. He died in Salt Lake City in 1963. *Encyclopedia of Mormonism*, vol. 4 (New York: Macmillan, 1992), appendix 1. Also, see Edward L. Kimball and Andrew E. Kimball Jr., *Spencer W.*

Kimball: Twelfth President of the Church of Jesus Christ of Latter-day Saints (Salt Lake City: Bookcraft, 1977), 208–10.

91. In various permutations, these thoughts express the sentiments of large numbers of members I interviewed in Mexico in 1975 and who had the good faith and trust to disclose their personal lives to me.

7

SAN MARCOS MORMONS EMBRACE TEMPORAL PROGRESS AND DEVELOPMENT

This chapter reviews Mormons' basic ideas about progress and development and examines some of the startling ways in which they were applied in San Marcos. Temporal pursuits joined spiritual ones in the Saints' quest for a better life. We look at literacy, cultural change, membership core, leadership stability, institutional support, and the Church's further organizational development in Mexico.

Early on, beginning with a small core of first-generation members and later expanding to include hundreds, the Saints in San Marcos developed a Herculean desire to become a literate people and to alter their culture to be consistent with the moral and behavioral tenants of the restored gospel. These changes did not come easily. Nevertheless, in the process, the Saints survived the Mexican civil war, eventually received significant institutional support from Church headquarters in Salt Lake City, and then saw the culmination of everyone's efforts in the creation of stakes (an organization, similar to an archdiocese, that embraces numerous congregations or wards). Finally, a culminating prize came to the Mormon congregations throughout the land—the construction of their most sacred edifices, their temples.[1]

When reflecting on their own history, Mormons frequently cite the Lord's statement that "by their fruits ye shall know them" (Matthew 7:20). Frequently, this invites people to examine their inner spiritual ability to distinguish good from evil and rise to a higher plane of existence.[2] However, from the beginning, the general Mormon population has also understood Christ's dictum to link temporal accomplishments with spiritual insights in a hoped-for trajectory of progress and development.[3] Eternal progress begins here and now. Thus, most Mormons understand the fruits to which the Lord referred to as involving the totality of a people's life.[4]

The Lord forcefully buttressed this idea when he focused on his people's need to acquire knowledge and intelligence, which Mormons understand to be the basis for obtaining wisdom, a most desirable godly trait: "Whatever principle of intelligence we attain unto in this life, it will rise with us in the resurrection. And if a person gains more knowledge and intelligence in this life through his diligence and obedience than another, he will have so much the advantage in the world to come" (D&C 130:18–19). Moreover, the Lord adds the following challenge: "It is impossible for a man to be saved in ignorance" (D&C 131:6).

With such admonitions, it is unsurprising that Mormons have adopted a predilection for work—work to acquire spiritual authenticity, work to obtain temporal wellbeing, work to gain an education, work to create and enjoy all the positive technological and scientific advances consistent with a Christ-centered life, work to acquire intelligence and knowledge and apply them to daily life in homes and communities. These fruits are not only desirable, they are harvestable. However, they don't just fall off the trees of life to be picked up with little effort. They must be cultivated, nourished, sought after, and engaged with tremendous desire and energy. Work. Indeed, Mormons have developed a gospel of work, a gospel to "make evil-minded men good and to make good men better,"[5] and to improve their conditions of life along the way.

In a practical sense, aside from trying to learn to live within a gospel culture, for illiterate and semiliterate members of the Church in Mexico, a natural, indeed, pressing need was to pursue an education, to become literate so that as a minimum they could read and understand the faith's sacred texts and have greater economic security from which to provide for their families. It was a daunting task.

LITERACY AND THE MORMON IDEA OF PROGRESS AND DEVELOPMENT

Humanity had a long, rough, and circuitous road to become literate. In the beginning, ambitious people had to invent writing symbols to express their oral capabilities, a complex system of communication itself being an astral feat. The desire to communicate symbolically was so intense that it appears that self-taught "linguists" developed independent scripts at least four times in human history: in Mesopotamia, Egypt, Mesoamerica, and China.[6] In the early years, Mormons even developed their own phonemic "Deseret Alphabet" as a means to help the Church's disparate members from a plethora of nationalities learn English.[7]

Developing a language script is one of the seminal achievements of humankind. Learning how to use it, even getting permission to use it, almost rivals the linguistic creation itself. During the European Middle Ages, religious authorities proscribed teaching, knowing, or even talking about a written language if it involved learning to read the Bible, which would be too disruptive of traditional authority.[8] Later, when the access issue was resolved through the Reformation, only those with economic means had the wherewithal to learn to read the Bible or anything else. For the vast majority of humanity, work in the fields began at around six years of age. Learning a language script was not necessary for survival even if one had energy after a day's work to think about wanting to. Such was the situation among numerous early Mormons in Mexico, including many of the first members of the branch of the Church in San Marcos.

Joining the Church ruptured the tradition of illiteracy. Contrary to the Catholic elite in medieval and later times, The Church of Jesus Christ of Latter-day Saints *wanted* its members to read and study its sacred texts. Accordingly, many early Mormons—Anglo as well as Mexican—learned their alphabets and how to use them to sound out words by studying the Book of Mormon and their other revered texts.[9]

Following up on these learning biases, the Church, from its beginning, invested enormous resources in institutions to help educate its members— elementary schools, high schools, junior colleges, and universities—thereby fostering an ethic of not only acquiring an ability to read and write but also of pursuing voluminous opportunities during a lifetime of learning.

By the turn of the twentieth century, there were at least three elementary schools functioning in the Anglo-American Mormon colonies in Chihuahua. Soon, in Colonia Juárez, the Church even constructed an academy for secondary studies. Later, as the membership among ethnic Mexicans grew in central Mexico, the Church moved to establish and maintain schools there until the Mexican public education system improved substantially.[10]

In central Mexico, member-led foundational initiatives began before any general Church educational efforts were undertaken. In 1944, Bernabé Parra and his friends set the mold for all that followed,[11] cementing among themselves and Mormons in other congregations in central Mexico the idea that it was God's will to become educated, which meant, at a minimum, the ability to read and write.[12] Beginning in Parra's San Marcos home in 1944 with six students, by 1959 the first LDS-related school for ethnic Mexicans had 211 elementary students in much enlarged scholastic quarters.[13]

These and subsequent efforts have immensely helped members of the Church in their efforts to improve their lives temporally and spiritually, aiding, in particular, San Marcos members in countless ways to become greater contributors to the Church; more faithful adherents to its doctrines of salvation; and more substantial social, economic, political, and moral contributors to the communities in which they live.

Success, popular proverbs tell us, has many fathers, while *failure* is an orphan. The San Marcos "Church School," founded in 1944 and morphed into Héroes de Chapúltepec in 1961, has at least two conflicting accounts of parentage: the one that Bernabé Parra and Amalia Monroy have advanced, and an alternative one that Agrícol Lozano Bravo has put forth. Let us briefly consider each.

BERNABÉ AND AMALIA AND THE SAN MARCOS SCHOOL

As we have seen, Bernabé Parra transmuted from an ambitious but illiterate *campesino* to a politically astute businessman who unselfishly lent his talents and resources to building up the community of Mormons in San Marcos. Along the way, he became not only literate but also one of the area's greatest sponsors of literacy—and not just for Mormons. For example, while he was president of San Marcos's Department of Public Works (*obras materiales*), he used his position to guide the building of a public school in the community. In his honor, community officials installed a commemorative plaque at the municipal (county) magistrate's office next to the now old school.[14]

For Parra's role, he had married well when he united with Jovita Monroy. Without the overarching cultural influence of the Monroy family and its resources on his developing life, it is hard to imagine how he could have become so accomplished. Ambition, latent talent, conviction of the truthfulness of the Restoration, and opportunity combined to make Parra a towering influence among Mormons and beyond. One of the best expressions is the "Church School" in San Marcos, a work to which Parra dedicated himself as an excommunicated Mormon, a status he endured for a decade (ca. 1936–46).

Parra's great respect for his mother-in-law Jesusita frequently brought to his mind her educational hopes for her progeny. As early as 1915, Jesusita had expressed her longings to mission president Rey L. Pratt. "I must procure a place," she said in her letter, "where I may educate my little granddaughter, my little Conchita, the jewel of my dear son, as also Carlota."[15] Writing just a month following the Zapatista execution of her son Rafael, Jesusita, still in deep mourning, was nevertheless already looking ahead generationally, even to the yet unborn, attempting to give them the best launch she could into the future.

In the spring of 1944, Bernabé Parra had not forgotten Jesusita's sentiments when his mistress Amalia Monroy took him to a window in their home that gave a view of the town's public school. Throngs of unkempt children shouting obscenities (*groserías*) at each other were milling about. "I cannot send our children to school there," she must certainly have expressed. Until then, Amalia had homeschooled her two boys, then about ages seven and five, but knew she had to turn them loose to pursue a formal education. But where? Not there![16]

Putting together his sons' needs and Amalia's desires, Bernabé was easily convinced. They began looking for a Church member to employ as a private teacher for their children and a few other elementary-aged youngsters. They would use their home as a base.

The couple settled on Luis Gutiérrez, a relative of Bernabé's and the brother of Nicolás Gutiérrez, whom Parra had supported on a mission,[17] a particularly studious soul who read "many books."[18] Apparently, Nicolás's brother Luis was cut out of the same mold. Parra paid him sixty pesos a month for his teaching services.[19] Later, Luis Gutiérrez, writing not only as a beneficiary of welcomed employment but as an astute observer of the local educational scene, spoke of Bernabé, and by implication of Amalia, as being "full of charity for humanity."[20]

The "Parra School," which later was called the "Church School" and which finally became known as Los Héroes de Chapúltepec, began on 29 March 1944 with six students meeting in the home that Parra shared with Amalia. The six were Benjamín Parra, Bernabé Parra Jr., Enrique Montoya, Calixto Cruz, Felipa Cruz, and Virgilio de la Vega, although others are mentioned as having joined quickly thereafter.[21] Accordingly, the following year the school enrolled forty-five students, increasing in size to over two hundred students by 1959.

Bernabé and Amalia paid Luis Gutiérrez's salary, purchased the necessary curriculum materials, and provided the space. More students began applying for admission. Parra could see the bills mount and, eight months following the beginning of the first classes, in December of 1944 he tendered a formal application through mission president Arwell L. Pierce to the LDS Church's education department for incorporation into its system of educational oversight and support.[22] Over the next seventeen years, the Church offered piecemeal funding from time to time and underwrote the cost of a school building on land that Parra donated, but not until 1961 did it take on the full costs of maintenance and operations.[23]

Clearly, observers had seen the need,[24] but Church and Mexican bureaucracies and decision-making centers were both cautious and arcane. The result? With only occasional contributions from the Church during the seventeen-year interregnum, Parra, the Monroys, the Villaloboses, other members, the students, and students' parents raised the money to operate their school. They organized a "school board" (*patronato escolar*) to meet Mexican legal requirements so their elementary school graduates would be accepted into the government's secondary schools, held fundraisers of every kind, charged tuition, assessed members fifty centavos a week as a kind of "school tax," and for seventeen years accepted the continued donations of Parra, Benito Villalobos, and the Monroys.[25]

Part of the Church's delay in embracing a good idea was its quandary about the pressing educational needs of its members throughout Mexico, many of whom, at the time, were illiterate. Anything the Church did in San Marcos would likely need to be generalized. Could the Church sustain the cost, and if so, what expenditures elsewhere would need to be curtailed in order to do so? What about the Church's other burgeoning worldwide needs? Internally, various decision-making groups had disparate views.[26]

Another element in the delay directly involved the Mexican government. Given that civil war–era proscriptions against religiously sponsored schools were still in force, how could the Church work legally in educational matters, or quasi-legally—or even extra-legally—but with political support? All these matters had to be worked out, culminating finally in the formation of a separate entity funded by the Church to sponsor the effort. The Sociedad Educativa y Cultural S. A. was born[27] and, modeling its efforts on the San Marcos School, soon established, maintained, and operated more than thirty elementary schools in Mexico for Mormon children and others who, depending on behavior and moral conduct, qualified to attend.

A CONTRASTING VIEW ON THE SAN MARCOS SCHOOL: AGRÍCOL LOZANO BRAVO'S ROLE

For twelve years, from about 1935 to 1947, long before he was set apart as the first bishop of the Ermita Second Ward and later ordained a patriarch,[28] Agrícol Lozano Bravo was the San Marcos Branch president. By all accounts, he excelled in aiding the Saints and supporting his large family of thirteen children, a significant majority of whom became not only lifetime Mormons but distinguished themselves in their Church service and in education and other ways. Whether from genes, culture, accidental opportunity, or purposeful design, Agrícol Lozano Bravo and his wife, Josefina Herrera Hernández, created one of the most significant pioneer families in the history of the Church in Mexico. Most of these families' patriarchs and matriarchs had humble origins that they overcame through a monumental desire to excel once they had accepted the gospel. This desire appears to have been a perpetual guidance to the Lozano Herrera extended family.

Agrícol Lozano Bravo was San Marcos's branch president when the Church excommunicated Bernabé Parra. He was branch president when President George Albert Smith visited San Marcos and restored Parra's priesthood after Arwell L. Pierce had rebaptized him. He was in San Marcos when the "Church School" began.

In his 1974 interview with Gordon Irving, Lozano Bravo wanted it known that the role generally accorded to Bernabé Parra with the school (summarized previously) is unwarrantedly placed.[29] Indeed, Lozano Bravo took credit for a series of events that got the school founded and then had the Church take over its maintenance and operations under the fictive guise of an independent Sociedad Educativa y Cultural S. A.

According to Lozano Bravo, his efforts began during the reign of Mexico's president Lázaro Cárdenas del Rio (1934–40). A number of San Marcos members, unmoved by the economic nationalism and agrarian reform policies that Cárdenas espoused[30] (a return to the rhetoric of the Revolution) and frightened by their president's welcoming León Trotsky and other Russian socialists into Mexico, approached branch president Lozano Bravo with a special request. Would he get a school started for their children? Caught up in the propaganda that Cárdenas was a communist and was working to establish communism as the country's prevailing ideology and that he would use the schools to infiltrate these scary ideas into the minds of the children, some San Marcos Mormons wanted an alternative educational venue for their youngsters.[31]

The branch president consulted with his counselors, Ezequiel Montoya and Nicolás Gutiérrez, and they were thrilled with the idea. Lozano Bravo then traveled to Mexico City to solicit the support of mission president Arwell L. Pierce (1941–50). Pierce told him to create an official request (*solicitud*), signed, notarized, and with supporting documents (all translated into English), to be sent to Salt Lake City. Pierce would then write a cover letter and send it off. Clearly, the request was in line with Pierce's own assessment of the educational needs of the Mexican Saints.

The Church authorized the school on the following basis: Headquarters would pay 50 percent of the cost of construction and sustaining the school, with the other 50 percent coming from branch members and users of the school's services. A quota of 50 centavos per person weekly was established for branch members. This was the first LDS church-sponsored school in the whole of Mexico outside of the Mormon colonies in Chihuahua and Sonora.

Parra's role was to grease the skids with governmental authorities. Because of his political acumen, he was highly successful, and on this count, Lozano Bravo paid Parra great compliments. However, the first classes, Lozano Bravo affirms, were not held in the Parra home but rather in the Monroy home, where they used the hall where sacrament meeting was held and a few additional rooms, doing so until a new school was constructed.³²

WHICH VIEW PREVAILS?

Without detracting from Agrícol Lozano Bravo's heroic service to the Church over many decades, clearly there are many inconsistencies in his recollections about the school, even accounting for his being seventy-eight when Gordon Irving interviewed him in 1974. All other accounts stipulate that the school moved from the Parra home to the old, then decrepit, LDS church building that the Mormons had constructed years before. Classes continued in that venue until the Church constructed a new school in 1957, funded entirely from headquarters, on adjacent land Parra donated for that purpose.

Construction for the new school commenced on 24 January 1955 and terminated in 1957 with the inaugural celebration occurring on 11 July of that year. Mexican government and public school officials and members of the Church attended.³³ All during the construction, the school's 171 elementary students continued to meet in the old chapel and its adjacent classrooms.³⁴

By the mid-1940s, when the idea of a school was circulating, sacrament meetings and other church gatherings had long ceased to be held in the Monroy home. These meetings had all moved to a first and then a second church building the Saints had constructed from their own will, grit, and ingenuity, with little funding from Salt Lake City. Thus, Lozano Bravo's claims that the Monroy home rather than the Parra home was the seat of first educational encounter for a few Mormon children is clearly in error.

Despite Lozano Bravo's initiative as early as 1940 during the Cárdenas administration and fully four years before anyone else was talking about a San Marcos School, he seemed to concentrate his views on the early 1960s, when the Church did indeed take over the San Marcos School, as we have already seen. Lozano Bravo paid scant attention to the twelve years that preceded the takeover.

Lozano Bravo's efforts probably were influential to the Church eventually assuming responsibility for the school. It is less likely that these efforts coincided with the private initiative, funding, and support that Bernabé Parra and others generated in 1944 and sustained for twelve subsequent years.

EDUCATION AND INSTITUTIONALIZATION

In terms of *consequence*, it matters less who did what than the fact that these efforts furthered the moral, ethical, and educational development of Mormon children in San Marcos in the mid-twentieth century when the Mexican school system was highly dysfunctional. Those who benefitted from the school's existence and, indeed, their descendants for several generations will unlikely forget the educational trek that began under private initiative and humble circumstances more than three quarters of a century ago.

Returning to the general role of education in the life of Mormons, one sees the gospel infusing a longing among members to progress and develop and improve their personal lives as well as their capability to serve others. The Church is now in its sixth generation in Mexico, and each generation appears to have made improvements over the preceding one consistent with opportunity and enhanced desire. In English, the hackneyed phrase "pulling yourself up by your bootstraps" suggests a fierce longing to progress that does not necessarily await institutional help, governmental or church. Yet hundreds of thousands of Mexico's Saints whose pioneer forebears did indeed pull themselves up by their bootstraps are now beneficiaries. They have the example of Mexico's Mormon pioneers in addition to the benefits of enhanced governmental educational services and the Church's continued educational emphasis, such as through its Perpetual Education Fund, to foster children's capabilities to integrate with a developing economy.[35]

In each successive generation, Mexican Mormons have availed themselves of opportunities that increasingly have come their way. Accordingly, despite the Church's completely closing the educational initiatives in 2013 that nurtured the San Marcos School[36] into becoming perhaps the best elementary school in the Tula Hidalgo municipality, launching hundreds of children into a better life, San Marcos children still push on to excel. It is a pattern throughout the Church in Mexico.[37]

Among Mormons, with notable individual exceptions, greater religiosity is associated with higher levels of education, thus facilitating the institutionalization of a faith where people think of "progress and development" as including improvements in their relationship with God.[38] All this facilitates the process by which institutionalization associated with greater spiritual integrity occurs.[39]

CULTURAL CHANGE

Wherever and whenever the gospel of Jesus Christ has implanted itself in societies, it has done so on a bed of prescriptions and proscriptions—people's cultures[40]—that already orient individual lives. The gospel does not exist as an isolated and independent social construct. It embeds itself in and, in important ways, alters the customary beliefs, social forms, and material traits of a given people who otherwise might define themselves independently by national, racial, ethnic, or social groups. Over time, the struggle is for the people of each generation to discover the purity of the gospel and progressively define their lives in terms of a "gospel culture" that takes precedence in key areas over their inherited secular cultures.[41]

National or folk cultures tend to be a powerful warp on people's thinking, encouraging them to believe that what they do and say and how they do and say it (not to mention the reasons behind both) are, if not totally God's will, then certainly the best that humankind can offer. It can be a trap, convincing people to think that what they are is the epitome of God's will for them and that all other humans are inferior. From this cauldron of self-deceit and arrogance, the Lord takes people as they are, embedded in whatever way in the cultures of their times, and through His teachings—His gospel—seeks to make them into new beings of faith and commitment, adherents to a new culture, a gospel culture informed by "a distinctive way of life."[42]

That the gospel has flourished well in diverse cultures and times attests to its possibility of being a faith for nearly all cultures,[43] the most likely exception being the trajectory that leads people to become rabid, fundamentalist terrorists.[44] However, even under the best of circumstances, sometimes the possibility and the practice of developing a gospel culture are hard to match up. Gospel living requires cultural liberation from the confines of some aspects of whatever ethos has embraced it to the expansiveness of a culture that focuses people's attention on the concept of eternal life and how to obtain it. It matters less what people wear and eat or whether they sport facial hair or play soccer or football than what they are doing about God's commandments. They have to decide what entails obedience, righteous living, modesty in dress and behavior,[45] and kindness to one another in a community striving toward a Zion where knowledge and wisdom combine to produce a people who can live with God. That, it appears, is what happened to the Mormons' fabled city of Enoch.[46]

As the gospel spreads among nations and cultures in modern times, which national culture should prevail? Until a half-century ago or less, the prevailing thinking among North American Mormons of Anglo-European descent was that they had it, that they truly embraced a gospel culture. In some ways they certainly did. However, they confused a lot of ephemeral baggage for the gospel.[47] People in several other cultures have done the same. It has taken time to weed out ephemerality so that gospel tendencies in all cultures that direct people's attention to Christ-oriented behavior, obedience, and progress are magnified in light of the Restoration.

In addition to understanding the doctrines of salvation and the Atonement of Christ, Mormons in all nations and cultures, as they work to embrace their faith, will progressively see the gospel as a binding cultural overlay of their respective national identities. Thus, with constant and careful attention to the essentials that unite them, Mormons can proudly be Mexicans, US Americans, Brazilians, Japanese, Russians, Angolans, Filipinos, or whatever nationality and be less concerned about what separates than what ties them to Jesus Christ and makes them eligible for the array of blessings the gospel promises the faithful.

CULTURAL CONSTANCY, CHANGE, AND INSTITUTIONALIZATION

Aside from cultural ephemeralities that may be alien to a gospel culture rather than simply an interesting but unimportant expression of human living, all cultures appear to have laudable elements that may tap into the primordial instincts of people who see themselves as children of God. As an illustration, the Mexican practice of ancestral bonding would certainly seem to qualify. For twenty-first-century Anglo-American Mormons in the United States, such powerful bonding sentiments usually require the surrounding walls of a sacred temple.

Ancestral bonding in Mexico is played out publicly the first and second of November of each year (the Day of the Dead), wherein families link with their deceased through storytelling and graveside visiting in the various *panteones* throughout the land. However, it is more. Recall that as soon as the Monroy children emerged from the waters of their baptism, they immediately wanted to reenter and be baptized for their nearly always-thought-about progenitors. Recall that at their martyrdom, Rafael Monroy and Vicente Morales were said to have even prayed for their yet unborn descendants. The idea of ancestral and descendant links rises to such a level of importance in Mexican culture that it may approach universal religiosity.[48] That is certainly a cultural constant easily aligned with a gospel culture.

All these things aside, change toward embracing a gospel culture is a fundamental aspect of becoming a people truly embedded with God. Most faithful Mormons just keep trying, the perhaps trite but nevertheless penchant question frequently surging in their minds, "What would Christ have us do?" For the early members in San Marcos, this change required their painful attention to the Savior's teachings about chastity and sexual morality. It required them to address backbiting and rumormongering. They had to address their alcohol problem in light of the Mormons' Word of Wisdom (D&C 89) and the constant need to be caring for one another in all conditions of life. Magnificent people rise to these challenges of change. Many in San Marcos rose grandly.

Among Mormons, the doctrine of repentance is a powerful motivator for cultural change and renewal toward gospel living. At least it ought to be.[49] The Saints in San Marcos worked long and hard at it, and, despite their stumbling and frequently awkward passage, many arrived to a point where the gospel was a complete part of them. On such a foundation, the Church in San Marcos became institutionalized, proceeding through a process by which its doctrines, mission, policies, vision, action guidelines, codes of conduct, central values, and eschatology associated with the Restoration became integrated into the culture of leaders and members and sustained through time by an organizational structure.

MEMBERSHIP CORE AND LEADERSHIP STABILITY

A frequently voiced folk proverb in English reads, "When the going gets tough, the tough get going," meaning that when situations become mortally menacing or difficult, the strong rise to the challenge and work harder to meet it.

Any new beginning for the Church that enjoys "tough members" truly is a godsend. For one thing, they do not wilt in the face of the nearly inevitable persecution. For another, they work doubly hard to inculcate the norms and values of their new faith, to change their lives, their attitudes, and their beliefs toward embracing a gospel culture, even when it becomes more difficult than they may have anticipated at their individual baptisms.

Almost inevitably, Mormon pioneers in every land have suffered varying degrees of persecution, including, in San Marcos, the martyrdom of native leaders. Every pioneer, whether the first member in a given locality or the first of a family anywhere, nearly always faces hard decisions about what she or he will give up in order to accept and pursue the new life that has captured heartfelt sentiments.

In the face of persecution, those who retain a decision to change religiously and culturally find their nerves steeled and resolve hardened. They work overtime to teach their children and grandchildren not only gospel basics but the cultural traits of honesty, hard work, fidelity, rectitude, doing good to others, forgiving enemies, and becoming educated, all of which form a part of what they feel ought to be associated with the gospel culture they are trying to learn and adopt. There is a lack of warring "Hatfield and McCoy" families,[50] with their spiraling retribution and revenge that not only corrodes the heart and damages the soul but costs human lives and produces societal disintegration.

A strong membership core profoundly blessed San Marcos, particularly in the lives of the Monroy family, and more particularly in the person of Jesusita Mera, one of the grandest matriarchs whom the author has had the pleasure of encountering. When Jesusita's daughters started investigating the Church, she did not disown them. At first, she objected to their time with the foreign missionaries, but then she examined the evidence and joined the Church, resolving "never to be defeated." When her son was lost to an execution squad, she collapsed in despair but shortly arose to give direction, support, moral example, and physical strength to others. Faced with running from her persecutors or standing her ground so that the Church would have a fighting chance in San Marcos, she chose the latter, eventually earning the respect of thoughtful townspeople of whatever degree of persuasion. She took in orphans not even of her bloodline. She used her financial resources to help many others.

Although from a relatively privileged class economically, Jesusita spent her years building up others rather than climbing a figurative rameumptom[51] to cast aspersions on the "lesser people," a nearly universal social-class practice that allegedly makes the privileged feel good about themselves. Jesusita moved as quickly as she could into a gospel culture and taught others by precept and word to do likewise. In part because of her "ministry," other strong families emerged—Montoyas, Villaloboses, Moraleses, Parras, and Gutiérrezes. There were others.

With a strong core in place, members in the San Marcos Branch resisted the overtures of Mormon schismatics, in part because the members had pushed gospel learning in the early years. Some members learned to read and write by studying the Book of Mormon. Others aggressively sought out all the literature the Church had published in Spanish and studied it. Some learned English in order to expand the literature they could consume. They held testimony meetings under all kinds of circumstances, using the time not only to express their heartfelt convictions but also to tell what they had or were learning about gospel principles. Strong people do this hard work because it is their inclination to know for themselves what their hearts tell them is true. This also gave impetus to the school that the Mormons established so that, along with academic learning, their children could learn proper moral behavior and something of how the gospel of Jesus Christ ought to be expressed in members' homes, in their communities, and in their church.

Institutionalizing the gospel in any locale becomes infinitely more probable if strong members bless its efforts from the beginning. San Marcos members, all their personal faults and trials notwithstanding, in many ways created a laudable mold from which others could emerge with accelerated progress.

INSTITUTIONAL SUPPORT AND OUTCOMES

A survey of Christian churches in the United States lists thirty-five denominations (which includes numerous subpersuasions) with membership of over 2,500 each.[52] The same publication lists 313 religions for the same region if one counts as doctrinal bases belief in one god, many gods, no god, or god as represented by animal spirits, alien groups, or psychoactive substances. It is likely that other countries have similar nearly unfathomable variations, particularly in Mexico, where storefront churches pepper the urban landscape everywhere.

Within Christianity, one also sees great variation with respect to centralized direction. For example, among the Churches of Christ[53] central direction is nonexistent. The Churches' byline emphasizes that they "are undenominational and have no central headquarters or president. . . . Each congregation . . . is autonomous, and it is the Word of God that unites us into One Faith."⁵⁴

Regarding a centralized guiding hierarchy, The Church of Jesus Christ of Latter-day Saints is a polar opposite of the Churches of Christ. Composed mostly of lay clergy at local and regional levels who come from bewildering varieties of life, it is a president-prophet and a council of twelve Apostles, aided by scores of other "General Authorities," that hierarchically direct local leaders and therefore the whole Church. Through semiannual general, regional, and "stake" conferences, seminary classes, institute programs, myriad publications on leadership and administration of church affairs, the Internet (https://www.lds.org; in Mexico, https://www.sud.org.mx), leadership training seminars, symposia, and sometimes even region-wide training gatherings, these authorities attempt to maintain a steady hand on the Mormon faith worldwide. In particular, they work to build a unified understanding of doctrinal matters as the faith increasingly spreads across cultures, nationalities, languages, and ancestral customs.

Aside from fundamental doctrinal issues, the centrally directed Church of Jesus Christ of Latter-day Saints strives for its members to have a common understanding of being "disciples of Christ." Accordingly, numerous teachings emanate from headquarters on social, spousal, and parental relations and ancestral attachments as well as personal conduct and other categories designed to inculcate a gospel culture among Mormons. The rapid increase in the number of Mormon temples (Mormons' most holy edifices, which now number more than 150 worldwide) that foster these teachings and inculcate conviction and testimony in members' hearts are the apex of spiritual institutional support.

Absent such a central direction and support, the Church in its tens of thousands of localities could develop different practices and even beliefs on a range of issues depending on ethnic, family, ancestral, language, and national ties and local leadership prerogatives. It therefore would likely fragment into numerous subdenominations and lose the coherence it mostly now enjoys. In the days of nonattention from central headquarters in Mexico, in part because of a civil war and the Cristero uprising, we have already seen how divergent groups emerged (e.g., Margarito Bautista and the Third Convention).

Mission president Rey L. Pratt was the central link between headquarters in Salt Lake City and local members in the early years of the Church in San Marcos. He was a spectacular personality in his dedication to the Mexican

Saints and in his ability to communicate with them. Fairly, one may say that through him the Church had an affectionate following, partly for the restored gospel it embodied but also partly for Rey L. Pratt himself. Because of his position as mission president and the direction his superiors gave him, we may call Pratt's service "institutional support." Such support tided the Saints through transitions amidst local leaders' personal shortcomings and failures. It gave them comfort through their tragedies and persecution. "The Church cares about us."

PRATT'S INSTITUTIONAL SUPPORT

Pratt's institutional support marshalled and directed local missionaries, placed foreign missionaries on the scene when possible to teach and disseminate doctrines of the Restoration, and sent Agustín Haro and other leaders from more mature branches in San Pedro Mártir and Ixtacalco on various rescue missions to Church members in San Marcos. The teachings, the priesthood ordinances, and, to some extent, even new patterns of social interaction came to San Marcos via institutional support.

There was more. In my mind's ear, I hear Pratt saying, "You want to build a chapel? OK, I'll see if I can get funding for the metal roof."

"I can't visit you now, but you can expect a letter of support and instructions from me every week. Follow them carefully and heed the words of your branch president."

"Be careful not to be misled by designing men. Follow the prophet. We are working hard to get more material to you in your native Spanish so that you may be better instructed, especially during times when we cannot be with you."

"Love one another as Christ loves you. Do good to each other. Support one another through your trials and tribulations."

CONSTRUCTION PROGRAMS

Later, the central Church constructed a new church building and school for the San Marcos Saints, aided them in their educational pursuits, and instituted helpful programs to assist the poorer members in their sometimes-desperate search for food. It established "health missionaries" to work on public health and maternal and infant care through the local Relief Societies and to train young sisters in the rudiments of these fields.[55]

Photo 23. New LDS chapel, San Marcos, Hidalgo, 1974. Courtesy of Laura Smith.

One of the underlying assumptions of the Mormon way of life is that, aside from understanding the doctrines of salvation, the gospel is best understood through the prism "By their fruits ye shall know them" (Matthew 7:20). For Mormons, this does not extend a license to savage people with whom one disagrees, as is so often done in the name of Christ among various religious persuasions and their political offshoots.[56] Rather, it is a call to help one another reach each person's potential as a child of God. Accordingly, the phrase vigorously persuades Mormons to engage in "good causes" and to extend a helping hand to those in need; to help them grow and develop spiritually, physically, and socially; and to prepare themselves to be economically productive citizens wherever they live.[57]

A clean, functionally appropriate edifice in which to worship and engage in other activities to improve members' spiritual and social lives gives evidence that "the Church is here to stay." It encourages people to redouble their commitments. It helps the Church to become institutionalized.

AGRICULTURAL AND HEALTH SERVICES PROGRAM

The agricultural and health services program gained traction in San Marcos with the Church school there. Less than a decade after the Church assumed funding for the school, it launched a complementary agricultural and health services missionary program (1973) that Dr. James O. Mason and his associates Mary Ellen Edmunds and Edward Soper had put together.[58] Someone had noticed that in San Marcos and environs (as elsewhere in Latin America among some of the Church membership) prenatal and postnatal care for mothers and infants did not meet "church standards." Infant morbidity and childhood mortality rates were alarmingly high.

In 1972, many people in San Marcos, young and old, had died from typhoid fever. A disease called *sarna* (insect transmitted) was a scary concern—"purple eruptions in the skin, like boils, which eventually could become fatal."[59] Laura Smith, a health services missionary, notes, "Other major concerns were diarrhea, gripa, stomach pains, fevers and diabetes. Many sisters and investigators were also interested in prenatal, infant and child care."[60] The agricultural and health services missionaries gained enthusiastic traction.

Institutional support that put health services missionaries in San Marcos to work on medical and nutritional problems among members and their friends created a vehicle. However, it did not "start the engine" or give minute guidance on how to drive. The missionaries had to figure that out for themselves. In San Marcos and the surrounding region, the pattern was to select young female members from each branch of the Church and train them as assistants. Then, on a weekly basis, the missionaries traveled from village to village, made contact with their assistants—who, by then, had already made appointments with interested people—and together went about the task of improving the health of the members. In 1975, the author visited a Relief Society meeting in Santiago Tezontlale where the sisters were vigorously discussing materials that the health services missionary and her assistant had taught them about.

During the 1970s, considerable enthusiasm for health services existed among Mormons and their friends in the state of Hidalgo. In some of the meetings, scores of people—mostly women—showed up. Never mind that some of them were illiterate. They could speak and hear and learn orally. They must

Photo 24. Health Services missionary aides, San Marcos, Hidalgo, training day, 1974. Courtesy of Laura Smith.

have, because in a few years public health indicators among Church members improved greatly.

This was an ambitious outreach program to help members and others help themselves. In Hidalgo, health services missionaries worked in Church branches in Pachuca, Tulancingo, Ciudad Sahagún, Tepatepec, Guerrero, San Lucas, Santiago Tezontlale, Tezontepec, San Marcos, Conejos, and Ixmiquilpán. They also extended their activities to areas where formal branches had not yet been organized, including Atotonilco, Cruz Azul, El Carmen, Iturbe, Magdalena, Presas, San Lorenzo, San Miguel Vinho, Tlahuelilpan, Totonico, Tula, and Zimapán.[61]

A membership better informed on matters of health and nutrition appears to give people both the strength and the will to extend themselves in their new faith. Institutionalization is thereby enhanced.

ORGANIZATION OF STAKES

The pinnacle of local organization among Mormons is the "stake," with its affiliated (usually six to twelve) local congregations called "wards" and "branches." A transformation from a branch to a ward and a district to a stake requires considerable institutional support for initiation and maintenance. One of the most ambitious efforts of which this author is aware occurred in central Mexico in November 1975. Fifteen new stakes and ninety-six wards were created in a single day, including a San Marcos Ward (now affiliated with the Tula Mexico Stake).

Mormons view this massive creation of new stakes as a truly Herculean effort. Elder Howard W. Hunter, then of the Council of the Twelve Apostles, his assistant Elder J. Thomas Fyans; and four "regional representatives" interviewed more than two hundred priesthood bearers as possible new leaders. They "set apart" (conveyed) the mantle of authority and responsibility to "45 members of stake presidencies, 288 members of bishoprics for 96 wards, 36 members of 12 branch presidencies, and about 150 high councilors."[62]

In San Marcos and elsewhere, Church support from headquarters has aided, bolstered, guided, reprimanded, and sustained the members. It is hard to imagine that in just a few generations the members could have accomplished so much without it.

Building on a bedrock of repentance—fitfully, despondently, hopefully, and eventually successfully—San Marcos members turned their attention to bettering their temporal lives in the here and now and to taking personal responsibility for as much of their lives as they could. As an example, they rejected the old adage of "If God wills it" (*Si Dios lo quiere*), so culturally ingrained during centuries of apathy and defeatism born of myriad forces, some extremely oppressive. They became temporal-development activists with a long, generational view as they worked to become literate and provide opportunities for their children to excel educationally.

Regarding personal accountability, strange expressions such as "The book fell away from me" were replaced with phrases like "I dropped the book"[63] as people took more responsibility for some of the problems they got into or that happened to them. People began to believe that not everything was out of their control, that they could take initiatives to solve problems and better their lives. Mormonism was a natural ally of such thinking. Thus, with a strong membership core such as the Monroy family and Bernabé Parra, members could adapt their culture to be more consonant with a Zion people, and the central Church could give assistance that helped to accelerate the temporal development of its members in San Marcos.

True, In San Marcos, the Church's institutionalization took time, but it ultimately had proper personnel and a proper trajectory to bring it about. The Mormons there have now accelerated their exceptional progress. Not surprisingly, the region has produced a relatively large number of local, mission, and area leaders for the Church and one General Authority. Many of these individuals have served the Church not only in Mexico but worldwide. What the genes of the martyrs have bequeathed is the subject of the next chapter.

NOTES

1. As of this writing, thirteen temples have been constructed in Mexico: Ciudad Juárez, Colonia Juárez, Guadalajara, Hermosillo, Mérida, Mexico City, Monterrey, Oaxaca, Tampico, Tijuana, Tuxtla Gutiérrez, Veracruz, and Villahermosa.

The first, Mexico City, was constructed in 1983; the last, Tijuana, in 2015. "Statistics," *Temples of The Church of Jesus Christ of Latter-day Saints*, http://www.ldschurch temples.com/statistics/units/mexico/.

2. See Robert L. Millet, "'By Their Fruits Ye Shall Know Them,'" in *The Sermon on the Mount in Latter-day Scripture*, ed. Gaye Strathearn, Thomas A. Wayment, and Daniel L. Belnap (Provo, UT: Religious Studies Center, Brigham Young University; Salt Lake City: Deseret Book, 2010), 215–29.

3. The classic case to how this linkage on progress, development, and religious conditions played out in early Protestant Christianity is Max Weber, *The Protestant Ethic and the Spirit of Capitalism*, trans. Talcott Parsons and Anthony Giddens (London: Unwin Hyman, 1930).

4. See Dean L. Larsen, "Self-Accountability and Human Progress," general conference talk, April 1980, https://www.lds.org/general-conference/1980/04/self-accountability-and-human-progress?lang=eng.

5. David O. McKay, *Millennial Star*, October. 1961, 469, cited by Royden G. Derrick, "By Their Fruits Ye Shall Know Them," LDS general conference, October 1984, https://www.lds.org/general-conference/1984/10/by-their-fruits-ye-shall-know-them?lang=eng.

6. See, for example, Stephen Chrisomalis, "The Origins and Coevolution of Literacy and Numeracy," in *The Cambridge Handbook of Literacy*, ed. D. Olsen and N. Torrance (Cambridge: Cambridge University Press, 2009), 59–74.

7. Stanley S. Ivins, "The Deseret Alphabet," *Utah Humanities Review* 1 (1947): 223–39.

8. In general, see A. G. Dickens and John M. Tonkin, eds., *The Reformation in Historical Thought* (Cambridge, MA: Harvard University Press, 1985).

9. Illustrative for Anglos is Ammon Mesach Tenney, 1844–1925, whose story was written by LaMond Tullis and can be found at http://www.sud.org.mx/ammon-meshach-tenney?lang=spa-mx. Illustrative for Mexican members are Luis Cayetano Maldonado Medina, Pedro Martínez Cid, Benito Torres Sandoval, and Juan Serafín Camacho Reyes, whose stories are at http://sud.org.mx in the portal Historia de la Iglesia en México, Historias de Pioneros Mexicanos. (As of this writing the web page is temporarily unavailable due to a platform change. Once up, searching by names will reveal biographical vignettes about each person.)

10. Barbara E. Morgan, "Benemérito de las Américas," 89–116.

11. Clark V. Johnson, "Mormon Education in Mexico," ch. 3.

12. For a strong argument of San Marcos being the model, see Clark V. Johnson, "Mormon Education in Mexico," chap. 3. The effects of education generally on a

society are reviewed by John W. Meyer, "The Effects of Education as an Institution," *American Journal of Sociology* 83, no. 1 (July 1977): 55–77.
13. Johnson, "Mormon Education in Mexico," 75.
14. Minerva Montoya Monroy, email with photo attachment to LaMond Tullis, 21 September 2016.
15. María Jesús Mera Vda. de Monroy to President Rey L. Pratt, 17 August 1915.
16. Johnson, "Mormon Education in Mexico," 65–66. Bernabé Jr. has his father taking the initiative after looking out the window of the apartment over his store. Bernabé Parra Monroy, oral history, 17.
17. Bernabé Parra Monroy, oral history, 13.
18. Bernabé Parra Monroy, oral history, 17.
19. Johnson, "Mormon Education in Mexico," 66.
20. "Historia de la escuela Héroes de Chapúltepec," Church History Library, 1.
21. "Historia de la escuela Héroes de Chapúltepec," Church History Library, 2; and Johnson, "Mormon Education in Mexico," 66. Bernabé Parra Jr. remembers the first students as being himself, his brother Benjamín, Felipa Cruz, Calixto Cruz (in 2008 president of the Tuxtla Gutiérrez temple), Virgilio Reinoso, Moisés Barrón, Virginia Barrón, and Enrique Montoya. Parra Monroy, oral history, 18. The notes from the "Historia de la escuela Héroes de Chapúltepec," 1, are probably more reliable. In sixty-eight years of Bernabé Jr.'s memory, names from several years may well have morphed into that first year. Minerva Montoya Monroy informs us that, as far as her ancestors are concerned, the first student was Enrique Montoya, not Alfonso Montoya, as stated in other sources. Email to LaMond Tullis, 21 September 2016.
22. Mexican Manuscript History, Church History Library, under the date of 31 December 1944.
23. Joseph T. Bentley, interview by Richard O. Cowan and Clark V. Johnson, 9 March 1976 and reported in Johnson, "Mormon Education in Mexico," 73–74.
24. Arwell L. Pierce, president of the Mexican mission from 1941–1950, authorized the text of one of the final paragraphs of his annual mission report, which reads, "The Branch at San Marcos, Hidalgo, has made formal application for a Church School. We believe that several church schools should be established in well-selected places so that our Mexican children may be trained in Church ideals and faith by LDS teachers." Mexican Mission Manuscript History, report of 31 December 1944, LDS Church Archives. For more on the singular role that Pierce played in the Mexican Mission, see LaMond Tullis, "A Shepherd to Mexico's Saints: Arwell L. Pierce and the Third Convention," 127–57.

25. Johnson, "Mormon Education in Mexico," 70–73.
26. Johnson, "Mormon Education in Mexico," ch. 4.
27. Johnson, "Mormon Education in Mexico," ch. 4. Clark Johnson has studied the internal workings of the LDS Church and its relationship with the Mexican government in regards to multiple actors and complex decisions giving rise to the creation of the Sociedad Educativa y Cultural S.A.
28. Biographical information listed under "Familia Lozano," "Mormones en México," *Sapienslds* (blog), 23 December 2013, http://sapienslds.blogspot.com/2013/12/mormones-en-mexico-recopilacionpor.html.
29. Agrícol Lozano Bravo, oral history, interview by Gordon Irving, typescript, Mexico City, 1974, LDS Church Archives, 8.
30. For a scholarly treatise of this period, see Marjorie Becker, *Setting the Virgin on Fire: Lázaro Cárdenas, Michoacán Peasants, and the Redemption of the Mexican Revolution* (Berkeley: University of California Press, 1995).
31. Agrícol Lozano Bravo, oral history, interview by Gordon Irving, 8–9.
32. Lozano Bravo, oral history, 8–9.
33. Johnson, "Mormon Education in Mexico," 74.
34. Johnson, "Mormon Education in Mexico," 77.
35. See Gordon B. Hinckley, "The Perpetual Education Fund," *Ensign*, May 2001, 52–53; and John K. Carmack, *A Bright Ray of Hope: The Perpetual Education Fund* (Salt Lake City, UT: Deseret Book, 2004).
36. The influence of the Church's flagship school in central Mexico is discussed by Barbara Morgan, "The Impact of Centro Escolar Benemérito de las Américas, A Church School in Mexico," *Religious Educator* 15, no. 1 (2014): 145–67.
37. From 2011 to 2013, I visited scores of Mexican-member homes whose children confirmed others' widespread observations that "progress and development" have now become a near universal aspiration among Mormons in Mexico.
38. Stan L. Albrecht and Tim B. Heaton, "Secularization, Higher Education, and Religiosity," *Review of Religious Research* 26, no. 1 (September 1984): 43–58. Stan L. Albrecht, "The Consequential Dimension of Mormon Religiosity," *BYU Studies* 29, no. 2 (1989): 57–108. In this, Mormons are an anomaly. The dominant tendency among many other faiths is noted by Michael Shermer, *How We Believe: Science, Skepticism, and the Search for God* (New York: William H. Freeman, 1999), especially 76–79.
39. The process by which the Church's doctrines, mission, policies, vision, action guidelines, codes of conduct, central values, and eschatology associated with the Restoration

of the gospel becomes integrated into the culture of its leaders and members and sustained through time by its organizational structure.

40. That culture profoundly shapes the evolution of societies whether they are in stasis or change is amply demonstrated in the symposium that Harvard University's Weatherhead Center for International Affairs conducted in 1999, which emerged as a book by Lawrence E. Harrison and Samuel P. Huntington entitled *Culture Matters: How Values Shape Human Progress* (New York: Basic Books, 2000). Frequently, some traditional values do not change commensurate with other values that underpin an evolving culture, which, for this monograph, highlights the constant struggle people have in finding and living a gospel culture as their convictions of its necessity grow. For a discussion in secular terms, see Ronald Inglehart and Wayne E. Baker, "Modernization, Cultural Change, and the Persistence of Traditional Values," *American Sociological Review* 65 (February 2000): 19–51.

41. Arturo DeHoyos and Genevieve DeHoyos, "The Universality of the Gospel," *Ensign*, August 1971, 9–14.

42. Dallin H. Oaks, "The Gospel Culture," *Ensign*, March 2012, 42.

43. See Tullis, *Mormonism: A Faith for All Cultures*.

44. For a disturbing discussion of general implications, see Samuel P. Huntington, *The Clash of Civilizations and the Remaking of World Order* (New York: Simon & Schuster, 1996).

45. A stellar discussion from a young Jewish woman is worthy of everyone's attention. Wendy Shalit, *A Return to Modesty: Discovering the Lost Virtue* (New York: The Free Press, 2000).

46. See the Mormon canonical text the Pearl of Great Price, Moses 7.

47. A robust discussion of elements of this conundrum is by Wilfried Decoo, "In Search of Mormon Identity: Mormon Culture, Gospel Culture, and an American Worldwide Church," *International Journal of Mormon Studies* 6 (2013): 1–53.

48. Samuel M. Brown, in his article "Believing Adoption," *BYU Studies Quarterly* 52, no. 2 (2013): 45–65, especially in the last two pages, argues that on generational bonding the early Mormons in New York, Ohio, Illinois, and Missouri had cultural sentiments more akin to those I have described for Mexico than for contemporary US Anglo-American Mormon culture.

49. Dallin H. Oaks, "Repentance and Change," *Ensign*, October 2003, 37–40.

50. Refers to a feud between two families—Hatfield and McCoy—of the West Virginia and Kentucky areas that lived along the Tub Fork and Big Sandy River. They were engaged in a blood feud so adversarial that it has entered the lexicon of America

folklore as an example of disintegration and loss over issues of justice, family honor, and revenge. At least twelve members of these two families were killed in revenge clashes. See Otis K. Rice, *The Hatfields and McCoys* (Lexington: University Press of Kentucky, 1982).

51. According to the Book of Mormon, a *rameumptom* was a high tower or stand that socially and economically privileged individuals could climb and from which they could look down on the poor masses as they recited rote prayers of thanksgiving for their privileged status (Alma 31). This ancient practice is most likely found in every society.

52. "35 Largest Christian Denominations in the United States," last updated 30 June 2008, http://undergod.procon.org/view.background-resource.php?resourceID=000087.

53. The Churches of Christ emphasize that they are *un*affiliated with the denominational church known as "The United Church of Christ."

54. "The Churches of Christ," www.church-of-christ.org.

55. Lori Smith, interview by LaMond Tullis, Orem, UT, 3 June 2014.

56. As an example and for a discussion of the comments of Pastor Robert Jeffress of the First Baptist Church of Dallas, Texas, about Mormons as "cultists," see Darius A. Gray, "Wherefore by Their Fruits Ye Shall Know Them," published 14 October 2011 and updated 14 December 2011, http://www.huffingtonpost.com/darius-a-gray/mitt-romney-mormon_b_1011759.html.

57. A fine example of this is seen in a 1980 BYU devotional address by David B. Haight, a member of the Church's Quorum of the Twelve Apostles. "By Their Fruits Ye Shall Know Them," 7 December 1980, http://speeches.byu.edu/?act=viewitem&id=673.

58. For general information, see David Mitchell, "Agricultural and Health Services Missionaries: A New Way to Serve the Whole Man," *Ensign*, September 1973, 72.

59. Lori Smith (health services missionary), "Notes on San Marcos, Mexico," 3 June 1974–1 January 1975, 2, copy in author's possession.

60. Lori Smith, "Notes on San Marcos, Mexico." Sarna, if treated, is rarely fatal. It is likely that those who died "of it" did so from ancillary complications around the infection sites. See "Sarna," Center for Young Women's Health, http://youngwomenshealth.org/2005/10/06/sarna/

61. Smith, "Notes on San Marcos, Mexico," 1.

62. "Fifteen New Stakes Created in Mexico City," *Ensign*, January 1976, 94–95.

63. The passive expression (*Se me cayó el libro—The book fell away from me*) sounds strange in English because, in this case, one among a multitude, the book was responsible for its collision with the floor, not the person who held it.

8

THE GENES OF THE MARTYRS

People who elect martyrdom over renunciation live life beyond the moment. They look forward a hundred or even a thousand years as they view their place in life as being neither just here and now nor theirs alone but one tied to cohorts, followers, and descendants through generations. Within the Mormon community, willing-if-necessary martyrs think of their unborn descendants, which follows the principles in the sixth lecture on faith delivered at the School of the Prophets at Kirtland, Ohio.[1] In this sixth lecture, it was taught that no sacrifice is too much or oblation too demanding if one lives by faith. However, it does produce a question: How would the martyrs' lives affect their descendants even to the end of time? This matter was probably front and center with Rafael Monroy and Vicente Morales, however unarticulated in their minds, as they knelt in prayer moments before their execution, asking the Lord to watch over their loved ones and those yet to be born. Mormons do not seek martyrdom. However, as historical accounts show us, some will choose it on their own terms if required.

VICENTE MORALES

Vicente Morales's only potentially living child was still in utero but successfully saw the light of day nine weeks after the firing squad had killed Morales.[2] As a single mother, Eulalia raised her daughter, Raquel, in San Marcos within the supporting social fabric of the community of Mormons, who banded together to overcome their discord and work on their substantial personal failings as they continued to face the onslaught of community contempt. With this help, mother and daughter got through the rest of the civil war and beyond as they enjoyed the blessings of the Church, which carried on (however fitfully) under a succession of new branch presidents.

While growing up, Raquel regaled in the stories of her father. She loved to hear about him joining the Church in Cuautla and about his missionary service when full-time missionaries were withdrawn from the country. She liked to hear of her father's work as a bricklayer and a ranch hand for Rafael Monroy and of his service as a counselor in the San Marcos Branch presidency. She loved the story of his steadfast refusal to renounce his faith even potentially to save his life. This family story has since entered the consciousness of six generations of descendants of Vicente Morales. In each one, the faithful service of many individuals has been exemplary.

Vicente's genes and his legacy to the Church thus lived on in his daughter, Raquel, who lived most of her forty-nine years in San Marcos. Raquel served a two-year mission (1937–39) in Monterrey and then spent an additional six months in service to members in Ozumba at a time when the branch there was undergoing great stress from Margarito Bautista's apostate group. In Ozumba, Raquel further fortified her commitments to the Church.

Joined in union with Antonio Roberto Saunders barely a month prior to his own baptism, Raquel and Antonio had three children: two boys and one girl. Through the girl, Ruth Josefina Saunders Morales, not only did Vicente's genes pass to a sixth generation as of this writing, but so did his fidelity in the Church. With Ruth's marriage to Benito Villalobos Vásquez—from another of the great families from San Marcos—genes, culture, and religious conviction combined to create scores of faithfully committed descendants. These, with others of his posterity, had produced by 2012 twenty-four missionaries, two Area Seventies, one mission president, one stake president, four Relief Society presidents, ten Young Women and Primary presidents at stake and ward levels, and numerous others invested in the religious, humanitarian, and educational foundations of the faith.[3] In figurative response to the townspeople's previous comments to Eulalia in 1915 ("See, that is what you get for being a Mormon"), someone could now say on Vicente's and Eulalia's behalf, "See, this is what we have given you."

As Morales faced his executioners with his convictions unbowed and his testimony resolute, one wonders if his hopes for his family's future might have embodied the following aphorism derived from 3 John 1:4: "My greatest blessings are to see my children walk uprightly before the Lord."[4] If so, he is not disappointed.

RAFAEL MONROY

In unpredictable ways, Rafael's genes have moved down through the ages. Aside from his union with Maclovia Flores Pérez, which led to the birth of a daughter and a son, and his marriage to Guadalupe Hernández, which gave him a daughter, Rafael had a "sentimental union" with Alejandra Cornejo, which produced two daughters; however, both died in infancy.[5]

Rafael's legitimate daughter, Concepción (Conchita) Monroy, did not marry until late in life and did not have children.[6] Accordingly, Monroy's only possibility of having descendants was through his common-law union (prior to his marriage to Guadalupe Hernández) with Maclovia Flores. They had a three-year love affair that created the two children who survived to pass on Rafael's genes.

What happened to Maclovia and her children? Following Rafael's marriage to Guadalupe Hernández in 1909, Maclovia worked at the hacienda El Cedó for a while but then fled to her ancestral village and a hoped-for warm parental and extended family embrace there. She took her children with her. Although Rafael seemingly reflected about his son, Luis, and daughter Gerarda,[7] he apparently made no effort to contact them. The record does not disclose if he sent their mother any support. In due course, probably in part out of economic necessity, Maclovia entered a common-law union with Santos Ortiz, with whom she had two more children.[8] Thus the years passed until September 1915.

Symptomatic of the nonfunctioning of intervillage communication during wartime, Maclovia did not hear of Rafael's July 1915 execution until September, around two months later. Shocked and saddened beyond recovery, she quickly fell gravely ill from an undetermined malady that within ten months took her life. She was twenty-seven. Her death left Rafael's Luis and Gerarda not only motherless but, in a practical sense, orphans.[9] Luis was eleven, Gerarda nine.

Stepfather Santos Ortiz did not want to keep Luis and Gerarda.[10] Aside from not being his children, he perhaps felt he could not care for someone else's progeny amidst the unremitting and grinding poverty that characterized his life. He had the two young daughters that Maclovia had borne him, and they would be a sufficient challenge for him to support. At least, they were all he wanted to sustain.

Blood ties were powerful in rural Mexico, where people generally viewed children as a precious gift from God. Accordingly, Maclovia's maternal aunts immediately stepped in to retrieve the children their niece had borne when she was living with Rafael Monroy. Oddly, however, an uncle ended up with the children. Guadalupe Pérez, one of Maclovia's half brothers who lived alone and had no children of his own, took Maclovia's Luis and Gerarda to his home.

Although sundry maternal aunts would alternatively give attention to Luis and Gerarda, it was natural that Maclovia's half brother Guadalupe Pérez should take the lead. He had always had a close relationship with her. Indeed, he had brought her the news of Rafael's execution and on numerous other visits had apparently brought some little gift to ease her deprivations and to cheer up her youngsters. Of all Maclovia's relatives, her children knew their uncle Guadalupe best. Thus, when the widower Santos Ortiz said, "Take them," the children had no reluctance in hoping to find sustenance and love in Guadalupe Pérez's home. We do not know if Maclovia's two daughters by Ortiz would also have left had their impoverished father given them the opportunity, though in time, one of them, Alfonsa, did go to live with Jesusita.

Guadalupe's economic condition was probably similar to Santos Ortiz's. However, without a wife, partner, or children of his own, he had fewer places for his scarce resources to reach. He was happy to share what he had with his niece and nephew. In retrospect, it was not much. One of Luis's grandsons remarked that the children "had a life of suffering and poverty at his side."[11]

The arrangements with Guadalupe Pérez worked well for the children for a couple of years. However, by the time Gerarda was eleven, not even the single Guadalupe—who spent a significant portion of his modest resources on Maclovia's children—could make ends meet, in part because he could see that the bright and aspiring Gerarda needed more opportunities, especially educational ones, than he could provide. Perhaps there were other reasons, too, like how to deal with a budding female teenager. In any event, he must have put out a call for help, which surfaced among Gerarda's aunts, who began to look for options. One was to place Gerarda with a family in Tula, where she could further her education beyond simple primary school.[12] Before this idea got much traction, a market event intervened that changed the lives of many people.

Several of Gerarda and Luis's maternal aunts made their living following the Mexican *tiangui* tradition of traveling from village to village and selling their wares, comestibles, clothing, artifacts, services, or whatever conceivably would bring in currency. They would sell these from portable street stands or booths that, one day a week, could line a village street for about a quarter mile. One village on their 1917 circuit was San Marcos, Hidalgo.

Selling in Mexico's rural villages in the early twentieth century was not only a transaction but also a scene of conversational art. Commentary, gossip, and informational chats were in some areas the principal ways people got their news and perhaps even validated their lives, at least at the household level. On one occasion, the aunts were chatting with a customer when the subject of Rafael Monroy came up, with the aunts no doubt adding that their family had two of his children under its care. Was their listener a Monroy sympathizer or antagonist, perhaps with the raw feelings of the civil war—which had not yet ended—still front and center in her life? Either way, it did not matter. As the conversation unfolded, the aunts learned that the Monroys still had two ranches, a store, and an ample home, and except for their psychological despair, they were in every other way relatively well-off despite the repeated Zapatista sackings.

Eventually returning to their homes to prepare for another round of selling on their market circuit, the aunts reported their findings to Guadalupe Pérez. Would the Monroys be willing to accept Gerarda into their home? The children's uncle must have quickly grasped the implication of this because nearly immediately he made arrangements to take the eleven-year-old girl to San Marcos to meet her paternal grandmother, Jesusita, and aunts Jovita, Guadalupe, and Natalia.[13]

The meeting must have gone well. The Monroys not only accepted Gerarda into their home as one of their own but they also would have taken Luis had his uncle Guadalupe been willing. Later, Jesusita took in Alfonsa Ortiz, one of Gerarda's two half sisters, also treating her as a daughter.

Through Maclovia's daughters, the Monroys developed a strong relationship with Maclovia's son, Luis, who never joined the Church but who was always supportive of and sympathetic to the Mormons. In fact, he raised his five children within the social fabric of Mormon life. His daughter Cresencia Maclovia (still alive in 2014 and named after her grandmother) was Rafael's first descendant to serve a mission.[14] The children's uncle Guadalupe Pérez, who never faltered in his attention to Gerarda even though she was living in the Monroy household, ultimately joined the Church.[15]

Grandmother Jesusita's first official act was to change Gerarda's name to Amalia.[16] Three generations later, many members of the Church in San Marcos continued to remember Amalia Monroy with affection. One of the reasons was that through her (and her brother, Luis) Rafael's genes continued to course the veins of descendants, scores of whom have not only been faithful members of the Church but also rendered powerful service among the Saints throughout Mexico and even the world, including occupying positions in some of the Church's regional and general councils.

In December of 2006, a posterity gathering took place in Salt Lake City, Utah, among descendants of Rafael Monroy and the missionary W. Ernest Young. The organizers had hoped that representatives of the Vicente Morales family would also be able to attend. Financial considerations worked against them, but they sent their warm regards and thanks for the invitation. President James E. Faust of the Church's First Presidency sent a congratulatory letter (Elder Faust had used the execution story in one of his general conference talks). Most of those in attendance were descendants of Luis Monroy, although two grandsons of Amalia through her son Benjamín Parra were also there (David Parra and Hugo Parra).

A grand gathering of thirty-four souls congregated to not only celebrate their forebears but also reflect in gratitude about the circumstances that had brought them to that moment. A great-grandson of Rafael's, José Luis Montoya Monroy, read the names of the families descended from Rafael and commented that more than two hundred of Rafael's posterity were then working in the Church in one or more capacities. Many on the list were either then serving or had served missions.

Among them was Hugo Montoya Monroy, one of Rafael Monroy's great-grandsons (through his mother) and a great-grandson (through his father) of another of the founding families in San Marcos. On 4 April 2015, at age fifty-five, Montoya Monroy was sustained as a member of the First Quorum of the Seventy, one of the general councils of the Church.

Montoya Monroy came to his new calling with impeccable credentials, which for years had set a standard for members of his extended Monroy and Montoya families. Most recently, he had been serving as an Area Seventy in Mexico and as the Church's area auditor for Mexico. In this latter position, an observer who had watched his work over a number of years remarked:

> [Hugo] did a superb job of improving the integrity of the handling of Church finances throughout Mexico. As you probably know, this is particularly important in areas where the lay leaders are not used to handling money, and where it can be a temptation. It was amazing to me to see how he improved the audits and was able to quickly identify and focus on those areas of most concern. . . . I would venture to say that no volunteer in the Church did as much to professionalize the systems and upgrade the oversight of the financial affairs of the Church in Mexico as did Elder Montoya. His attention to detail and his understanding of how all this fit in the Lord's purposes were really impressive.[17]

Moments before his execution, Rafael Monroy knelt in prayer—not to petition the Lord to save his life but to ask for blessings for his posterity, even until the end of time. So far, it is doubtful that he would be disappointed.

NOTES

1. N. B. Lundwall, comp., *A Compilation Containing the Lectures on Faith as Delivered at the School of the Prophets at Kirtland, Ohio* (Salt Lake City: N. B. Lundwall, 1943). At least sixteen versions of this volume are held in BYU's Harold B. Lee Library.
2. Raquel Morales Mera was born on 27 September 1915. Monroy Mera, "Como llegó el evangelio," 33.
3. LaMond Tullis to Elder Daniel L. Johnson, 4 November 2012.
4. The scripture reads, "I have no greater joy than to hear that my children walk in truth."
5. Hugo Montoya Monroy to LaMond Tullis, email, 3 March 2014.

6. María Concepción Monroy de Villalobos, oral history interview by Gordon Irving, 1974, typescript, James Moyle Oral History Program, Church History Library. At a postchildbearing age, Concepción married Benito Villalobos.
7. Rafael's family was very opposed to the union, which occurred when he was twenty-six and Maclovia was fifteen. The family reports fragmentary evidence that, occasionally, he affectionately mentioned the children he had with Maclovia. Hugo Montoya Monroy to LaMond Tullis, email, 3 March 2014.
8. Maclovia began living with Santos Ortiz, by whom she gave birth to two daughters, Juliana and Alfonsa. Interestingly, Alfonsa was later raised with the Monroy family, who changed her name to Dolores. Montoya Monroy to Tullis, email, 3 March 2014.
9. Montoya Monroy to Tullis, email, 3 March 2014. Maclovia died on 26 August 1916 at age twenty-seven. Guadalupe Pérez, Maclovia's half brother, gave her the news about Rafael's execution. Guadalupe Pérez looked after the children for a time and later also joined the Church.
10. Montoya Monroy to Tullis, email, 3 March 2014.
11. Montoya Monroy to Tullis, email, 3 March 2014.
12. "Historia de Rafael Monroy."
13. Montoya Monroy to Tullis, email, 3 March 2014.
14. Minutes of a meeting of descendants of Rafael Monroy with descendants of W. Ernest Young held in Salt Lake City, Utah, 28 December 2006, 5.
15. Montoya Monroy to Tullis, email, 3 March 2014.
16. Montoya Monroy to Tullis, email, 3 March 2014.
17. Richard Thomas to LaMond Tullis, email, 30 August 2014. At the time, Thomas was serving as the executive secretary to the Church's Area President for Mexico, Daniel L. Johnson.

AFTERWORD

Chronicling and interpreting other people's lives is as formidable as it is interesting. Although the objective records (diaries, letters, journals, oral histories, publications, and interviews) frequently give a writer a good orientation to "who, what, when, and where," infrequently do they offer direct evidence as to "why." For example, why did Rafael Monroy and Vicente Morales not cave in to the demands of their executioners and renounce their faith, thereby possibly saving their lives? We assume it was because of their convictions about the veracity of the restored gospel and their concern about having an honorable relationship with God. However, we cannot know for sure what actually did go through their minds. But based on all the evidence we have seen, we have tried to interpret their likely thoughts. It is a challenge one sees throughout this monograph. Readers will necessarily judge for themselves whether the analyses offered here hit the mark on questions of "why."

Entering people's lives, as is done in this monograph, is both an emotional and scholarly experience. I have been distressed at life's slights to some, the shortcomings of others, and the downright malevolent designs of several.

Similarly, I have rejoiced over the tenacity of the faithful, their incessant desire to make the best of themselves, their condition in the light of Christ's teachings, and their caring concern for one another during times of ultimate trial. If this monograph proves to be a faithful and honest portrayal of their life journeys, as I have endeavored to make it be, I will be forever grateful.

BIBLIOGRAPHY

"35 Largest Christian Denominations in the United States." http://undergod.procon.org/view.background-resource.php?resourceID=000087.

Albrecht, Stan L. "The Consequential Dimension of Mormon Religiosity." *BYU Studies* 29, no. 2 (1989): 57–108.

———, and Tim B. Heaton. "Secularization, Higher Education, and Religiosity." *Review of Religious Research* 26, no. 1 (September 1984): 43–58.

Bailey, David C. *Viva Cristo Rey!: The Cristero Rebellion and the Church-State Conflict in Mexico.* Austin: University of Texas Press, 1974.

Balderas, Eduardo. "How the Scriptures Came to Be Translated into Spanish." *Ensign*, September 1972, 26–29.

Barr, Alwyn. *Texans in Revolt: The Battle for San Antonio, 1835.* Austin: University of Texas Press, 1990.

Bautista, Margarito. *La evolución de México: sus verdaderos progenitores y su origen; el destino de América y Europa.* México: Talleres Gráficos Laguna, 1935.

Bazant, Jan. *Alienation of Church Wealth in Mexico: Social and Economic Aspects of the Liberal Revolution 1856–1875.* New York: Cambridge University Press, 2008.

Beecher, Dale F. "Rey L. Pratt and the Mexican Mission." *BYU Studies* 15, no. 3 (Spring 1975): 293–307.

Benbow, Mark E. "All the Brains I Can Borrow: Woodrow Wilson and Intelligence Gathering in Mexico, 1913–1915." *Studies in Intelligence: Journal of the American Intelligence Professional* 51, no. 4 (December 2007): 1–12.

Bennett, Richard E. "'Line upon Line, Precept upon Precept': Reflections on the 1877 Commencement of the Performance of Endowments and Sealings of the Dead." *BYU Studies* 44, no. 3 (2005): 39–76.

———. "'The Upper Room': Latter-day Saint Temple Work during the Exodus and in Early Salt Lake Valley, 1846–1854." Presidential Address, Mormon History Association Conference, San Antonio, Texas, 7 June 2014.

———. "'Which Is the Wisest Course?': The Transformation in Mormon Temple Consciousness, 1870–1898." *BYU Studies Quarterly* 52, no. 2 (2013): 5–43.

Bennett, Wendell Clark. *The Tarahumara, an Indian Tribe of Northern Mexico*. Chicago: University of Chicago Press, 1935. Updated with the collaboration of Robert M. Zingg. Glorietta, NM: Rio Grande Press, 1976.

"Biografía de Mamá Jesusita Mera, narrada por Minerva Montoya Monroy." Typescript, five pages, n.d. Copy provided by Hugo Montoya Monroy, 1 March 2014.

Brown, Samuel M. "Believing Adoption." *BYU Studies Quarterly* 52, no. 2 (2013): 45–65.

Cajero, Mateo. *Historia de los otomíes en Ixtenco*. 2nd ed. Bristol, England: University of the West of England, Bristol, 2009.

Carmack, John K. *A Bright Ray of Hope: The Perpetual Education Fund*. Salt Lake City: Deseret Book, 2004.

Ceballos, Armando, and Dina De Hoyos. "Nefi de Aquino Gutiérrez: heredero de una historia de fe en Santiago Xalitzintla, Puebla." Typescript, three pages, 2014.

Chrisomalis, Stephen. "The Origins and Coevolution of Literacy and Numeracy." In *The Cambridge Handbook of Literacy*, edited by D. Olsen and N. Torrance, 59–74. New York: Cambridge University Press, 2009.

Christensen, Clint. "Lonely Saint in Mexico: Desideria Quintanar Yáñez (1814–1893)." In *Women of Faith in the Latter Days*, vol. 1, edited by Richard E. Turley Jr. and Brittany A. Chapman. Salt Lake City: Deseret Book, 2011.

"Churches of Christ," www.church-of-christ.org.

Cornejo de Trujillo, Florencia. Interview by LaMond Tullis, San Marcos, Hidalgo, 20 May 1975.

Corrés, Jaime Ballón, Carlos Martínez Assad, and Pablo Serrano Álvarez, eds. *El siglo de la Revolucón Mexicana*. 2 vols. Mexico City: Instituto Nacional de Estudios Históricos de la Revolución Mexicana, Secretaria de Gobernación, 2000.

Cosío Villegas, Daniel. *Historia moderna de México: el Porfiriato—vida económica*. Mexico City: Editorial Hermes, 1994.

——— et al. *Historia general de México*. Mexico City: El Colegio de México, 2009.

Decoo, Wilfried. "In Search of Mormon Identity: Mormon Culture, Gospel Culture, and an American Worldwide Church." *International Journal of Mormon Studies* 6 (2013): 1–53.

DeHoyos, Arturo, and Genevieve DeHoyos. "The Universality of the Gospel." *Ensign*, August 1971, 8–14.

Díaz, José, and Ramón Rodríguez. *El movimiento cristero: sociedad y conflicto en los Altos de Jalisco*. Mexico City: Editorial Progreso, 2002.

Dickens, A. G., and John M. Tonkin, eds. *The Reformation in Historical Thought*. Cambridge, MA: Harvard University Press, 1985.

Duffy, John-Charles, and Hugo Olaiz. "Correlated Praise: The Development of the Spanish Hymnal." *Dialogue: A Journal of Mormon Thought* 35, no. 2 (Summer 2002): 89–113.

Encyclopedia of Mormonism, vol. 4. New York: Macmillan, 1992, appendix 1.

"Fifteen New Stakes Created in Mexico City." *Ensign*, January 1976, 94–95.

Galvin Rivera, Flavio. "El concubinato actual en México." https://revistas-colaboracion.juridicas.unam.mx/index.php/rev-facultad-derecho-mx/article/view/30097/27172.

García Martínez, Leticia Dunay. "Una guerra inevitable: el noreste de Tamaulipas frente a los Estados Unidos, 1840–1849." Master's thesis, El Colegio de San Luis, A. C. San Luis Potosí, S. L. P., February 2013.

Gilly, Adolfo. *The Mexican Revolution*. New York: W. W. Norton, 2005.

Gómez, Fernando. *La Iglesia de Jesucristo de los Santos de los Últimos Días y las convenciones lamanitas: de la oscuridad a la luz*. Mexico City: Museo de la Historia del Mormonismo en México, 2004.

———. "The Myth about Margarito Bautista's 1935 Book." Paper presented at the Mormon History Association's forty-ninth annual conference in San Antonio, Texas, 7 June 2014.

Gonzales, Michael J. *The Mexican Revolution, 1910–1940*. Albuquerque: University of New Mexico Press, 2002.

Gray, Darius A. "Wherefore by Their Fruits Ye Shall Know Them." *Huffington Post*, 14 October 2011.

Grim, Brian J. *The Price of Freedom Denied: Religious Persecution and Conflict in the Twenty-first Century*. New York: Cambridge University Press, 2011.

Griswold del Castillo, Richard. *The Treaty of Guadalupe Hidalgo: A Legacy of Conflict*. Norman: University of Oklahoma Press, 1990.

Grover, Mark L. "Execution in Mexico: The Deaths of Rafael Monroy and Vicente Morales." *BYU Studies* 35, no. 3 (1995–96): 7–28.

Guynn, Beth Ann. "A Nation Emerges: 65 Years of Photography in Mexico." The Getty Research Institute, http://www.getty.edu/research/tools/guides_bibliographies/photography_mexico/.

Haenn, Nora. "The Changing and Enduring Ejido: A State and Regional Examination of Mexico's Land Tenure Counter-Reforms." *Land Use Policy* 23 (2006): 136–46.

Haight, David B. "By Their Fruits Ye Shall Know Them." *BYU Speeches*, 7 December 1980, https://speeches.byu.edu/talks/david-b-haight_fruits-ye-shall-know/.

Harrison, Lawrence E., and Samuel P. Huntington, eds. *Culture Matters: How Values Shape Human Progress.* New York: Basic Books, 2000.

Henrichsen, Kirk. "Preliminary Screenplay Outline Notes," 19 March 2014. Copy provided by Hugo Montoya Monroy, in author's possession.

Hernández, Trinidad. Interview by LaMond Tullis, Santiago Tzontlale, Hidalgo, 27 May 1975.

Hill, Bradley Lunt. Email to LaMond Tullis, 21 February 2014.

Hinckley, Gordon B. "The Perpetual Education Fund." *Ensign*, May 2001, 51–53.

"Historia de la escuela Héroes de Chapúltepec." Typescript, 1944. Church History Library, Salt Lake City.

"Historia de Rafael Monroy." Linaje Monroy en el estado de Hidalgo, México. https://sites.google.com/site/linajemonroy/rafael-monroy-mera/historia-de-rafael-monroy.

Huntington, Samuel P. *The Clash of Civilizations and the Remaking of World Order.* New York: Simon & Schuster, 1996.

Inglehart, Ronald, and Wayne E. Baker. "Modernization, Cultural Change, and the Persistence of Traditional Values." *American Sociological Review* 65 (February 2000): 19–51.

Ivins, Stanley S. "The Deseret Alphabet." *Utah Humanities Review* 1 (1947): 223–39.

La invasión a Veracruz de 1914: enfoques multidisciplinarios. Mexico City: Secretaría de Marina-Armada de Mexico, Secretaría de Educación Pública, Instituto Nacional de Estudios Históricos de las Revoluciones de México, 2015.

Jarrard, Jack E. "Martyrdom in Mexico." *Church News*, 3 July 1971.

Johnson, Chalmers. *Revolutionary Change.* 2nd ed. Stanford, CA: Stanford University Press, 1982.

Johnson, Clark V. "Mormon Education in Mexico: The Rise of the Sociedad Educativa y Cultural." PhD diss., Department of History, Brigham Young University, 1977.

Joseph T. Bentley Papers. MSS 848, box 5, folder 1. L. Tom Perry Special Collections, Harold B. Lee Library, Brigham Young University, Provo, Utah.

Katz, Friedrich. *El Porfiriato y la Revolución en la historia de México: una conversación.* Mexico City: ERA, 2011.

Kimball, Edward L., and Andrew E. Kimball Jr. *Spencer W. Kimball: Twelfth President of the Church of Jesus Christ of Latter-day Saints.* Salt Lake City: Bookcraft, 1977.

Kinder, Gordon. "Religious Literature as an Offensive Weapon: Cipriano de Valera's Part in England's War with Spain." *The Sixteenth Century Journal* 14, no. 2 (Summer 1988): 223–35.

Labastida, Horacio. *Belisario Domínguez y el estado criminal: 1913–1914.* Mexico City: Siglo XXI Editores, 2002.

López de Santa Anna, Antonio. *The Mexican Side of the Texas Revolution, 1836.* Translated with notes by Carlos E. Castañeda. Austin, TX: Graphic Ideas, 1970.

Lozano Bravo, Agrícol. Oral History Interview by Gordon Irving, OH389. Typescript. Church History Library, Salt Lake City.

Lozano Herrera. *Historia del mormonismo en México*. Mexico City: Editorial Zarahemla, 1983. Second edition, Editorial Villicaná, 1984.

———, Agrícol. Interview by LaMond Tullis. Mexico City, 31 May 1975.

Lundwall, N. B., comp. *A Compilation Containing the Lectures on Faith as Delivered at the School of the Prophets at Kirtland, Ohio*. Salt Lake City: N. B. Lundwall, 1943.

Martín Moreno, Francisco. *México mutilado*. Mexico City: Editorial Santillana, 2004.

Martínez Hoyos, Francisco. *Breve historia de la Revolución Mexicana*. Madrid: Ediciones Nowtilus, S. L., 2015.

"Martirio en México." Linaje Monroy en el Estado de Hidalgo, México. https://sites.google.com/site/linajemonroy/rafael-monroy-mera/martirio-en-mexico.

Matthews, Robert J. "The Fulness of Times." *Ensign*, December 1989, 46–51.

McAllen, M. M. *Maximilian and Carlota, Europe's Last Empire in Mexico*. San Antonio: Trinity University Press, 2014.

McLynn, Frank. *Villa and Zapata: A History of the Mexican Revolution*. New York: Carroll and Graf, 2000.

Mera Vda. de Monroy, Jesús. Letter to Rey L. Pratt, 27 August 1915. https://sites.google.com/site/linajemonroy/rafael-monroy-mera/como-llego-el-evangelio-restaurado-a-san-marcos.

Mexican Mission Manuscript History. Reports of 31 December 1944, 14 September 1955, 18 November 1955, and 12 March 1959. Church History Library, Salt Lake City.

Mexico in Transition: The Diplomatic Papers of John Lind, 1913–1931. Microfilm reel 1, UPA Collection from LexisNexis, 2005.

"Mexico Revolutionary Paper Money Catalog." ATSNotes. http://www.atsnotes.com/catalog/banknotes/mexico-revolution.html.

Meyer, Jean. *The Cristero Rebellion: The Mexican People between Church and State, 1926–1929*. New York: Cambridge University Press, 1976.

———. *La Cristiada: The Mexican People's War for Religious Liberty*. Garden City Park, NY: Square One Publishers, 2013. Spanish language edition published by Fondo de Cultura Económica (Mexico), 2006.

Meyer, John W. "The Effects of Education as an Institution." *American Journal of Sociology* 83, no. 1 (July 1977): 55–77.

Millet, Robert L. *A Different Jesus? The Christ of the Latter-day Saints*. Grand Rapids, MI: Eerdmans, 2005.

"Minutes of a Meeting of Descendants of Rafael Monroy with Descendants of W. Ernest Young." Reunion held in Provo, Utah, on 28 December 2006. https://docs.google.com/viewer?a=v&pid=sites&srcid=ZGVmYXVsdGRvbWFpbnxsaW5hamVt b25yb3l8Z3g6NjU5MDVjNmJkMmE1NjZlYg.

Mitchell, David. "Agricultural and Health Services Missionaries: A New Way to Serve the Whole Man." *Ensign*, September 1973, 72–74.

Monroy, Rafael. Letter to W. Ernest Young in Tucson, Arizona, ca. June 1915. Read by José Luis Montoya Monroy at a Monroy descendants' reunion in Provo, Utah, 28 December 2006. https://sites.google.com/site/linajemonroy/home/archivos.

Monroy de Villalobos. Interview by LaMond Tullis. San Marcos, Hidalgo, 17 and 19 May 1975.

———, María Concepción. Oral History Interview by Gordon Irving, 1974. Typescript. James Moyle Oral History Program. Church History Library, Salt Lake City.

Monroy Mera, María Guadalupe. "Como llegó el evangelio restaurado al pueblo de San Marcos, Tula de Allende, estado de Hidalgo," 1944; addendum, 1962. Transcription of the author's manuscripts by Minerva Monroy, 1990s, https://sites.google.com/site/linajemonroy/rafael-monroy-mera/como-llego-el-evangelio-restaurado-a-san-marcos. Copies of the originals in Spanish are available in the Church History Library in Salt Lake City and BYU's Harold B. Lee Library in Provo, Utah.

———. Diary of María Guadalupe Monroy Mera, selections excerpted by Minerva Montoya Monroy and reported to LaMond Tullis in email, 21 September 2016.

Montoya, Jorge. Interview with LaMond Tullis. San Marcos Hidalgo, 17 May 1975.

Montoya Cruz, Ezequiel. Oral History Interview by Gordon Irving, 1974, OH 725. Typescript. James Moyle Oral History Program, Church History Library, Salt Lake City.

Montoya Gutiérrez, Daniel. Oral History Interview by Gordon Irving, 1974, OH 723. Typescript. James Moyle Oral History Program, Church History Library, Salt Lake City.

Montoya Monroy, Hugo. Email to LaMond Tullis, 3 March 2014.

Montoya Monroy, Minerva. Email to LaMond Tullis, 21 September 2016.

Montoya Ortíz, Ezequiel. Interview with LaMond Tullis. San Marcos, Hidalgo, 20 May 1975.

Morgan, Barbara E. "Benemérito de las Américas: The Beginning of a Unique Church School in Mexico." *BYU Studies Quarterly* 52, no. 4 (2013): 89–116.

———. "The Impact of Centro Escolar Benemérito de las Américas, a Church School in Mexico." *Religious Educator* 15, no. 1 (2014): 145–67.

Murphy, Thomas. "'Stronger than Ever,' Remnants of the Third Convention." *Restoration: The Journal of Latter-day Saint History* 10, no. 1 (1998): 1–12.

Oaks, Dallin H. "The Gospel Culture." *Ensign*, March 2012, 40–47.

———. "Repentance and Change." *Ensign*, October 2003, 37–40.

Odekirk, Sally Johnson. "Mexico Unfurled: From Struggle to Strength." *Ensign*, January 2014, 36–43.

Orozco H., María Elena. *Tarahumara: una antigua sociedad futura*. Chihuahua, Mexico: Subcomité Especial de Cultura de COPLADE del Gobierno del Estado de Chihuahua, 1992.

Parra de Pérez, Elena. Interview by LaMond Tullis. Mexico City, 25 May 1975.

Parra Monroy, Bernabé, and Irma Soto Ledezma de Parra. Oral History Interview by Stephen G. Boyden, Kirk Henrichsen, and Clinton Christensen. Salt Lake City, 3 October 2008, OH 4221. Church History Library, Salt Lake City.

Pérez de Villalobos, Violeta. Interviews by LaMond Tullis. San Marcos, Hidalgo, 15, 16, 17, and 19 May 1975.

Pérez Parra, María Elena. Interview by LaMond Tullis. San Marcos, Hidalgo, 21 May 1975.

Pratt, Parley P. *A Voice of Warning and Instruction to All People; Or, an Introduction to the Faith and Doctrine of the Church of Jesus Christ of Latter-day Saints.* Salt Lake City: Deseret News, 1874.

Pratt, Rey L. Diary, vol. 8.

———. In Conference Report, April 1920, 87–93.

———. "A Latter-day Martyr." *Improvement Era* 28 (June 1918): 720–26.

———. Letter to Jesús Mera Vda. de Monroy, 28 October 1915. https://sites.google.com/site/linajemonroy/rafael-monroy-mera/como-llego-el-evangelio-restaurado-a-san-marcos.

Reséndez Cruz, Albino. Oral History Interview by Gordon Irving, Mexico City, 1974, OH 716. Church History Library, Salt Lake City.

Reséndez Fuentes, Andrés. "Battleground Women: Soldaderas and Female Soldiers in the Mexican Revolution." *The Americas* 51, no. 4 (April 1995): 525–53.

Rice, Otis K. *The Hatfields and McCoys.* Lexington: University Press of Kentucky, 1982.

Rojas, Luis Manuel. *La culpa de Henry Lane Wilson en el gran desastre de México.* Mexico City: Compañía Editora "La Verdad," 1928.

Rojo Mendoza, Reynaldo. "The Church-State Conflict in Mexico from the Mexican Revolution to the Cristero Rebellion." *Proceedings of the Pacific Coast Council on Latin American Studies* 23 (2006): 76–96.

Romney, Marion G. Letter to the First Presidency of the Church of Jesus Christ of Latter-day Saints, 9 December 1959. Joseph T. Bentley Papers, box 5, folder 1. L. Tom Perry Special Collections, Harold B. Lee Library, Brigham Young University, Provo, Utah.

Ruíz, Ramón Eduardo. *The Great Rebellion: Mexico, 1905–1924.* New York: W. W. Norton, 1980.

Santos, Richard G. *Santa Anna's Campaign against Texas, 1835–1836.* 2nd ed. Salisbury, NC: Documentary Publications, 1981.

"Sarna." Center for Young Women's Health. http://youngwomenshealth.org/2005/10/06/sarna/.

Saunders Morales de Villalobos, Ruth Josefina. Letter to LaMond Tullis, 11 February 2014.

Severance, Frank H. "The Peace Conference at Niagara Falls in 1914." *Buffalo Historical Society Publications* 18 (1914): 3–75.

Shalit, Wendy. *A Return to Modesty: Discovering the Lost Virtue.* New York: The Free Press, 2000.

Shermer, Michael. *How We Believe: Science, Skepticism, and the Search for God.* New York: William H. Freeman, 1999.

Sion, Denia. Interview by LaMond Tullis. San Marcos, Hidalgo, 19 May 1975.

Smith, Lori. Interview by LaMond Tullis. Orem, Utah, 3 June 2014, with subsequent correspondence 8 and 11 August 2014.

———. "Notes on San Marcos, Mexico," 3 June 1974–1 January 1975. Copy in author's possession.

Stojanovich, Ljudmila, and Dragomir Marisavljevich. "Stress as a Trigger of Autoimmune Disease." *Autoimmunity Reviews* 7, no. 3 (January 2008): 209–13.

Summers, Lionel M. "The Divorce Laws of Mexico." *Journal of Law and Contemporary Problems* 2, no. 3 (1935): 310–21.

Sweetman, Jack. *The Landing at Veracruz: 1914.* Annapolis, MD: Naval Institute Press, 1968.

Talmage, James E. *The Great Apostasy: Considered in the Light of Scriptural and Secular History.* Salt Lake City: Deseret Book, 1978.

———. *Jesus the Christ: A Study of the Messiah and His Mission according to Holy Scriptures both Ancient and Modern.* Salt Lake City: Deseret Book, 1931.

Trujillo Linares, Emilio. Interview by LaMond Tullis. San Marcos, Hidalgo, 19 May 1975.

Tuck, Jim. *The Holy War in Los Altos: A Regional Analysis of Mexico's Cristero Rebellion.* Tucson: University of Arizona Press, 1982.

———. *Pancho Villa and John Reed: Two Faces of Romantic Revolution.* Tucson: University of Arizona Press, 1984.

Tullis, LaMond. "Ammón Meshach Tenney, 1844–1925: amigo de los pueblos amerindios y rescatador de los santos SUD del centro de México." http://www.sud.org.mx/ammon-meshach-tenney?lang=spa-mx.

———. "Los colonizadores mormones en Chihuahua y Sonora." http://www.sud.org.mx/historia-de-la-iglesia-en-mexico/articulos/los-colonizadores-mormones-en-chihuahua-y-sonora.

———. "Desideria Quintanar de Yáñez, 1814–1893. http://www.sud.org.mx/historia-de-la-iglesia-en-mexico/pioneros-articulos/una-solitaria-pionera-mexicana.

———. Letter to Elder Daniel L. Johnson, 4 November 2012.

———. "El Libro de Mormón en español: la primera traducción y cómo llegó a México," http://www.sud.org.mx/el-libro-de-mormon-en-espanol.

———."La misión del apóstol Moses Thatcher a la Ciudad de México en 1879," http://www.sud.org.mx/historia-de-la-iglesia-en-mexico/articulos/la-mision-del-apostol-moses-thatcher-a-la-ciudad-de-mexico-en-1879.

———, ed. *Mormonism: A Faith for All Cultures.* Provo, UT: Brigham Young University Press, 1978.

———. *Mormons in Mexico: The Dynamics of Faith and Culture.* Logan: Utah State University Press, 1987.

———. "Los Primeros: Mexico's Pioneer Saints." *Ensign,* July 1997, 46–51.

———. "La reapertura de la Misión Mexicana en 1901." http://www.sud.org.mx/historia-de-la-iglesia-en-mexico/articulos/la-reapertura-de-la-mision-mexicana-en-1901.

———. *A Search for Place: Eight Generations of Henrys and the Settlement of Utah's Uintah Basin.* Spring City, UT: Piñon Hills Publishing, 2010.

———. "A Shepherd to Mexico's Saints: Arwell L. Pierce and the Third Convention." *BYU Studies* 37, no. 1 (1997–98): 127–57.

———. "Writing about the International Church: A Personal Odyssey in Mexico." *Journal of Mormon History* 42, no. 4 (October 2016): 1–30.

"Two Members Died Courageously for the Truth." *Church News*, 12 September 1959.

Ulloa Ortiz, Pito. "La lucha armada" In Daniel Cosío Villegas et al., *Historia general de México.* Mexico City: El Colegio de México, 2009, 757-821.

Villalobos, Saúl. Interview with LaMond Tullis. San Marcos, Hidalgo, 21 May 1975.

Villalobos Rodríguez, Benito. Interviews with LaMond Tullis. San Marcos, Hidalgo, 16, 17, and 19 May 1975.

Villalobos Vásquez, Efraín. "Church Schools in Mexico." In *Mormonism: A Faith for All Cultures*, edited by F. LaMond Tullis, 126–34. Provo, UT: Brigham Young University Press, 1978.

———. Interview with LaMond Tullis. Mexico City, 27 May 1975.

Villegas, Daniel Cosío, ed. *Historia de la Revolución Mexicana.* Mexico City: El Colegio de México, 1977–1984.

Walser, William. Oral History Interview by Gordon Irving, 1976. James Moyle Oral History Program, Church History Library, Salt Lake City.

"Weapons Used in the Mexican Revolution." History Wars Weapons. www.historywarsweapons.com/weapons-used-in-mexican-revolution.

Wells, Allen, and Gilbert M. Joseph. *Elite Politics and Rural Insurgency in Yucatán, 1876–1915.* Stanford, CA: Stanford University Press, 1996.

Widtsoe, John A. *Priesthood and Church Government in the Church of Jesus Christ of Latter-day Saints.* Salt Lake City: Deseret Book, 1954.

Wilson, Henry Lane. *Diplomatic Episodes in Mexico, Belgium and Chile.* Garden City, NY: Doubleday, Page & Company, 1927.

Womack, John. *Zapata and the Mexican Revolution.* New York: Alfred Knopf, 1969.

Young, Brigham. "Letter to Elder B. Morris Young, Honolulu, Hawaiian Islands, 23 October 1873." In *Letters of Brigham Young to His Sons*, edited by Dean C. Jessee. Salt Lake City: Deseret Book, 1974.

Young, W. Ernest. *The Diary of W. Ernest Young.* N.p.: W. Ernest Young, 1973.

INDEX

A

accountability, 149
agricultural and health services program, 147–48
ancestral bonding, 28, 46n32, 140–41, 155–61
Ángeles, Tomás, 21
anger, 70
anti-American hysteria, 54–57
anticlerical legislation, 110–13

B

baptisms for the dead, 28, 46n32, 140–41
"Battle Hymn of the Cristeros," 126n75
Bautista, Margarito, 14n58, 86, 100, 103, 104–6, 123n46

C

Calles, Plutarco Elías, 110–11
Calles Law, 110–13
Carrancistas, 54, 58–59, 64n36, 76–77, 79
caskets, 75–76, 80–81n4
caudillos, 89, 90
Cerón, Marcelino, 113–14
chapel construction, 100–101, 109, 145–46
chastity, 89, 98–99, 102–3, 114–17, 127n82
Churches of Christ, 143–44
coffins, 75–76, 80–81n4
conscription, 39–40, 50n62
construction programs, 100–101, 109, 145–46
Cornejo, Alejandra, 157
Cristero rebellion, 95, 109, 126n75
Cruz Corona, María Manuela, 102–3
cultural change, 139–41, 152–53n39, 153n40
currency, 59, 63n24, 64n34, 74

D

dead, ordinances for, 28, 46n32, 140–41
development. *See* temporal progress and development
disease, 147
divorce, 102–3
Doctrine and Covenants, 36, 49n50

E

Edmunds, Mary Ellen, 147
education, 4–6, 131–38, 143
Espinoza, Othón, 104
Estrada, Asención (Don Chon), 121n28

F

Flores, Jesús, 36
Flores Pérez, Maclovia, 6–7, 16n20, 157–58, 162n7, 162n8, 162n9
forgiveness, 78. *See also* repentance
fortitude, 141–43
Fyans, J. Thomas, 148

G

García, Juan, 37
Garff, Louis, 43–44n14
González, Pedro, 59, 77
González, Plácida, 11
Gutiérrez, Casimiro, 11, 40–41, 75–76, 79, 88–90, 94
Gutiérrez, Luis, 133–34
Gutiérrez, María Petra, 10–11
Gutiérrez Sánchez, Margarita, 103, 124n55

H

Haro, Agustín, 12, 17n26, 36–37, 120n10
Haro, Trinidad, 40
health services program, 147–48
Hernández Ávalos, Guadalupe, 7–8, 9, 16n20, 20, 30, 32
Los Héroes de Chapúltepec, 131–35
Herrera Hernández, Josefina, 135

Huerta, Victoriano, 23, 24, 44–45n18, 55
Huish, Willard, 24–25
Hunter, Howard W., 148
hymnals, 35, 48n48

I

institutionalization of Church, 85–87, 109, 119
institutional support, 143–45
intelligence, 130. *See also* temporal progress and development

J

Jiménez, Dimas, 90
Juárez, Benito, 53, 61n8
Juárez, Isaías, 110, 113

K

knowledge, 130. *See also* temporal progress and development

L

language, written, 131
Law Reforming the Penal Code, 110–13
Lind, John, 44–45n18
literacy, 130–32
Lozada, Tomasa, 95
Lozano, Sabino, 113–14
Lozano Bravo, Agrícol, 113–14, 135–37
Lyman, Richard R., 106–7, 127n90

M

Madero, Francisco, 23, 24, 44n18, 57
Mairet, Juan, 95
Martínez de Estrada, Dolores, 121n28
Mason, James O., 147
Maximilian, Archduke, 3–4, 15n7
McVey, Natalia, 24. *See also* Monroy Mera, Natalia
McVey, Roy Van, 24, 43n13, 56, 78, 92, 106
Melchizedek Priesthood Handbook, 49n51

INDEX

Mera, Juana, 94
Mera Martínez, Eulalia, 11–12, 13, 30, 32, 97, 99, 123n37, 156
Mera Pérez de Monroy, María Jesús (Jesusita)
  attends regional conference, 101–2
  background of, 4–5
  baptism of, 9, 32
  considers leaving San Marcos, 78
  and conversion of Monroy family, 20, 30
  and death of Jesús Sánchez, 24
  education of, 15n10
  following executions, 73
  fortitude of, 142–43
  importance of education to, 133
  and marriage of Jovita to Bernabé Parra, 97–99
  moves to San Marcos, 7
  persecution of, 54
  rebukes Zapatistas, 74–75
  takes food to family in prison, 67
  takes in Eulalia Mera Martínez, 11–12
  Zapatistas raid store and home of, 66–67
Mexican Revolution
  Carrancistas regain advantage in, 76–77
  challenges facing Church during, 38–41
  conscription during, 50n62
  and death of Sánchez, 22–24
  displacement caused by, 11
  evacuations ordered due to, 33–34
  neutrality recommended during, 23, 39–40, 50n63
  reaches San Marcos, 57–60
  social-class nature of, 10, 68–69
  Zapatista-Villista alliance during, 14n3
missionary work
  renewed in Hidalgo, 19
  in San Marcos, 95, 100
  socioeconomic status and success in, 47n36
  of Vicente Morales, 11, 17n29, 37–38

Monroy, Pablo L., 2–4
Monroy Espejel, Cresencia Maclovia, 160
Monroy family
  arrest and torture of, 66
  attends San Pedro Mártir conference, 25–28
  baptism of, 28–32
  Bernabé Parra Gutiérrez's relationship with, 91
  considers leaving San Marcos, 77–78
  and death of Jesús Sánchez, 24–25
  persecution of, 32–33, 53–54, 61n10
  social standing of, 30
Monroy Flores, Gerarda (Amalia), 6–7, 114–19, 126n79, 133, 157–60
Monroy Flores, Luis, 6–7, 157–58, 159–60
Monroy Hernández, María Concepción (Conchita), 8–9, 38, 39, 157
Monroy Mera, Guadalupe, 13n1
Monroy Mera, Isauro, 76, 79, 94, 122n31
Monroy Mera, Jovita
  arrest and torture of, 66
  baptism of, 9, 28–32
  education and employment of, 4, 46–47n35
  following executions, 73
  health issues of, 80, 92–93
  investigates church, 20
  marriage of, 97–99
  moves to San Marcos, 7
  and Parra's infidelity, 114–15, 126n79
Monroy Mera, María Guadalupe
  arrest of, 59, 63n24, 66, 67
  attends San Pedro Mártir conference, 26–28
  baptism of, 9, 28–32
  following executions, 73
  investigates church, 20
  marital status of, 43n10
Monroy Mera, Natalia
  arrest of, 66
  and arrest of Guadalupe Monroy, 59, 63n24
  attends San Pedro Mártir conference, 26–28

Monroy Mera, Natalia (*continued*)
  baptism of, 24, 39
  education and employment of, 4, 46n35
  flees San Marcos, 92
  following executions, 73
  marriage of, 43n13
  moves to San Marcos, 7
  persecution of, 56
  returns to Mexico, 106
Monroy Mera, Pablo, 7
Monroy Mera, Rafael
  accusations against, 58–59
  arrest and torture of, 66, 67–68
  attends San Pedro Mártir conference, 26–28
  baptism of, 28–32
  Bernabé Parra Gutiérrez's relationship with, 91
  called as branch president, 34–36
  challenges facing, 38–39
  children and employment of, 6–8
  conversion of, 9–10
  Daniel Montoya Gutiérrez's ties to, 100
  declines invitation to join Zapatistas, 60
  descendants of, 157–61
  education of, 4–6
  entertains Carrancista officers, 59, 64n36
  events following execution of, 73–80
  execution of, 1–2, 68–69, 72n12
  factors influencing execution of, 51–52, 60n3, 69–71
  family of, 2–4
  justifications for execution of, 65
  marriage of, 16n20, 162n7
  motivations of, 163
  municipal authority of, 64n37
  persecution of, 54
  Zapatistas raid store and home of, 66–67, 70
Monroy Vera, José Jesús Silvano, 4–6, 7
Monroy Vera, Praxedis, 4
Montoya, Enrique, 117
Montoya Gutiérrez, Daniel
  assumes leadership of San Marcos Branch, 89–90, 99–100
  attends regional conference, 102
  comes out of hiding, 77
  comforts Bernabé Parra Gutiérrez, 93
  divorce of, 102–3
  helps Monroy and Morales women, 76, 81n8
  marriage of, 124n55
  and new chapel construction, 101
Montoya Monroy, Hugo, 161
Montoya Monroy, José Luis, 160
Montoya Monroy, Minerva, 13n1, 121n28
Morales Guerrero, Vicente
  arrest and torture of, 66, 67–68
  birth of, 16n25
  conversion of, 10–11, 17n27
  descendants of, 156–57
  events following execution of, 73–80
  execution of, 1–2, 68–69
  factors influencing execution of, 51–52, 60n3, 69–71
  justifications for execution of, 65
  marriage of, 11–12
  missionary work of, 11, 17n29, 37–38
  motivations of, 163
Morales Mera, Raquel, 13, 156
murals, 109, 125n71

O

Ortiz, Alfonsa, 160, 162n8
Ortiz, Santos, 157, 158, 162n8
Otomíes, 17n25

P

Páez, Abel, 86, 100, 110, 113, 123n46
Páez, Juan, 38
Parra Gutiérrez, Bernabé
  assumes leadership of San Marcos Branch, 89, 91–94, 108–10
  attends Monroy family baptisms, 30
  baptism of, 32
  comes out of hiding, 79
  and contention in San Marcos Branch, 95

INDEX

Parra Gutiérrez, Bernabé (*continued*)
    fathers child with Eulalia Mera Martínez, 97
    and illness of Jovita Monroy, 92–93
    leaves to find employment, 96–97
    legacy of, 113
    marriage of, 97–99
    and new chapel construction, 100–101
    release and subsequent fall of, 113–19
    returns to San Marcos, 77
    and San Marcos School, 131–36
    teaches gospel to family, 121n28
Parra Mera, Elena, 97, 99, 122–23n37, 126–27n81
Parra Monroy, Benjamín, 127n89
Pearl of Great Price, 36, 49n50
Pérez, Amado, 38
Pérez, Guadalupe, 158–59, 160, 162n9
persecution, 32–33, 51–57, 61n10, 79–80, 142
photography, 2–4
Pierce, Arwell L., 135, 151n24
Plan de Ayala, 57
plural marriage, 108, 127n90
Pratt, Rey L.
    attends regional conference, 101, 102
    attends San Pedro Mártir conference, 26
    and baptism of Monroy family, 28–29, 32
    and Casimiro Gutiérrez's assumption of leadership, 88, 90
    corresponds with Monroy, 37, 38–39
    institutional support of, 144–45
    leaves Mexico, 33–34
    and local leadership development, 109–10
    returns to Mexico, 93–94
    and trouble with Margarito Bautista, 104
    as witness to Monroy baptisms, 16n23
progress and development. *See* temporal progress and development

R

rameumptom, 142, 154n51
La Reforma, 79, 81n21
repentance, 98–99, 102–3, 115–17, 141
resilience, 141–43

revenge, 70
Reyes, Andrés, 58, 65
Reyes Molina, General, 67, 68, 70
Robles, Cándido, 99
Rodríguez, Francisco, 36, 38, 39, 40, 54
Rosales, Ángel, 37, 39, 89
Rosales, Gabriel, 76, 79, 120n10
rumormongering, 65

S

Sánchez, Felix, 24
Sánchez, Jesús, 19–25, 42n3, 42n4, 42–43n6
Sánchez Villalobos, Maclovio, 79, 113
Sánchez Villalobos, Margarito, 76, 81n4
San Marcos
    anti-American hysteria in, 55
    chapel construction in, 100–101, 109
    institutionalization of Church in, 85–87
    Mexican Revolution reaches, 57–60
    missionary work in, 95, 100
    Monroy family considers leaving, 77–78
    Mormon refugees in, 40–41, 54
    opposition to Mormonism in, 51–52
    people return to, following war, 106
    persecution in, 53–54, 61n10, 79–80
    regional conference held in, 101–2
San Marcos Branch
    activities of W. Ernest Young in, 42n3
    Agrícol Lozano Bravo as president of, 135
    Benito Villalobos Sánchez assumes leadership of, 103–4
    Bernabé Parra Gutiérrez assumes leadership of, 91–94, 108–10
    Casimiro Gutiérrez assumes leadership of, 75–76, 79, 88–90
    Daniel Montoya Gutiérrez assumes leadership of, 89–90, 99–100
    leadership succession in, 87–88
    Rafael Monroy called as president of, 34–36
    Rey L. Pratt returns to, 93–94

San Marcos Branch (*continued*)
  spirit of contention in, 94–95
  spiritual growth in, 41
  support for, 36–39
San Marcos School, 131–38
San Pedro Mártir Branch conference, 25–28
Saunders, Antonio Roberto, 156
Saunders Morales, Ruth Josefina, 156
Sirrine, Seth E., 19–20
Smith, George Albert, 114
Sociedad Educativa y Cultural S. A., 135
Soper, Edward, 147
"spontaneous violence," 69
stakes, organization of, 148–49

T

Tarahumaras, 72n15
temporal progress and development, 129–31
  cultural change and, 139–41, 152–53n39, 153n40
  institutional support and, 143–45
  literacy and, 130–32
  San Marcos School and, 131–38
  through agricultural and health services program, 147–48
  through construction programs, 145–46
  through organization of stakes, 148–49
  through strength of Church members and leaders, 141–43
Third Convention movement, 86, 104, 122n29, 123n46
Tolteca cement factory, 55–56
Toluca conference, 33
tough Church members, 141–43

V

Vera López, Porfiria, 2–3
Villalobos, Bernardo, 76, 80–81n4
Villalobos, Efraín, 117, 127n89
Villalobos Sánchez, Benito, 103–4, 108, 156
Villistas, 14n3, 58, 59, 63n28

W

Wilcken, August, 19
Wilson, Henry Lane, 23, 44n18, 55
Wilson, Woodrow, 23, 44–45n18, 55
wisdom, 130. *See also* temporal progress and development
work, 130
written language, 131

Y

Yáñez, José, 20, 22
Young, Brigham, 127n82
Young, Brigham Morris, 127n82
Young, W. Ernest
  activities of, in San Marcos, 42n3
  and conversion of Monroy family, 9, 16n23, 19–20, 22, 25–26, 28
  corresponds with Monroy, 37
  and death of Jesús Sánchez, 24–25
  Monroy sisters visit, 32

Z

Zapata, Emiliano, 57, 69, 71, 72n14
Zapatistas
  arrest and torture Monroy and Morales, 66
  execute Monroy and Morales, 1–2, 68–69
  go on defensive, 76–77
  Jesusita Mera Pérez rebukes, 74–75
  justify executions of Monroy and Morales, 65
  mission and organization of, 14n3, 57–58, 63n28, 72n14
  motivations of, in executing Morales and Monroy, 69–71
  raid Monroy store and home, 66–67
  seen as national heroes, 71
  support for, 45n27

ABOUT THE AUTHOR

F. LaMond Tullis has been a professor of political science and associate academic vice president at Brigham Young University (BYU). He is a specialist in Latin American studies and has written multiple works on The Church of Jesus Christ of Latter-day Saints in Latin America, especially Mexico. Tullis received his master's degree in political science from Brigham Young University, and his doctorate from Harvard University. He has been a visiting fellow at the London School of Economics, the University of Sussex's Institute of Developmental Studies, and Princeton University's Center of International Studies at its Woodrow Wilson School of Public and International Affairs. Among the books written by Tullis are *Lord and Peasant in Peru*; *Politics and Social Change in Third World Countries*; *Modernization in Brazil*; *Mormons in Mexico: The Dynamics of Faith and*

Culture; *Unintended Consequences: Illegal Drugs and Drug Policies in Nine Countries*; *Handbook of Research on the Illicit Drug Trade*. Tullis was also the general editor of *Mormonism: A Faith for All Cultures*. He has also written multiple articles published in *BYU Studies Quarterly*, *Dialogue*, *Southern California Historical Quarterly*, and *Journal of Mormon History* related to The Church of Jesus Christ of Latter-day Saints in Latin America. His articles in Spanish about the Church in Mexico are published on lds.org.mx in the portal "Historia de la Iglesia en México."